CUBAN STUDIES 17

ADVISORY BOARD

ANTONIO BENÍTEZ-ROJO, Literature, Amherst College
COLE BLASIER, Political Science, University of Pittsburgh
CLAES BRUNDENIUS, Economics, University of Lund
JORGE I. DOMÍNGUEZ, Government, Harvard University
RICHARD FAGEN, Political Science, Stanford University
EDWARD GONZALEZ, Political Science, University of California, Los Angeles
ROBERTO GONZÁLEZ ECHEVARRÍA, Literature, Yale University
IRVING LOUIS HOROWITZ, Sociology, Rutgers University
FRANKLIN W. KNIGHT, History, Johns Hopkins University
WILLIAM M. LEOGRANDE, Political Science, American University
LEVÍ MARRERO, History and Geography, Puerto Rico
JULIO MATAS, Literature, University of Pittsburgh
JOSÉ A. MORENO, Sociology, University of Pittsburgh
ROLLAND G. PAULSTON, Education, University of Pittsburgh
LISANDRO O. PÉREZ, Demography, Florida International University
LOUIS A. PÉREZ, JR., History, University of South Florida
JORGE F. PÉREZ-LÓPEZ, Economics, U.S. Department of Labor
ALEJANDRO PORTES, Social Relations, Johns Hopkins University
SERGIO ROCA, Economics, Adelphi University
ENRICO MARIO SANTÍ, Literature, Cornell University
IVAN A. SCHULMAN, Literature, University of Illinois
HAROLD D. SIMS, History, University of Pittsburgh
ANDRÉS SUÁREZ, Political Science, University of Florida
HUGH THOMAS, History, University of London
NELSON P. VALDES, Sociology, University of New Mexico

CUBAN STUDIES 17

CARMELO MESA-LAGO, Editor

CENTER FOR LATIN AMERICAN STUDIES
University of Pittsburgh
UNIVERSITY OF PITTSBURGH PRESS

CUBAN STUDIES

Carmelo Mesa-Lago, Editor
Harold D. Sims, Book Review Editor
June S. Belkin, Assistant Editor

Manuscripts in English or Spanish may be submitted to the Editor, *Cuban Studies,* Department of Economics, 4M38 Forbes Quadrangle, University of Pittsburgh, Pittsburgh, PA 15260, USA. Maximum length is forty pages, double-spaced, including tables and notes. Please submit two copies and include an abstract of no more than 200 words. Either the MLA or APA reference style is acceptable. *Cuban Studies* will not accept work that has been published, or is under consideration, elsewhere.

Back issues of volumes 1–15 of *Cuban Studies,* when available, may be obtained from the Center for Latin American Studies, 4E04 Forbes Quadrangle, University of Pittsburgh, Pittsburgh, PA 15260, USA.

Published by the University of Pittsburgh Press, Pittsburgh, Pa., 15260
Copyright © 1987, University of Pittsburgh Press
All rights reserved
Feffer and Simons, Inc., London
Manufactured in the United States of America

Library of Congress Catalog Card Number 75-649635
ISBN 0-8229-3562-7
US ISSN 0011-2631

Contents

Preface ix

Sex, Gender, and Revolution
Virginia R. Domínguez and Yolanda Prieto, Guest Editors

Introduction 3
Virginia R. Domínguez and Yolanda Prieto

Sex, Gender, and Revolution: The Problem of Construction and the Construction of a Problem 7
Virginia R. Domínguez

Images of Women in Pre- and Postrevolutionary Cuban Novels 25
Lourdes Casal, edited by Virginia R. Domínguez

Cuban Women and the Struggle for "Conciencia" 51
Marifeli Pérez-Stable

Cuban Women in the U.S. Labor Force: Perspectives on the Nature of Change 73
Yolanda Prieto

Afro-Cubanism

The Geographic, Ethnologic, and Linguistic Roots of Cuban Blacks 95
Jorge Castellanos and Isabel Castellanos

"Los negros brujos": A Reexamination of the Text 111
Edward J. Mullen

Research Notes

The U.S. House of Representatives and Policy Toward Cuba: A Study of Political Attitudes 133
Manuel R. Gómez

Comparative Performance of Large Cuban Sugar Factories in the 1984 "Zafra" 141
Willard W. Radell, Jr.

Debate

Analyzing Cuban Planning: A Response to Roca 159
Andrew Zimbalist

Planners in Wonderland: A Reply to Zimbalist 167
Sergio G. Roca

Reviews 175

Recent Work in Cuban Studies 201

Contributors 249

Sumario

Prefacio ix

Sexo, género y revolución
Virginia R. Domínguez y Yolanda Prieto, Editores Invitados

Introducción 3
Virginia R. Domínguez y Yolanda Prieto

Sexo, género y revolución: El problema de la construcción y la construcción del problema 7
Virginia R. Domínguez

Imágenes de la mujer en las novelas cubanas pre- y post-revolucionarias 25
Lourdes Casal, redactado por Virginia R. Domínguez

La mujer cubana y la lucha por la "conciencia" 51
Marifeli Pérez-Stable

Las mujeres cubanas en la fuerza laboral de los EE.UU.: Perspectivas sobre las condiciones del cambio 73
Yolanda Prieto

Afro-cubanismo

Raíces geográficas, etnológicas y lingüísticas de los negros cubanos 95
Jorge Castellanos y Isabel Castellanos

"Los negros brujos": Una reconsideración del texto 111
Edward J. Mullen

Notas de investigación

La cámara de representantes de los EE.UU. y la política hacia Cuba: Un estudio de actitudes políticas 133
Manuel R. Gómez

Rendimiento comparativo de los ingenios grandes en Cuba durante la zafra de 1984 141
Willard W. Radell, Jr.

Controversia

Análisis de la planificación cubana: Respuesta a Roca 159
Andrew Zimbalist

Planificadores en el país de las maravillas: Réplica a Zimbalist 167
Sergio G. Roca

Reseñas 175

Estudios recientes sobre Cuba 201

Colaboradores 249

Preface

Cuban Studies 17 is the second hardback edition published by the University of Pittsburgh Press as part of its Pitt Latin American Series. These comprehensive annual volumes replace the semiannual journal, *Cuban Studies/Estudios Cubanos* (1975–1985).

The 1987 edition features a collection of four essays on "Sex, Gender, and Revolution" under the guest editorship of Virginia R. Domínguez and Yolanda Prieto. Each article examines some aspect of gender inequality in a process of revolutionary transformation. Virginia Domínguez establishes a theoretical framework with a discussion of the ideological limitations inherent in the study of gender in specific cultural and historical discourses. "Images of Women in Pre- and Postrevolutionary Cuban Novels," excerpted from the 1975 doctoral dissertation of Cuban-born writer, social psychologist and activist Lourdes Casal, views pre- and postrevolutionary Cuban society through the eyes of Cuban novelists and attempts to test hypotheses concerning changes in the society's images of women. Marifeli Pérez-Stable briefly reviews the status of women before the revolution as a prelude to discussing the integration of women into Cuban society, including their entry into the Cuban labor force, and looking at the contradictory trends in the development of egalitarian relations between men and women. The fourth essay, by Yolanda Prieto, examines Cuban women in the U.S. labor force and attempts to shed light on the significant behavioral change regarding women and work that has taken place among Cubans in the United States.

"Afro-Cubanism" presents two articles. Jorge Castellanos and Isabel Castellanos describe the geographic, ethnologic, and linguistic roots of Cuban blacks including a discussion of the many tribal, clan, regional or political terms used to refer to Cuban slaves. Edward Mullen suggests that the text of Fernando Ortiz's work, *Los negros brujos,* be reexamined to discover its multiple levels of meaning through an inquiry into the facts of the book's publication, sources, and major themes.

In "Research Notes," Manuel R. Gómez gives the results of interviews he conducted with foreign policy aides of legislators serving on the Committee on Foreign Affairs of the U.S. House of Representatives; the topic was U.S. policy toward Cuba. Willard W. Radell, Jr., analyzes the 1984 Cuban sugar harvest to determine whether factory size affects efficiency.

This edition's "Debate" is between Sergio G. Roca and Andrew Zimbalist on the subject of Cuban planning. Also included in this volume are reviews of current books and the traditional cataloging of publications related to various aspects of Cuban Studies. We are grateful to Frank Joseph Shulman, of the University of Maryland–College Park Libraries, for information on dissertations dealing with Cuba.

Carmelo Mesa-Lago
June S. Belkin

SEX, GENDER, AND REVOLUTION

Virginia R. Domínguez and Yolanda Prieto, *Guest Editors*

Introduction

A radical revolution, by its very nature, questions the bases on which hierarchical differences have rested in the past. Understanding the roots in inequalities is a precondition for changing them. Has the Cuban Revolution addressed the question of gender differentiation? Has it dealt with gender issues in a sufficiently radical way? How sufficient is sufficient? And how radical is radical? The answers to these questions in the literature on Cuba range from praise to strong criticism. The problem with these answers is that they generally originate outside of Cuba and carry cultural and ideological baggage that must be understood on its own terms.

This collection of essays cannot transcend the limitations of the ideological discourse in which its authors participate, but it can allow for further understanding of the Cuban case by being ideologically self-critical. The work is clearly not the product of contemporary Cuban thinking: it is published in the United States; its two guest editors, though born in Cuba, have not lived there for years; and its contributions are from Cuban-born academics trained in the United States primarily after the resurgence of the women's rights movement in the late 1960s.

The article by Virginia Domínguez deals precisely with the consequences of ideological limitations in the construction of a gender problem. The discussion about gender presupposes the existence of both male and female. However, it is almost always assumed that "gender" issues are "women's" issues. Perhaps this is because women, being "invisible" in the past, have become the object of study now. But this has epistemological *and* political consequences. Marking women for special attention ends up perpetuating the assumption that men are people first and males second, whereas women are always females first and rarely, if ever, just people. Thus, we find books, articles, and pamphlets on "women in Cuba." Why is it that there is so little—other than Oscar Lewis's work—on "men in Cuba"? What, after all, is gender? Domínguez attempts to alert us to the ideological limitations inherent in the rootedness of the study of gender in specific cultural and historical discourses, and to explore, nonetheless, some of the potential epistemological benefits that can follow from such awareness.

Lourdes Casal's essay, "Images of Women in Pre- and Postrevolutionary Cuban Novels," edited by Domínguez, documents the images of women present in Cuban literature both before and after the Revolution. As an assessment of the effect of the Cuban Revolution on longstanding social inequalities, Casal's detailed analysis of characters, expectations, and language use examines the interaction between images of women with images of men, of sexual inequality with racial inequality, and of gender with class position. We are especially pleased to include this material here. Others have explored the dynamics in the relationship between literature and society, but none before Casals, to our knowledge, have used it as their primary tool for analyzing cultural and ideological baggage in the actual process of transforming Cuban society. The sample compares the last decade before the Revolution with the first decade after the Revolution.

Marifeli Pérez-Stable takes the analysis beyond the first decade of the Revolution. Her contribution on Cuban women and "conciencia" addresses the struggle for women's equality in Cuba within the limitations imposed by dependent socialism. Will material difficulties and economic expediency indefinitely postpone the socialist vision of full equality among human beings in Cuba? Are deeply rooted cultural beliefs in gender differences masked by apparently circumstantial, rational considerations when decisions affecting women are made by a mostly male leadership? Are Cuban women—along with Cuban men—consciously developing strategies to move closer to that socialist vision of equality?

The Cuban Revolution had, and continues to have, an impact on many who rejected it and left Cuba. In that sense, Cubans outside Cuba are to some extent part of the revolutionary process. The article by Yolanda Prieto attempts to clarify a paradox. The Cuban Revolution challenged the traditional place of women in Cuban society by bringing them out of their homes to take jobs. Prerevolutionary Cuban society had regarded salaried employment for women with disfavor. The Revolution sought to incorporate women into the labor force. Many Cubans who left the island have pointed to the changes in the role of women as one reason they left their country. However, Cuban women in the United States today have the highest labor force participation rate among all Hispanic and native U.S. women in the country. How is this behavior justified by both Cuban men and women under different circumstances in the United States? Can we assume that this change either reflects or engenders further changes—at the ideological and cultural level—concerning sex and gender in the Cuban-American community?

The essays in this first section of *Cuban Studies 17* aim to address these questions in the spirit of constructive criticism. We seek to raise questions more than to offer definitive answers. Perhaps more than anything, we seek to outline the parameters of what we consider to be issues in the construction of gender in the transformation of postrevolutionary Cuban society.

VIRGINIA R. DOMÍNGUEZ

Sex, Gender, and Revolution: The Problem of Construction and the Construction of a Problem

ABSTRACT

A discussion of the ideological limitations of discourse—in which the "object" created makes sense only within that discourse, and the construction of which has epistemological consequences—provides a theoretical basis for examining the way North American feminists have variously redefined their feminist agendas. It also weighs the potential benefits of the insights of North American feminism to an analysis of sex discrimination, if it exists, in Cuba. Sample texts on and about postrevolutionary Cuba illustrate both the existence of an analytic problem and the range of difference in how the problem is construed.

RESUMEN

La discusión sobre las limitaciones ideológicas del discurso—en la cual el "objeto" tiene sentido solamente dentro de dicho discurso, la construcción del cual tiene a su vez consecuencias epistemológicas—provee una base teórica para examinar las varias maneras en que las feministas norteamericanas han redefinido su agenda feminista y asimismo pondera los beneficios potenciales de los discernimientos del feminismo norteamericano al análisis del problema de discriminación sexual, si el mismo existiera, en Cuba. Textos de muestra sobre y acerca de la Cuba post-revolucionaria ilustran tanto la existencia de un problema analítico como el alcance de la diferencia en la forma en que se interpreta el problema.

Sex and *gender* are words that have come into vogue over the past fifteen years, but what do they really refer to? We know that they now carry semiotic baggage, that they attract some readers and alienate others. But what is perhaps most ironic about them is that the attraction and the alienation both rest on the same assumption: that these are often code words indexing feminist women writing about women and a historically and socially constructed system whereby men dominate and subordinate women. It is a common assumption, reflecting the recent history of various feminist movements, but it is also a dangerous one.

Do *sex* and *gender* apply only to women? Internationally renowned scientist Evelyn Fox Keller recounts an incident when a former professor, having heard of her work on gender and science, asked her to tell him just what it was that she had learned "about women." "I tried to explain," she writes, " 'It's not women I am learning about so much as men. Even more, it is science.' The difference is important, and the misunderstanding (not his alone), revealing."[1] If it takes two to tango, why do we see only one of the two?

Invisibility is a phenomenon women have long experienced and some, especially in recent years, have come to recognize. When a schoolbook presents the history of a country, city, or institution in terms of the actions of men who held acknowledged positions of power or who acquired the posthumous status of heroes—but not in terms of the women in that country, city, or institution—women are made invisible. When, in the past, publishing houses failed to accept manuscripts written by women, except under male pseudonyms, women writers became invisible. When newspapers report on the activities of men in their news sections but relegate the reporting of women's activities to the "style," "lifestyle," and/or "family" sections of their papers, women become highly visible in the home and highly invisible in politics, science, business, and industry.

The irony is that the more women have called into question the roots of that invisibility, the more we talk about gender in a way that frequently makes men invisible. Linguistic marking and partial consciousness-raising produce a dangerous kind of male invisibility. Margaret Randall writes books about women in Cuba, but where are the books about men in Cuba?[2] Jorge Domínguez's *Cuba: Order and Revolution* includes a short section on women and the Revolution in a chapter on political culture, and "women" appears as an entry in the book's index, but there is neither a section on men and the revolution nor an entry in the index simply labeled "men."[3] The apparently liberal, profeminist act of marking women for special attention ends up perpetuating the longstanding assumption that men are people first and males second, whereas women are always females first and rarely, if ever, just people.

How, in fact, does one write about gender distinctions without falling for the built-in ideological trap of just focusing on the position of women in society and giving little more than lip-service to the construction and perpetuation of men *as men*? And what is at issue in discussing gender with regard to a society whose otherwise radical revolution was not especially concerned with gender? In the former, we are confronted with the ubiquitous power of our own gender ideology, captured and disseminated by the power of marked words. In the latter, we are confronted with the epistemological and ethical dilemma of recognizing the reality of variations and differences in gender ideology—the way people think about gender, the importance they attribute to it, and the extent to which they think about it—and yet proceeding to ask culturally inappropriate questions.

This article itself illustrates its own problem. It does not—indeed cannot—transcend the limitations of the ideological discourse in which I participate, but it can and must allow for further understanding of the Cuban case by being ideologically self-critical. What I write here is clearly not a product of contemporary Cuban thinking. While I was born in Cuba, I have not lived there for years. Moreover, I was trained in the United States primarily after the resurgence of the women's movement in the late 1960s, and I participate in a contemporary Euro-American academic discourse that has given increasing legitimacy to the analysis of gender over the past decade. I do not apologize for that; I simply consider it necessary to state it. The topics I bring together in this essay make sense to me, but I am a Cuban who has been deeply influenced by my experience of North American society since the 1960s—a phenomenon that the Grupo Areito's perceptive and pioneering document *Contra Viento y Marea*[4] suggests is part of our collective Cuban-American experience. The question is, how can we become more culturally self-aware, and what can we learn that would shed light both on Cuba and on the construction and reproduction of gender relations in society?

What does North American feminism have to contribute to contemporary Cubans' understanding of their own society? How would various North American schools of feminist thought construe the object of study—circumscribe a "problem," identify related issues, cope with the epistemological and ethical problem of seeing what the natives do not see—and still argue for its validity? What I intend here is an exposition and analysis of the possibilities that come into being in the internal dynamics of different ideological discourses. Is there sex discrimination in contemporary Cuba? Who thinks there is? What are its outlines? To what is it connected? What are its roots, and what is its significance in and outside Cuba? Exploring the varying directions suggested by different forms of North American feminism has the advantage of helping place contemporary Cuba's gender ideologies along a continuum, and avoiding the all too easy tendency to either condemn or glorify.

The Etiology of Criticism

In a review of three recent publications on women in Cuba—Inger Holt-Seeland's *Women in Cuba,* Margaret Randall's *Women in Cuba—Twenty Years Later,* and Elizabeth Stone's *Women and the Cuban Revolution: Speeches and Documents by Fidel Castro, Vilma Espín and Others*—Lois Smith and Alfred Padula diplomatically point out that "there is a price to be paid for [taking an] uncritical approach."[5] First, they argue, "It diminishes the credibility of what are impressive and certifiable advances of women in Cuba," but more importantly they find the "aura of self-congratulation and satisfaction"[6] dangerous and counterproductive. They explain, "The socialist regime has succeeded in getting young women into the work force and into the universities and technical institutes in record numbers. It is urging them to be ambitious and then blocking their career paths at mid-level."[7] Then comes a reference to the Nicaraguan experience and the specter of criticism of the Cuban Revolution. They end with the comment:

The Nicaraguan revolution is now famous for its assertive, self-confident and high-ranking women. If the Cuban revolution cannot promote its own women, cannot perceive the need to open up a new plateau of power to them, it faces the danger of reduced international prestige, i.e. being overtaken by Nicaragua as a model for socialism-feminist development, and more significantly, may well find that in simultaneously pushing women ahead, and holding them back, it has created a very serious and self-destructive social problem.[8]

Smith and Padula imply in their review that theirs is a more critical approach, and consequently that their criticism is potentially useful both to feminism and the Cuban Revolution. But what interests me the most about their comments is the juxtaposition of their call for critical analysis with reference to Cuba and their cavalier references to women in Nicaragua. It might be unfair to fault a short review essay for failing to elaborate on casually made points, but the contrast in how Smith and Padula deal with Cuba and with Nicaragua is so startling that it calls attention to itself. Nicaragua sounds like utopia for feminists; Cuba, like the last failed experiment.[9]

The contrast becomes even more suspect when compared to recent analyses of the situation in Nicaragua. According to Maxine Molyneux, for example, while the Sandinista revolution worked because it universalized the character of the opposition to Somoza, universalization of *goals* never entailed a loss of people's specific identities, including gender.[10] But what to do with the gender problem? How to use it on behalf of the revolution? Rather than make it the focus of attention, the Sandinista revolution took steps to "require the *subordination* of [women's] *specific interests* to the broader goals of overthrowing Somoza and establishing a new social order." Molyneux goes on to point out that this "raises an important question which lies at the heart of debates about the relationship between socialist revolution and women's emancipation . . . if women surrender their specific interests in the universal struggle for a different society, at what point are these interests rehabilitated, legitimated, and responded to by the revolutionary forces or by the new socialist state?"[11] Ironically she says that Nicaragua has "gone further than most Latin American governments (*except Cuba*) in recognizing both the strategic and practical interests of women."[12] Here Nicaragua looks like an ongoing, tentative experiment, and Cuba, like its moderately successful predecessor. That there might be ideological differences between these scholars I do not doubt, but of greater interest to me is how their divergent diagnoses of the situation in Cuba can be used to illustrate the extent to which the questions differ, how they are rooted in different assumptions about human nature, and their consequences for policy and practice.

Note, for example, that Smith and Padula (1) write about women, not about gender, (2) put a great deal of weight on rank and power, (3) seem to measure success in terms of the relative number of women in legitimately acknowledged positions of power, and (4) equate these assumptions with feminism. In contrast, Molyneux (1) writes about women but always in the context of gender, (2) puts a great deal of emphasis on distinguishing between mobilization and emancipation, (3) is impatient with those who measure success "by the privileging of economic criteria," and (4) considers the acknowledgment and analysis of sexual oppression, a critique of patriarchal family structures, and the emasculation of male power to be as important to feminism as the attainment of parity in rank and power in economic and governmental arenas.[13] The Smith-Padula line perceives the problem to be the economic and political disabilities of women, and it provides fairly clear—even quantifiable—criteria for measuring success or failure. Molyneux perceives the problem to be the difficulty in knowing what to do with gender interests so that legitimating them and attending to them would not just lead to sex segregation and the perpetuation of gender and class inequalities. It would be hard to come up with appropriate quantifiable measures of success or failure, and almost as hard to view the problem as anything but a multisided prism.

These are not just casual differences between scholars. Smith and Padula take what sounds very much like a liberal feminist line, while

Molyneux adopts and adapts the concerns of socialist feminists. The differences are deep and far-ranging, epistemological as well as practical. The liberal feminist's concern with equal opportunity for all, her/his campaign for explicit recognition of equal rights, and her/his gut-level rejection of sex segregation rest on a deep-rooted belief in the equal rationality of all human beings, viewed as individuals in search of self-fulfillment. The socialist feminist's commitment to try to develop a political theory and practice to eliminate the forms of oppression perpetuated by capitalism and made possible by continued blind acceptance of class and gender distinctions rests on the conviction that "the differences between women and men are not presocial givens, but rather are socially [and historically] constructed and therefore socially alterable."[14] Whereas the liberal seeks to affirm the dignity and equal worth of the individual, the socialist feminist seeks to identify the structures and mechanisms of group oppression and, thus, facilitate the search for alternatives.[15] It is not so much that one simply refutes the other, but rather that they talk past each other.

The same is true of "traditional Marxists" and "radical feminists." The traditional Marxist's concern is to destroy the capitalist mode of production which is seen as exploitative by definition, and find a nonexploitative alternative to put in its place. Note that such a statement need not mention women, men, sex, or gender at all. Equitable gender relations are neither the motivating force behind Marxist revolutions nor the special concern of postrevolutionary Marxist governments. But the relationship between men and women is definitely still construed as one of those covered by the umbrella phrase "the relations of production"—rooted in the existence and reproduction of a sexual division of labor that benefits the capitalist mode of production. The privileging of production in the analysis of society is well known. Of interest here is the possibility that it might result from, or lead to, the belief that human beings are never fully human unless they engage in productive activity. To note the extent to which men's and women's primary activities differ could, therefore, just as easily lead traditional Marxists to justify the subordination of women to men as it could compel them to urge women to join men in traditionally male productive acitivities or promote practical and ideological changes in the circumscription of productive activity. Reproduction is *not* the issue.

In contrast, the radical feminist is continuously concerned to show "that distinctions of gender, based on sex, structure virtually every aspect of our lives and indeed are so all-pervasive that ordinarily they go quite unrecognized."[16] Just as traditional Marxists privilege production in their analysis of society, so radical feminists privilege gender.

But because they stress gender, they ironically develop a near obsession with what Simone de Beauvoir once called "the facts of biology."[17] While radical feminists most strongly insist on distinguishing between sex (the biological properties of being male or female) and gender (the social attributes of being masculine or feminine), it is also the radical feminists who talk most about sex—about the facts of biology and the possibility, at times even the imperative, to develop alternative perceptions of "the facts of biology." To the radical feminist, the traditional Marxist is just as unenlightened as the liberal—both hang on to optimistic illusions that radical feminists have reason to see as a kind of false consciousness. Both largely limit their concern over inequalities between men and women to the areas of law and employment, whereas radical feminists demand examination of, and changes in, "personal relationships in the home, in bed, and even in our internalized perceptions of ourselves."[18]

There are, of course, variants on each theme and scholars who continue to seek better analytical approaches. My point, however, is simple: the recent development of feminist scholarship in North America and Western Europe make it clear that there is no such thing as *a* feminist position, *the* problem of the status of women in society, *a* set of feminist issues, or a particular relationship between socialism and feminism.

The Problematique of Issues

Consider four recent texts written in the English-speaking world about contemporary Cuba. What is or should be the issue in Cuba? What, if any, is the problem?

In *The Cuban Revolution: Twenty-Five Years Later*,[19] a product of Georgetown University's Cuba Project sponsored by the Center for Strategic and International Studies and coauthored by Hugh Thomas, Georges Fauriol, and Juan Carlos Weiss, the issue is "women." The authors devote almost a page (out of sixty pages of text) to a topic they label "women," in a chapter entitled "Social Dimensions." As with Margaret Randall and Jorge Domínguez, mentioned earlier, these authors provide no commensurate section on men.

But let us proceed with a close reading of this text. The section on women (under "Social Dimensions") is preceded by, and separated from, chapters labeled "Background," "Political Dimensions," "Economic Dimensions," and "Cultural Dimensions." The semantic distinctions drawn make women, or at least the issue of women, something outside the political, economic, and cultural realms. The radical feminist who has long pushed for an understanding of how "the personal is political" would, of course, find the Thomas-Fauriol-Weiss perspective dangerously naive.

Moreover, women get discussed in that part of "Social Dimensions" subtitled "The Balance Sheet, Part I: Improvements?" The question mark is a clue to the skepticism of the authors, and the following paragraphs confirm the line: "The transformation of Cuba's political and economic systems has been accompanied by profound changes in Cuban society," but "figures cited alone and out of context can be misleading."[20] The authors admit that "to a degree, the regime may take credit for several instances of social progress, particularly in extending basic services to a larger portion of the population," but add that "in many cases . . . the appearance of progress may be misleading."[21] Throughout they keep on arguing that "many of the improvements . . . had little to do with the revolution" and instead "were a continuation of trends present before 1959 . . . often due to improvements in technology or health care techniques."[22] The authors clearly have a hard time giving any kind of credit to the Revolution. Cuban socialism is presented as inept and at odds with feminism.

In the discussion of "women" itself, Thomas, Fauriol, and Weiss espouse the language and concepts of the classic Western liberal. The opening lines juxtapose the "theoretical" equality between men and women in Cuba today with their practical inequality. There is talk of rights, equality, freedoms, roles, and the status of women. The authors acknowledge that "the regime has made some efforts to improve the status of women," but insist that "equal and sometimes greater accomplishments in the status of women have been achieved elsewhere without a similar price being paid."[23] Their only use of, or reference to, data concerns labor force participation rates: "By 1979 the rate of female labor force participation reached only 31 percent, *a level attained or surpassed in other Latin American countries.*" There is no mention of sexuality, gender, women's interests, reproduction, self-fulfillment, the capitalist mode of production, biology, or oppression.

Jorge Domínguez's *Cuba: Order and Revolution* resembles the Thomas-Fauriol-Weiss report in its semantic structure, though it differs significantly in tone. It also marks women for special attention and leaves men the unmarked category. Women appear twice in the table of contents—first, in a section on the Cuban Women's Federation in a chapter on "Mass Political Participation," and second, in a section entitled "Women and the Revolution" in the chapter "Political Culture." Here and there where demographic or health statistics distinguish between males and females—as in an appendix on changes in the height of Cubans since the turn of the century—Domínguez includes parallel references to men and women.

Domínguez's tone is deliberately matter-of-fact, his goal a "balanced" depiction of the accomplishments and failures of the Cuban Revolution, and his method of argumentation a heavy reliance on historical and statistical data. Domínguez is at once openly appreciative of the efforts made by the Cuban government and diplomatically critical. For him, the issue is not simply women, but rather "women and the Revolution."

The problem with Domínguez is that he does not seem to be sure he knows just what the problem is. Thus, not surprisingly, the discussion is about women *and* the Revolution, and not about women *in* the Revolution, women *to* the Revolution, women *for* the Revolution, women *into* Revolution, or women *as* the Revolution. His language is most telling. Interspersed throughout both sections of the book are comments on what *feminists* would and would not like, even a reference to the women's liberation movement.

He seems, in fact, sheepish vis-à-vis feminists. Early in his discussion of the Federation of Cuban Women, Domínguez apparently wants to make it clear that he is not naive about the nature of the federation. He writes, "By international standards, the Cuban Women's Federation has been conservative. . . . [Federation president Vilma Espín] told a reporter for *Ms.* magazine who was covering the federation's second congress in 1974, that the Cuban women's revolutionary movement is 'feminine, not feminist' [and] attitudes that help 'keep women in their place' are common."[24] Likewise, in discussing women in positions of political power or authority, Domínguez remarks, "The only thing to cheer a feminist is the evidence of government commitment to expanding the role of women in politics."[25] These references are far from condescending. Both sections appear as serious attempts to explore issues Domínguez thinks U.S. feminists have correctly pointed out as in need of analysis and change. But his blanket labeling of feminists and the encyclopedic presentation of attitudinal and behavioral data still give the strong impression that he himself does not feel he knows what the feminist line is—even less that there might be significantly different feminist lines.

In fact, Domínguez organizes his material in terms of one underlying but persistent question—the role of women in society. It allows him to bring together references to Cuban politicians' public statements, attitude surveys of the population, and aggregate socioeconomic statistics. The concept ironically fits in well with at least some Cuban official discourse, though it sounds equally Parsonian. "The leaders of the revolution," Domínguez writes, "have been somewhat ambivalent about the role of women in society."[26] Castro, he remarks, may have proclaimed the need for "a revolution in the revolution" some years back, but Jorge Risquet, at the time minister of labor, was quoted in *Granma* in 1970 explaining "why women would be exempt from the anti-loafing law: 'Women have the job of reproducing as well as producing. They have to take care of the house, raise the children, and do other tasks along these lines, and this is not easy. From the political point of view, our people would not understand it if we were to treat women and men alike.' "[27]

Thus, when Domínguez reports on polls and surveys done in Cuba, it is to see what the population at large thinks—about participation of women in the labor force, in political institutions of power and influence, and in decision making at home and in the workplace; about sexual relations, young women's career goals and expectations, and the possibility of really doing something to bring about a sharing of domestic chores between husbands and wives. Issues and analyses that do not seem to be potential answers to the question posed about the role of women in society get little or no mention. The issue is in part the rights and freedoms under the law, but clearly not subordination or oppression and the mechanisms that perpetuate them, not the complicated dynamics between production and reproduction, and not gender distinctions.

Elizabeth Stone's lengthy introduction to *Women and the Cuban Revolution* offers yet a third conceptualization of the "object."[28] Like Thomas, Fauriol, Weiss, and Domínguez, for whom the issue is women, or women and the Revolution—not men, women and men, sex, or gender—Stone construes the object as "women and the Cuban Revolution," to which she devotes an entire short monograph.

The resemblance between Domínguez's subtitle (*Order and Revolution*) and Stone's book title is both telling and deceptive. Politically and academically, their goals differ. While Domínguez strives for calculated balance in his ambitious and encyclopedic analysis of the Cuban Revolution, Stone openly sets out to document its accomplishments and bring it support and recognition. Domínguez is a Cuban-born U.S. scholar seeking academic recognition for analytical acuity and completeness; Stone, a non-Cuban, is the managing editor of the politically oriented, left-of-center Pathfinder Press. Her analysis of women is very obviously placed within a favorable analysis of the Cuban Revolution and a conscious critique of capitalism.

Her language follows suit. Much of the analysis is structured around the theme of "struggle." Stone writes freely about the "oppression" of women and frames it all in the context of a "deepgoing revolution" against "capitalism." Much of the traditional Marxist epistemology is there, but so are elements of a socialist-feminist one. Both Stone's opening and concluding remarks make a point of addressing the overall nature of the Revolution. Throughout her piece, "capitalist property relations" appear as the real root of women's oppression, and the Revolution appears as the real motor behind "the struggle of Cuban women for equality." Writing about the prerevolutionary period, for example, Stone clearly puts the onus on capitalism and not on men, culture, or biology. After detailing how economic stagnation and a low level of industrialization make it nearly impossible for an uneducated, unskilled woman to get a job except as a domestic servant and blaming those conditions on "imperialist exploitation," Stone writes,

This legacy of social and economic backwardness was the greatest obstacle to women's equality. Real changes could only come about based on economic development and the integration of women into social production. Only with this could the deeply held prejudices about women's role be changed. This meant that changes in the situation of women in Cuba had to be made in stages, step by step, as the struggle against underdevelopment progressed.[29]

That Stone is intent on defending Cuba *and* what she sees as its adherence to traditional Marxism is especially obvious in her discussion of the Cuban family. Cubans, she argues, have taken very radical positions consistent with traditional Marxism—"the complete opposite of the reactionary 'profamily' forces in the U.S."[30] The implication is that Cubans have come under criticism from leftist circles outside Cuba, which equate a Cuban profamily policy with a conservative, antifeminist epistemology. Stone's defense says as much about her perspective as it does about the dynamic between the Cuban government and the international socialist and feminist community. She writes explicitly, "In all essentials the Cubans have acted in accord with the analysis of Marx, Engels, and Lenin on this question; . . . in his famous work, *The Origin of the Family, Private Property, and the State,* Engels puts forward the same goals the Cubans have stressed as being necessary to freeing women."[31] These are identified as "(1) ending the economic dependence of women on their husbands; (2) getting women out of the isolation of the home and incorporating them into the work force; (3) socializing household chores traditionally done by women through the use of public laundries, cafeterias, child care, and other public services; and (4) ending the *economic* chains that compel family members to remain together, so that relationships between people can be based on affection and not on economic necessity." It is noteworthy here that Stone should rely so much on Engels when so much work on gender and women has been done since Engels. It is not altogether uncommon, however, among traditional Marxists.

And yet, despite the heavy reliance on traditional Marxist analysis, Stone periodically lets on that she thinks there may be other valid issues as well. We note references to equality, to rights, to the need for "complete freedom for women," to a need for "greater self-confidence, a sense of their own worth and dignity, and more control over their lives."[32] When she says, with respect to the Revolution, that at the beginning of the process "there was nothing in Cuba resembling what we would today call a women's liberation movement" and that one of the accomplishments of the Revolution was that it "soon *brought about a massive awakening* of women,"[33] the implication is that the issue is more than figuring out ways to mobilize women so that they may contribute as much as men to the process of production. Proudly Stone reports that Cuban women have the right to abortion on demand, that "rape and violent crimes against women are nowhere near as prevalent in Cuba as they are in the United States," that "Cuba is also largely free of the omnipresent pornography that mixes sex with violence, which can be seen in U.S. films," that the means of contraception are "available and free," and that the 1975 Cuban Communist party thesis on the full exercise of women's equality "calls for using the same sexual standard for men and women."[34] On the other hand, the text offers little theoretical, analytical, or even practical elaboration on any of these issues relating sex and sexuality with power and reproduction.

In contrast, consider a two-part article entitled "Homosexuality, Homophobia, and Revolution: Notes toward an Understanding of the Cuban Lesbian and Gay Male Experience" recently published by Lourdes Argüelles and Ruby Rich.[35] Although the article was published in a journal "of women in culture and society," the issue is clearly not women, but rather the political manipulation of sexuality. Women, consequently, are not marked for special consideration, and men, consequently, are not invisible.

The Argüelles-Rich article analyzes and critiques its subject on two levels simultaneously. The authors appear as concerned with criticism of the Cuban Revolution "within North American gay academic and artistic circles and . . . segments of the Left"[36] as with evidence of continued repression against homosexuals in contemporary Cuba. The fact is that "thousands of homosexual men and women have migrated to the United States and to other capitalist nations since the start of the socialist revolution in Cuba in 1959," and that "this exodus has been interpreted as stemming almost exclusively from the homophobic nature of the Castro regime and a set of repressive policies that have purportedly rendered gay and lesbian expression on the island virtually impossible." Argüelles and Rich insist that this interpretation is simplistic, though the facts are correct, and that it is being manipulated in the United States for political purposes.

The authors walk a kind of tightrope, much as Jorge Domínguez does. They are concerned to address the interests of social and intellectual communities that are at least in part in odds with each other, but not to alienate them. Expressing concern with repression against homosexuals in Cuba incurs the risk of alienating Cuban government officials and many, if not most, Cuban heterosexuals; expressing concern over the criticism of revolutionary Cuba now heard in gay, lesbian, academic, and other sectors of the Left over the repression of homosexuality in Cuba incurs the risk of alienating gays and lesbians both in the United States and in Cuba. Argüelles and Rich are keenly aware of their dilemma. They write, "We are aware of the risks incurred by disseminating this study: giving ammunition to anti-Cuba lobbies and to strongly homophobic cliques on the island and risking the enmity of those Cuban émigrés who have long capitalized on this unexamined issue as a condemnation of the revolutionary process."[37] But they are clearly committed to the attempt, and applaud Cuban gays and lesbians who walk the tightrope with them. "The continual scapegoating of Cuban revolutionary homophobia," they write, "has made the growing number of progressive gay émigrés who criticize but also support the revolution into living contradictions: invisible to gay liberation forces but easy targets for the homophobic anti-Castro army in exile."[38]

From their explicit statements and analytic orientation, we deduce that Argüelles and Rich are themselves a kind of "living contradiction"—informed and guided by the historicity of a Marxist epistemology and its attention to the system of production, but committed to the legitimation of alternative forms of sexuality and the development of an analytic framework to explain what it has to do with gender. Capitalism and socialism form the backdrop here—not so much as competing ideological systems per se but rather as competing ideological systems confronting problems and contradictions generated by very similar, if not actually shared, assumptions about normative sexuality. Argüelles and Rich seem to be past the stage of debating the relative advantages and disadvantages of capitalism and socialism, and into an exploration of what their similarities might mean. For example, when they discuss prerevolutionary Cuba, they unwincingly blame capitalism for much of the *exploitative* nature of sexual relations in Cuba—in heterosexual as well as homosexual liaisons—and make a point of discussing "the commodification of homosexual desire in the Havana underworld and in the bourgeois homosexual underground during the prerevolutionary era."[39] But when they discuss postrevolutionary Cuba, they state equally assertively that socialism has also failed to prove itself a panacea for those seeking alternative forms of sexuality. The implication is that it is too facile to blame capitalism for the construction of gender distinctions, gender roles, or gender relations whether in pre- or postrevolutionary Cuba, and tempting but superficial to blame it for the empowering of sexuality as the mechanism for their perpetuation. Social expressions of sexuality and gender identity emerge throughout their work as human creations constructed historically by conditions at least in part independent of the ideology, as well as the practice, of both capitalism and socialism.

The Argüelles-Rich line is then to study not the history or political economy of sexual or gender relations, but rather the ways in which ideologically contradictory systems relate to, interpret, use, or try to change an aspect of society that neither system regards as constitutive of itself. Their approach is to take a very clear and strong position on the ethical dilemma I mentioned in the first few pages of this article—of recognizing the reality of variations and differences in sexual or gender ideology and yet feeling justified in asking culturally inappropriate questions. It is to allot sexuality a central place in the discussion of revolutionary change, gender ideology, and the struggle against oppression.

But what may, then, sound like a particularly enlightened perspective is still not a Cuban perspective. As Roger Lancaster has recently pointed out, "the danger of ethnocentrism here—of projecting *our* categories and understandings onto theirs—is particularly acute, for sexuality, like gender, is often taken as an a priori set of acts and categories, and therein enters what Mathieu has called 'the misleading light of the obvious.' "[40] Lancaster goes on to suggest that to move forward with our scholarly dialogue we must strive first for a richer understanding of "Latin folk categories of sexuality generally, and Cuban folk categories in particular."[41] I agree that research on, and sensitivity to, Cuban folk categories of sexuality and gender would enrich our understanding, but the question is still, our understanding of what? If it is of sexuality in the study of gender, it is not, or at least not necessarily, of production as the agent of continued inequality between the sexes, nor is it necessarily of legal rights and duties, oppression, or gender stratification. Lancaster is right, but he may not go far enough. Argüelles and Rich don't just run the risk of being ethnocentric; they are ethnocentric, but can we learn from their ethnocentrism?

The Problem of Construction

If earlier I suggested that North American feminism might have something to contribute to Cubans' understanding of their own society, it is because of the implications I find necessary to draw from the deconstruction of these texts. The simplest point to grasp is the fact of significant variation in how the issue is construed, but the most engaging is that it forces us to grapple with what it means to have that kind of variation.

Clearly, as Alison Jaggar has cogently argued in *Feminist Politics and Human Nature*,[42] much of the variation is the product of a lively academic and political discourse that has spanned the past two decades. Dissatisfaction with one formulation of "the problem" has frequently led to a reevaluation of the premises on which that formulation rests. The result has been a tendency for those holding new formulations of the problem to regard formulations that preceded them as simplistic, backward, and out-of-date. Radical feminists, despite their own internal debates, tend to become quite impatient with liberal feminists; socialist feminists find traditional Marxists simplistic and unthinkingly rigid.

But the variations say something as well about the nature of the "object"—that there is no object outside the discourse(s) which make it possible, that each objectification makes sense to discourse participants and that, by carving out part of a semantic map in a particular way, each objectification has epistemological consequences—making *certain* other perceptions possible and limiting the participants' ability to "see" alternative constructions of the object or, when shown alternatives, to accept them as equally valid. Were I writing about culture, we would all recognize the point as the fundamental principle behind the anthropological conception of culture. What makes it more challenging a problem is that much of feminism aims to improve things for women, not just contemplate differences. Tolerance for others' construction and treatment of "the problem" is rarely a characteristic of the classic anthropologist confronting another people.

Should socialist Cuba be treated any differently? The tendency has been to either praise or criticize, and each time to use criteria derived from intellectual and political life outside Cuba. So politicized is so much of that literature that Cubans have become suspicious of terms and concepts generated by a discourse external to Cuba and the other socialist countries. Vilma Espín's well-known remark in 1974 that the Cuban women's revolutionary movement was feminine, not feminist, fits the pattern. Feminism was at least then, in 1974, not something to be emulated in Cuba. Associated with the Western, capitalist, industrial countries, it came to be perceived in Cuba as a form of bourgeois decadence. But was she, is she, right? If we are willing to entertain all of the positions and texts discussed here as feminist ones, on what grounds could we validly argue that Cuba's stances over the years do not qualify as feminist?

We might be tempted to dismiss the problem as "pure semantics" or as food for philosophical debate alone. But is it? On what basis do we recommend specific government policies or grassroots activities? On what basis do we criticize our own system and turn to others as role models, or defend our progress and actions and criticize others? Without understanding the extent to which our construction of the problem differs, can we even begin to talk about the problem of sex or gender in revolutionary Cuba?

NOTES

1. Evelyn Fox Keller, *Reflections on Gender and Science* (New Haven, Conn.: Yale University Press, 1985), p. 3.
2. Margaret Randall, *Women in Cuba: Twenty Years Later* (New York: Smyrna Press, 1981).
3. Jorge Domínguez, *Cuba: Order and Revolution* (Cambridge, Mass.: Harvard University Press, 1978).
4. Grupo Areito, *Contra Viento y Marea* (New York, 1978).
5. Lois Smith and Alfred Padula, review of Ingere Holt-Seeland's *Women of Cuba*, Margaret Randall's *Women in Cuba: Twenty Years Later*, and Elizabeth Stone's *Women and the Cuban Revolution, Cuban Studies* 13, no. 2 (1983), 130.
6. Ibid.
7. Ibid.
8. Ibid.
9. My point is not that Nicaragua is doing more or doing things better than Cuba, but rather that Nicaragua is getting better press than Cuba, and this sheds useful light on the ideological foundations of criticism of gender stratification or sexual inequality. I should note that one of the reviewers of an earlier version of this essay points this out vividly in noting the contrast between what I quoted in reference to Cuba and Nicaragua and what this indidividual had heard, seen, and experienced: "Having spent some time in both Nicaragua and Cuba over the past year, I am less 'utopian' in my assessment of the situation of Nicaraguan women. In an interview with Vilma Espín, I found no lack of assertiveness on her part. . . . I might add that it is the Cubans and FMC in particular that have raised the power issue in special studies and in pressure on Fidel. The FMC finds power important."
10. Maxine Molyneux, "Mobilization without Emancipation? Women's Interests, the State, and Revolution in Nicaragua." *Feminist Studies* 11, no. 2 (1985), 227–54.

11. Ibid., p. 229.
12. Ibid., p. 250, emphasis added.
13. Ibid.; Here I am trying to point out the differences in their conceptualization, rather than the similarities. I think that Smith and Padula, if asked directly, might agree with Molyneux that Nicaragua has not solved its gender inequality problem. I doubt, nonetheless, that they would have much more in common, and I think we have much more to learn from examining their differences.
14. Alison Jaggar, *Feminist Politics and Human Nature* (Brighton, Sussex: Harvester Press, 1983).
15. One could well add that the socialist feminist assumption of a direct causal link between gender and capitalism may leave a socialist feminist conceptually unprepared for the existence of a gender problem in socialism. I think that this is one of the reasons so much attention is being paid to Cuba and Nicaragua. What happens if Cuba and Nicaragua do not succeed? Is the only possible interpretation of such "failure" the idea that the legacies of the past are just too strong to be easily eradicated? Could it not also say something constructively critical about the nature of contemporary socialism?
16. Jaggar, *Feminist Politics and Human Nature*, p. 85.
17. Simone de Beauvoir, *The Second Sex* (New York: Alfred A. Knopf, 1970).
18. Jaggar, *Feminist Politics and Human Nature*, p. 85.
19. Hugh Thomas, Georges A. Fauriol, and Juan Carlos Weiss, *The Cuban Revolution Twenty-Five Years Later* (Boulder, Colo., and London: Westview Press, 1984).
20. Ibid., p. 44.
21. Ibid., pp. 44–45.
22. Ibid., p. 45.
23. Ibid., p. 47.
24. Domínguez, *Cuba: Order and Revolution*, p. 268.
25. Ibid., p. 503.
26. Ibid., p. 494.
27. Ibid., p. 268.
28. Elizabeth Stone, ed., *Women and the Cuban Revolution: Speeches and Documents by Fidel Castro, Vilma Espín, and Others* (New York: Pathfinder Press, 1981).
29. Ibid., p. 7.
30. Ibid., p. 28.
31. Ibid., p. 27.
32. Ibid., pp. 29, 10.
33. Ibid., p. 5.
34. Ibid., pp. 20, 25, 26.
35. Lourdes Argüelles and B. Ruby Rich, "Homosexuality, Homophobia, and Revolution: Notes toward an Understanding of the Cuban Lesbian and Gay Male Experience, Part I," *Signs* 9 (1984), 683–99; "Part II," *Signs* 11 (1985), 120–36.
36. Ibid., pt. 1, p. 683.
37. Ibid., pt. 1, p. 685.
38. Ibid., pt. 1, p. 684.
39. Ibid., pt. 1, p. 687.
40. Roger Lancaster, comment on Argüelles and Rich's "Homosexuality, Homophobia, and Revolution: Notes toward an Understanding of the Cuban Lesbian and Gay Male Experience, Part II," *Signs* 12 (1986), 188.
41. Ibid., p. 191.
42. Jaggar, *Feminist Politics and Human Nature*.

LOURDES CASAL
edited by VIRGINIA R. DOMÍNGUEZ

Images of Women in Pre- and Postrevolutionary Cuban Novels

ABSTRACT

Excerpted from sections of Lourdes Casal's doctoral dissertation, this essay explores the ideological baggage about gender that Cubans have had to work with in attempting to transform Cuba from a capitalist to a socialist society. A comparison of the images of women and men in thirty pre- and postrevolutionary Cuban novels attempts to assess both the changes in perceptions about women and the ideological constraints on those changes. Included in the findings are demographic characteristics of the fictional societies portrayed in a sample of novels from the 1950s and 1960s, a detailing of the contexts in which change was evident, and a content analysis of expectations and relations between men and women before and after the Revolution, as reflected in Cuban fiction.

RESUMEN

Este ensayo, extraido de secciones de la tesis doctoral de Casal, explora el bagage ideológico sobre el sexo con el cual han tenido que trabajar los cubanos en su intento por transformar Cuba de una sociedad capitalista a una socialista. El mismo ofrece una comparación de las imágenes de hombres y mujeres en las novelas cubanas pre- y post-revolucionarias orientada a evaluar tanto los cambios en las percepciones acerca de las mujeres como las limitaciones ideológicas de tales cambios. En los resultados obtenidos se incluyen las características demográficas de las sociedades ficticias representadas en la muestra de novelas de las décadas de 1950 y 1960, una visión detallada de los contextos en los cuales se evidencia el cambio, y un análisis de contenido de las expectativas y relaciones entre hombres y mujeres antes y después de la revolución.

[Lourdes Casal, a writer, social psychologist, activist, and New York intellectual, died in 1982. In the midst of myriad academic projects, teaching responsibilities, and organizational commitments, she found the time to finish a doctoral dissertation she herself admitted was not mainstream social psychology. "Images of Cuban Society among Pre- and Post-Revolutionary Novelists" (New School for Social Research, 1975) attempted to analyze samples of Cuban novels "to derive a view of the pre-revolutionary social class structure and of racial and sexual inequality," and "to assess the extent of the changes introduced by the Revolution, as they are reflected in the novels" (p. 107). More important, it allowed Casal to draw simultaneously on her passion for literature, her changing views of the Cuban Revolution, her training as a social psychologist, and a personal sensitivity to racial and sexual inequalities heightened by her experience of the Civil Rights movement of the 1960s and her exposure to the rising feminist arguments of the late sixties and seventies. Ill health and overcommitment kept her from editing the work for publication and thus giving the broader scholarly community the opportunity to examine and digest her findings. I am, of course, aware that changes have taken place in Cuba in the ten years since the dissertation was completed, but still feel that the material Casal examined remains vastly understudied and that her findings offer a special window on the Cuban Revolution.

In presenting parts of that work here, I have taken on a task that is not without risks. One of Lourdes Casal's strengths was the ability, even the need, to integrate sources, methods, issues. For example, her study discusses images of women and of sexual inequality because it examines various inequalities—racial, social, and sexual. By excerpting those sections on women and sexual inequality, I do not mean to simplify what Casal obviously saw as a complex and interwoven reality; I have tried to keep the final product faithful to the spirit and argument of the dissertation as a whole.

The work presented here is a distillation, not a mere reproduction of any one chapter. I have tried, in effect, to piece together the article Lourdes Casal herself would have written based on her dissertation. The wording is largely intact, but I have excerpted and renumbered tables 16, 35, 36, 37, and 38 (here, 1–5), have removed some in-text references, and have rearranged the paragraphs taken from Casal's concluding chapter.

I would like to thank Marifeli Pérez-Stable, Lourdes Casal's literary executrix, for permission to print these excerpts.]

On Literature and Society

This study of pre- and postrevolutionary Cuban novels from the vantage point of the social psychologist aims to extract from such novels a detailed view of prerevolutionary Cuban society which is contrasted, at appropriate points, with available hard data. Also it attempts to test certain hypotheses concerning the extent to which the Revolution has introduced changes in the images of society presented in the novels.

The novelist is considered to be a privileged observer and recorder of society. Not that his viewpoint is necessarily the same as that of the sociologist (although in Spanish American countries the novelist has frequently been an amateur sociologist), but his works, insofar as they represent the image of society as seen by a participant observer in his time and locus, are basic documents for the sociologist and the social psychologist. Novels become especially valuable documents when formal systematic investigation of the society in question is limited or nonexistent.

It is not claimed here that the novelist's image of society is "objective." It is probably no more objective than that of any other member of the culturally privileged sectors of his society. But it can probably be assumed to be richer, more attentive to detail, more capable of registering nuances, of whose import the author himself may be partially or totally unaware.

Thus, in a sense, the study to be undertaken here is an analysis of the images of society prevailing in the social consciousness of pre- and postrevolutionary Cuban novelists. This kind of analysis is important because, as pointed out by Ossowski,

a. A view of the social structure which is widely held is an element in the social situation, and thus exerts an influence on the nature of human relations.
b. A way of perceiving the social structure which is more or less generally accepted in certain classes or milieux allows us to conclude which elements in the system of relationships seem particularly important in the eyes of their members. . . .
c. Finally, images of social structure, especially those which are socially determined, are important for us because they directly condition social ideologies and social programmes.[1]

M. C. Albrecht has indicated three possible sorts of connection between literature and society: literature as reflection, literature as social invention, and literature as a means of social control.[2] Without entering into a full theoretical discussion of this issue, a central one in the sociology of literature, one can defend the analysis of literary works in the task of describing a literate culture.[3] The most adequate model with which to conceptualize the relationship is probably one based on a reciprocal connection between society and literature.[4] Novels are seen, on the one hand, as reflections of society—that is, they mirror existing social reality—but they are also a medium through which norms and values are introduced or transmitted. Novels are not just images of the present but also anticipations of the future. In a literate culture, novels as well as other written materials are important sources of role models and ideal images that can have an impact upon shaping norms and behavior. In a revolutionary society, when the society's energies are devoted to altering not only prerevolutionary institutions and structures but also prerevolutionary attitudes and values, the written media must be seen as performing a resocializing function, together with the more massive visual and aural instruments specially suited for communicating with the nonliterate or semiliterate sectors of the population, such as TV, radio, billboards, posters, megaphones, not to mention mass mobilizations and recruiting by mass organizations.[5]

However, it must be recognized that the study of society in literature lacks a working methodology and an agreed-upon set of verification rules.[6] The present study integrates the use of quantitative, systematic analysis of the social data contained in the novels with various semi-quantitative and qualitative techniques in an attempt to do justice to the complexity of the materials faced.[7]

The Sample

Two target periods were selected: novels published between 1950 and 1958 (that is to say, the last nine years before the Revolution) and novels published between 1959 and 1967 (the first nine years after the Revolution).

The selection of the target periods of 1950–1958 and 1959–1967 was dictated by pragmatic considerations: first, the need to select a relatively brief span of time to insure manageability of the total number of novels, and second, given the current difficulties involved in securing Cuban materials, a relatively long period of time may elapse between publication date and accessibility; hence the 1967 end date. The list of all the novels published by Cuban authors within or outside of Cuba between 1950 and 1967 was compiled by means of existing Instituto del Libro catalogues, published bibliographies,[8] a survey of the book review sections of Cuban magazines, a survey of the Cuban literature sections of the Library of Congress, the University of Pittsburgh's Hillman Library and the New York Public Library. The resulting list consisted of 104 novels, 37 from the 1950–1958 period and 67 from the 1959–1967 period.

The following criteria were used in reducing this total of 104 novels to the final list of 57 eligible novels (18 for the prerevolutionary period; 39 for the postrevolutionary period):

1. Novels published by exiled writers were not included in the sample. Thus, for the postrevolutionary period, all novels published outside of Cuba were excluded. (This does not exclude novels published within Cuba by authors who later became exiles.)

2. Novels with historical settings far removed in time from 1959 were excluded. The pragmatic criterion followed was to include only novels dealing with pre- or postrevolutionary Cuban society and covering primarily the 1930s, 1940s, 1950s, and 1960s. If no explicit dates

were given, identification of timing was attempted on the basis of incidents, or other clues, and the novel was included if it depicted the above-mentioned target periods.

3. Similarly, novels not having a predominantly Cuban setting, either explicit or clearly discernible, were also excluded.

4. A number of novels listed in some of the sources mentioned above could not be located in any U.S. library. (The Library of Congress's search services were used.)

5. If a novel was not realistic (such as Virgilio Piñera's fantasy *Presiones y diamantes*) or presented extraordinary problems to those attempting to assess its plot or characters because of excessive complexities of narrative structure and language (for example, José Lezama Lima's *Paradiso*), it was also excluded.

6. Finally, novels best classified as detective novels or science fiction were excluded.

From the list of eligible novels, a random sample of fifteen novels from each period was drawn (see table 1).[9] The basic goal of the analysis was to fill in some gaps in our knowledge of prerevolutionary society, especially those gaps resulting from the scarcity of sociological and social psychological studies of prerevolutionary Cuba. In particular, there are few studies of sex-role stereotypes and attitudes prevalent in prerevolutionary society.

Revolutionary goals and values were assumed to be embodied in works published after the Revolution, partially as reflections of revolutionary changes, and partially because, in a revolutionary society, novels and other written works are instruments by means of which the new citizen is shaped. Several changes were hypothesized: social class consciousness should increase between pre- and postrevolutionary novels; also predicted were increases in black and female representation in the postrevolutionary sample; achievement imagery and references to values consistent with revolutionary ideology (egalitarianism, collectivism) were also expected to appear in postrevolutionary works.

Females in the Novels: Demographic Characteristics

It was hypothesized that, in agreement with the revolutionary emphasis on egalitarianism and increasing the access to resources by formerly oppressed groups, there should be an increase in female representation among the characters in postrevolutionary novels. Table 2 presents the percentage of males and females in the novels, broken down into pre- and postrevolutionary samples. Of the 1,756 characters present in the novels, 1,241 (70.7 percent) are male and 515 (29.3 percent) are female.

TABLE 1
Thirty Cuban Novels, 1950–1967

1950	Labrador Ruiz, Enrique	*La sangre hambrienta* [*Hungry Blood*]. 2d ed. Havana: Cruzada Latinoamericana de Difusión Cultural.
1951	Gómez, Francisco G.	*El burguesito recién pescado* [*The Recently Finished Petit-Bourgeois*]. Havana: Editorial Lex.
1952	Clavijo Tisseur, Arturo	*La maestra del pueblo* [*The Town Teacher*]. Manzanillo: Editorial El Arte.
	Ferrer, Surama	*Romelia Vargas*. Havana: Editorial Alonso.
1953	Iznaga, Alcides	*Los Valedontes* [*The Valedontes*]. Santa Clara: Universidad Central de Las Villas, Departamento de Relaciones Culturales.
1954	Esténger, Rafael	*El pulpo de oro* [*The Golden Octopus*]. Mexico City: Librería de Manuel Porrúa.
	Wen Maury, Jośe W.	*La noche de un martes 13* [*The Evening of a Tuesday 13th*]. Havana: Imprenta Pérez Sierra y Hermanos.
1955	Espinosa, Manuel	*¡Bastardo!* [*Bastard!*] Havana: Editorial Selecta.
	Tur Canudas, Angel	*La tierra y la viejecita* [*The Land and the Old Lady*]. Havana: P. Fernández y Cía.
1956	Serpa, Enrique	*La trampa* [*The Trap*]. Buenos Aires: Unión de Editores Latinos.
	Carpentier, Alejo	*El acoso* [*Hounding*]. Buenos Aires: Editorial Losada.
1957	Ortega, Gregorio	*Una de cal y otra de arena* [*Lime and Sand*]. Havana: Tipografía Ideas.
	Patiño Hernández, Antonio	*Ritmo de juventud* [*Youth Rhythm*]. Havana: Editorial Lex.
	Patiño Hernández, Antonio	"Una mujer y tres espejos" ["A Woman and Three Mirrors"]. Havana: Editorial Lex.
	De Boullon, Fernanda	*Lucha de razas* [*Race Struggle*]. Havana: Editorial Lex.
1960	Perera Soto, Hilda	*Mañana es 26* [*Tomorrow Is the 26th*]. Havana: Lázaro Hermanos.
1961	Desnoes, Edmundo	*No hay problema* [*No Problem*]. Havana: Ediciones Revolución.
1962	Arcocha, Juan	*Los muertos andan solos* [*The Dead Are Alone*]. 2d ed. Havana: Editorial Revolución.
	Piñeiro, Abelardo	*El descanso* [*Paid Vacation*]. Havana: Unión de Escritores y Artistas de Cuba.

	Sarusky, Jaime	*La búsqueda* [*The Search*]. Havana: Ediciones Revolución.
1963	Otero, Lisandro	*La situación* [*The Situation*]. Havana: Editorial Casa de las Américas.
	Soler Puig, José	*En el año de enero* [*In This January's Year*]. Havana: Editorial Unión.
1964	Feijóo, Samuel	*Juan Quinquín en pueblo mocho* [*Juan Quinquín in "Cut Off" Town*]. Santa Clara: Editora del Consejo Nacional de Universidades, Universidad Central de Las Villas.
	Soler Puig, José	*El derrumbe* [*The Collapse*]. Santiago de Cuba: Editora del Consejo Nacional de Universidades, Universidad de Oriente.
1965	Desnoes, Edmundo	*Memorias del subdesarrollo* [*Memories of Underdevelopment*]. Havana: Editorial Unión.
1966	Otero, Lisandro	*Pasión de Urbino* [*Urbino's Passion*]. Buenos Aires: J. Alvarez.
1967	Arenal, Humberto	*Los animales sagrados* [*The Sacred Animals*]. Havana: Instituto del Libro.
	Agüero, Luis	*La vida en dos* [*Split Life*]. Havana: Editorial Casa de las Américas.
	Granados, Manuel	*Adire y el tiempo roto* [*Broken Times*]. Havana: Editorial Casa de las Américas.
	Leante, César	*Padres e hijos* [*Parents and Sons*]. Havana: Unión Nacional de Escritores y Artistas de Cuba.

Note: The sample, consisting of fifteen prerevolutionary and fifteen postrevolutionary Cuban novels, was randomly chosen from the total list of eligible novels in each period.

Table 2 shows that there was a slight increase in the percentage of female characters, from 26.5 percent in prerevolutionary novels to 32.8 percent in the postrevolutionary sample. This difference was not found to be significant at the usual levels (CR = .50, df = 513, n.s.). Thus the hypothesis was not supported by the data. In other words, females are seriously underrepresented in fiction, when compared to the female proportion of the total population in the last prerevolutionary census. This underrepresentation is equally severe between pre- and postrevolutionary novels, with the overall ratio of male to female characters being 2.4:1. (The actual ratio in the Cuban population in the 1953 census was roughly 1.2:1.)

Thus, although similar hypotheses concerning lower-class representation and black representation in the novels did find empirical support, there does not seem to be a difference between pre- and postrevolutionary samples concerning the representation of females.

32 : LOURDES CASAL

TABLE 2
Male and Female Characters in Thirty Cuban Novels, 1950–1967

	Male		Female		
	N	%	N	%	Total
Prerevolutionary novels (1950–1958)	709	73.5	255	26.5	964
Postrevolutionary novels (1959–1967)	532	67.2	260	32.8	792
Total	1,241	70.7	515	29.3	1,756

Note: The sample included fifteen prerevolutionary and fifteen postrevolutionary novels, randomly drawn from the total list of eligible novels in each period.

Furthermore, it was hypothesized that female representation among characters with leading or important roles should also increase in postrevolutionary novels as compared with prerevolutionary ones. To test this hypothesis, the percentage of female representation among characters with leading or important roles was estimated. Importance of characters was indicated by their presence in plot summaries generated by the author and her reader-informants after reading each novel.[10] Percentages of women and men among the important characters were computed and average percentages for pre- and postrevolutionary novels were obtained. Results are summarized in table 3.

Table 3 indicates that female representation among important characters did not increase after the Revolution, as had been hypothesized. Actually, there was a small, nonsignificant, decrease in the average percentage of females among important characters, from 36.0 percent to 32.0 percent.

The failure of female representation to increase, whether among all characters or among important characters in particular, may have been due to a number of possible factors: the saliency of female equality as

TABLE 3
"Important" Characters in Thirty Cuban Novels, 1950–1967

	Average N	% Male	% Female
Prerevolutionary novels (1950–1958)	7.9	65.3	36.0
Postrevolutionary novels (1959–1967)	8.1	68.0	32.0

Note: The sample included fifteen prerevolutionary and fifteen postrevolutionary novels, randomly drawn from the total list of eligible novels in each period. Percentages are averages.

a revolutionary goal may have been lower than other aspects of the revolutionary program, at least for a group of overwhelmingly male authors—93 percent; the priority given to the cause of women during the early years of the Revolution may have been rather low, at least as compared to the importance of other status differences such as those based on class or race. Those were years of heightened class conflict and the energies of the revolutionary leadership were concentrated on carrying out basic changes in the structure of property and in the organization of production and the state apparatus. Postrevolutionary changes in female role and status have been slow and until fairly recently have mostly concentrated on the incorporation of women in the labor force, with positive but not earth-shaking results.

However, going back to the original hypotheses, there is some indication that analysis at the level of women as a group may be obscuring certain sectoral changes. Although females tend to be underrepresented in novels from both the pre- and postrevolutionary samples, this underrepresentation is less for the black female group than for the white female group for both samples. Table 4 indicates that black females represent a higher proportion of all females in the postrevolutionary sample, this value being the closest to the actual representation of blacks in the Cuban population according to the 1953 census.

Women's Occupations

In order to study the extent of sex-role stereotyping present in the novels, lists were prepared of all the different occupations in which

TABLE 4
Sex and Race of Characters in Thirty Cuban Novels, 1950–1967

	\multicolumn{5}{c}{Male}
	N	% Black	N	% White	Total
Prerevolutionary novels (1950–1958)	58	8.2	645	91.0	709[a]
Postrevolutionary novels (1959–1967)	91	17.1	428	80.4	532[b]
	\multicolumn{5}{c}{Female}
Prerevolutionary novels (1950–1958)	35	14.9	217	85.1	255
Postrevolutionary novels (1959–1967)	55	21.2	205	78.8	260

Note: The sample included fifteen prerevolutionary and fifteen postrevolutionary novels, randomly drawn from the total list of eligible novels in each period.
    a. Includes 6 Chinese.
    b. Includes 13 Chinese.

members of each of the four sex-race groups are depicted as engaged. It was found that white and black females were at a definite disadvantage as compared with the corresponding male groups in terms of the variety of occupations which were seen as available to them. Black females, in particular, being under the impact of double stereotyping (and, in reality, double discrimination) were the most restricted.

Table 5 presents an occupational and racial breakdown of females in the novels that will add further details to the material previously discussed. (The table excludes children and students.) White females are largely concentrated in the category of housewives. Still, even for white females in the novels, the percentage of women in the labor force is much higher than the average level of females actually in the labor force, which, in 1953, was less than 15 percent. It is interesting to note that the novels tend to overrepresent working women. It is possible that in these counts of total number of characters, more working women are included than actually are in the labor force because they are the ones more likely to enter into functional contacts with the dominant men, in the realm of "the street," while females in "the house" are highly invisible, unless they are members of the families of the male characters. The largest category of employment for both white and black females is in the area of service, although actual black female representation in the service field is three times the white representation. The second largest category of employment is in prostitution, accounting for roughly one out of ten women in the novels. Clerical and sales jobs seem to have been closed to black females in the novels, while, not surprisingly, more black than white females are included in the category of Afro-Cuban religion priestess (*santera*), spiritualist, healer.

Although nearly 5 percent of all females are listed as professionals, it must be pointed out that in the novels (as well as in reality), most female professionals are teachers—especially grade school teachers—or are engaged in other professional activity considered suitable for females (such as social work). Not one woman in the novels is a physician or a lawyer; none of them is in a situation in which she might give orders to males, except for male servants. All of the women who appear as managers or proprietors are in charge of very small or marginal businesses (such as a food delivery service, a small rooming house).

In summary, an analysis of the occupations of females in the novels shows a very restricted range of employment possibilities, and a predominance of lower-status occupations, especially among black females. A large proportion of women—especially white women—seem to be engaged in activities (keeping house or prostitution) mostly di-

TABLE 5
Occupations of Black and White Women in Thirty Cuban Novels, 1950–1967

	White N	White %	Black N	Black %
Managers and proprietors	7	1.9	1	1.1
Professionals	17	4.6	4	4.5
Paraprofessionals	0	—	1	1.1
Clerical and sales workers	18	4.9	0	—
Skilled or semiskilled workers	5	1.4	2	2.3
Agricultural workers	10	2.7	2	2.3
"Santeros," spiritualists, healers	3	.8	5	5.7
Service workers	40	10.9	30	34.1
Personal	39	10.6	28	31.8
Protective	0	—	0	—
Other	1	.3	2	2.3
Entertainers	3	.8	0	—
Prostitutes[a]	29	7.9	9	10.2
Unemployed workers	1	.3	1	1.1
Workers in other occupations	4	1.1	0	—
Workers in unspecified categories	62	16.8	19	21.6
Housewives[b]	170	46.1	14	15.9
Total	369	100.1	88	99.9

Note: The sample included fifteen prerevolutionary and fifteen postrevolutionary novels, randomly drawn from the total list of eligible novels in each period.
 a. Includes related activities.
 b. Includes kept women.

rected toward serving men's needs. Black women are presented as being incorporated into the labor force in much larger proportion than white women.

Image of Women in the Novels

Many aspects of the image of women that appear in novels are so close to common conceptions of the female role in other cultures that they will be dealt with only briefly here. (See table 1 for fuller bibliographical information.)

Females are commonly seen as under male tutelage (first fathers, then husbands), and they are considered explicitly or implicitly to be their husbands' property (Iznaga, 1952, p. 28; Feijóo, 1964, p. 83; Serpa, 1956, p. 15). Females *must* marry, since it is considered that a woman without a man is somehow incomplete and in a state of prolonged childhood and dependency; thus unmarried women in their thirties and forties may still be called "muchachitas," literally, "young girls" (Gómez, 1951, p. 38).

Once married, a woman is seen primarily as taking care of her husband's needs and, of course, those of her children. "The cardinal points" of a woman's life are husband, children, home (Perera, 1960, p. 122). Detailed descriptions of female activities are frequently provided throughout the novels: washing clothes, taking care of children (Iznaga, 1953, p. 122), sewing, cleaning the house (Labrador Ruiz, 1950, p. 108), washing dishes, making beds (Feijóo, 1964, p. 230), sewing, preparing food (Ortega, 1957, p. 63). Upper-class females and many middle-class females, instead of performing all these activities themselves, are described primarily as supervising the servants in performing them. If there are servants, the woman of the house is in charge of handling them, from hiring to firing to day-to-day supervision (cf. Perera, 1960).

The husband's needs take primacy over the wife's needs. Cuban women are described by the protagonist-narrator of *Memorias del subdesarrollo* (Desnoes, 1965) as "raised to please men as geese are raised to make foie gras" (p. 114). If there is a conflict between a woman's needs and her husband's, there is no question as to which should take precedence.

Thus Teresa, one of the protagonists of *Juan Quinquín en pueblo mocho* (Feijóo, 1964), renounces gratification of her need for friendship and companionship for the sake of her husband: "She was alone most of the time, almost the whole day. . . . At times she remained silent, tired, as if saddened by a remote pain. She wanted to see her father. . . . She needed a friend. . . . And then she laughed and thought 'I'm crazy; this is my world, right here in the mountains, next to Juan' " (pp. 80–81).

If there is a conflict about who could pursue advanced studies, again there is no question. The narrator of *La trampa* (Serpa, 1956) describes the role of the hero's wife: "He had counted on having María Teresa by his side; her support, her enthusiasm, even the smile with which she had resigned herself not to complete Philosophy and Letters, which was the doctorate to which she was attracted, to help him with his Law career" (p. 153).

Females are not supposed to become involved in politics; politics—even student politics—is considered a male preserve. For example, Clara, one of the characters in *Una de cal y otra de arena* (Ortega, 1957) is allowed to attend a meeting of the student leaders at her high school: "This was a new experience for her because, although she was usually aware of what was going on at the Students' Association, she had never participated in any of its activities" (p. 67). Even at this point, her participation is very limited indeed—nothing more than a tolerated spectator. When the strike finally comes, only males take over the high school building, and Clara's role is that of bringing food to the strikers.

The political and social position of women, as portrayed in fiction, is firmly rooted in historical realities. During the struggle against the Machado dictatorship in 1933, women from the middle and upper classes became involved in the revolutionary struggle by themselves or through their boyfriends (as illustrated in Ferrer, 1952; Serpa, 1956; Ortega, 1957). Women, when engaged in such activities, were nevertheless "protected by the males who insisted on keeping them away from the most risky tasks" (for example, Serpa, 1956, p. 129). Even in the anti-Batista struggle, a quarter of a century later, most of the women who helped in the underground were still in charge of "feminine" activities such as sewing flags and obtaining medicines. (But not all. Many women became active fighters in the rebel army. One of the protagonists of *El derrumbe* [Soler Puig, 1964] joins the rebels.)

However, the possibility of female involvement in politics, at any level, was seen as a departure from the feminine norm. Or, as one of the characters in *La trampa* (Serpa, 1956) phrases it, "He was happy that his daughter behaved as she did and not as any of those girls who are like tomboys, always talking idiocies and discussing social problems. . . . No, he had never liked, although he disguised it, to see women mixed up in politics, and even less in so-called revolutionary conflicts or afflicted with the Communist rash. Not even during the struggle against Machado" (p. 60).

To be active "in the street" was definitely against the norm: it was dangerous mostly because it could lead to gossip about the woman and perhaps to the loss of virginity. Virginity was seen as a prerequisite for upper- and middle-class marriages. At times, virginity is referred to in fiction as a marketable commodity. For example, it is because of Clara's steadfast refusal to give in to Machín's enticements, in *Una mujer y tres espejos* (Patiño Hernández, 1957) that she is rewarded with marriage (p. 190). Since virginity was extremely prized by men, for a lower-class woman it might be the only bargaining instrument she had to offer in exchange for marriage or at least care (see the story of Yolanda in *El derrumbe,* Soler Puig, 1964). If a lower-class woman lost her virginity, she was left resourceless; and she may have been forced to resort to prostitution or some covert form of it (or some job as a servant which was frequently the first step toward prostitution). For example, Lydia, a young lower-class female in *La búsqueda* (Sarusky,

1962) "had been raised by her parents in the cult of purity. . . . Virginity, sooner or later, is as much of an asset as a life insurance policy. . . . He would be able to breathe in peace the day he saw her going away married to an orderly, respectable, wealthy gentleman" (p. 55).

Among upper- and middle-class females, the preservation of virginity seems to have been tied to the concept of family "honor." The cultural code demanded "purity" during courtship, since the woman was expected to come to marriage as a virgin. Purity refers to the preservation of virginity; this did not prevent upper-class females from becoming specialists in the art of flirting and even of sexual teasing. There are many references to this pattern in *La situación* (Otero, 1963, p. 62). The latter behavior, although frequently described, was in direct contradiction to the image of the idealized female which was held as a cultural standard for upper-class females.

The "Idealized Female"

The image of the ideal woman, the model of femininity, described here is frequently found in the novels as an element in the sexual ideology of the middle and upper classes. Females are seen as somehow different and superior to men; they are purer, "cleaner," somehow not afflicted by the male's baser impulses (Labrador Ruiz, 1950, pp. 47–48). Females are fragile, and therefore worthy of special consideration (Feijóo, 1964, p. 58; Serpa, 1956, p. 103). Females are also more sensitive than men, being "pure souls" (Espinosa, 1955, p. 124). Females are easily frightened, they are weak and need the protection of men. For example, a female character in *No hay problema* (Desnoes, 1961) "pretended to be scared of insects to prove that she was feminine" (p. 156).

Indeed, the ideal female was supposed to be unconcerned with sex. Fear of sex was fostered in the upper- and middle-class females by all socializing agents from overprotective parents to the religious school. Thus a woman raised by nuns in *La trampa* (Serpa, 1956) is described as follows: "Lina reached adolescence with a deep aversion to anything sexual. . . . She judged that sexual relations were a sacrifice imposed on women by marriage and in the last analysis, a sin which can only be redeemed through maternity" (pp. 144–45).

This lack of interest in, or aversion to, sex by the "ideal female" led to a peculiar paradox in a sex-obsessed culture, whose machos measured their own value by their sexual prowess: the ideal woman was good for a wife, but not for pleasure. Or in the words of a middle-class character in *El descanso* (Piñeiro, 1962): "He had selected her to build a family, take care of the house, have children. For pleasure's . . . . sake you need some other kind of woman, who is not good for a wife" (p. 81).

This model of feminity did not apply to lower-class women: they were let loose by their families (Desnoes, 1965, p. 25); they could be "very lustful" (Ortega, 1957, p. 77); they had a lively sexuality and did not pretend to be "ladies" (Desnoes, 1961, p. 66), that is to say, they did not attempt to conform to the image of the ideal female we have been describing.

In view of the evidence reviewed in the novels, it is the tentative position taken here that the idealized views of the female that have been frequently presented as characteristic of the Iberian culture in general, and of the Cuban women in particular, must be considered as part of upper-class ideology. In fiction, it is the female of the upper and middle strata who is supposed to conform to the image of the ideal female.

The Macho

A discussion of the female image in Cuban novels, and especially of the ideal female, would not be complete without describing the image of the macho, Cuban version. In a sense, the image of the ideal female is the counterpart of the macho, its "negative," and therefore the two should be considered simultaneously, for the light that one can throw on the other. The image of the macho is taken here as the image of the ideal male, of what a really masculine man should be and do.

The macho is physically strong and courageous, worthy of his male attributes, quite literally, his genitalia. Thus, a lower-class father in *Los Valedontes* (Ignaza, 1953) who has just forced his son to swim naked in the river, explains to a friend: "Let him learn to be a *macho* as he grabbed his genitals with both hands, as if to give extra emphasis to his words" (p. 104). The true macho can face dangers without flinching, he is not afraid of perils, he is "hard." For example, a character in *Una de cal y otra de arena* (Ortega, 1957) describes a "true man" to a friend: "He was a true man! . . . Do you remember . . . when the police had us trapped . . . and we cleared our way through with our guns? I have never met anybody so cool" (p. 64). Or, in *El derrumbe* (Soler Puig, 1964) a father shames his son who is afraid of thunderstorms: "Coward, aren't you ashamed? you are already thirteen years old, you are already a man. And still afraid of a thunderstorm. You are a little woman!" (p. 39). Or as another character in *El derrumbe* phrases it: "To be a man is very hard, you must assert yourself, turn hard . . . live among beasts and like a beast" (p. 75).

The true macho sees engaging in any "female" activity as demeaning (Iznaga, 1953, p. 126). "Female" activities range from household duties to haggling; but by extension *machos* may not be tender or sensitive, may not write verses (Desnoes, 1961, p. 42).

What characterizes the macho above all else is his sexual power and how he conveys this to women. A true macho uses as many women as he has occasion to (Feijóo, 1964, p. 209), but he feels obliged to look at women provocatively in the streets, to whistle at them, to praise them ("piropear"), as he must prove his machismo (Desnoes, 1961, p. 141). If he is close to a woman, he must make advances; for example, "He attempted to kiss her so that she wouldn't be disappointed; he had to do it, so that the woman would know that she had a man by her side" (Soler Puig, 1964, p. 97).

The true macho can reach women sexually, even those who because of their profession (prostitutes) can be expected to be insensitive. For example, "That afternoon, he was more macho than ever, a true savage, Patricia became wild" (Soler Puig, 1964, p. 95). As opposed to the many constraints operating on females who are expected to remain at home until married, males are considered free, that is, they can pack up and roam the world if they wish (Labrador Ruiz, 1950, p. 52).

True machos do not accept quietly any challenge to their machismo. Thus in *La trampa* (Serpa, 1956), the leader of an action group suggests that a young member of the group should not participate because he was too "green"; the young man becomes extremely upset: "Bebo . . . screamed that he was as *macho* as anybody and that he was willing to demonstrate it at any time, in any way" (p. 107).

Machos respect one another and there seem to be definite rules governing macho interactions. For example, the macho gives his enemy a fair chance, defeats him honestly: "Men do not do that, they do not hit a defenseless enemy" (Feijóo, 1964, p. 260); machos are also expected to respect each other's women. However, the latter norm conflicts with the unrestricted exercise of his right (even duty) to conquer women. When these two norms collide, the latter seems to take precedence, for to be macho is to have power and one dimension of such power is to be able to possess any woman that the macho may really like (Feijóo, 1964, p. 209).

It seems likely that the rules governing macho interactions are remnants, residues of the code of chivalry from other times and other places. The operation of this code presupposes that two males dealing with each other are equals. Social class differences seem to invalidate the norm of mutual respect, and thus the right to conquer and to exert power takes precedence.

If the ideal female is all soul, the macho is all body. "They have the devil below their waist!" a common phrase goes. If the "ideal" female is all sensitivity and intuition, the macho is insensitive and tactless (Perera, 1960, pp. 16, 125). He is rational, objective, and tough, and to the ideal female's prolonged (almost perpetual) irresponsibility and dependency, we must contrast the image of the male as the responsible moral agent who must think, make choices, protect the women and take care of them.

It need not be emphasized here that in practice the macho was seen as having full rights to pursue women, regardless of his own marital status. A husband's adventures were not supposed to *harm* anybody (Arenal, 1967, p. 107). A wife's adventures would be intolerable because they harmed her husband's standing: being a cuckold was the worst of fates for a macho. Note that the double standard operated before marriage, during marriage, and after marriage: males not only were permitted to, but *had* to, engage in premarital sexual activities, while at least upper- and middle-class women were not expected to; males were allowed extramarital affairs, but women were not; and finally, even remarriage (after death of the husband) among upper- and middle-class women was somewhat frowned upon.

The macho ideology placed a high premium on being able to take a woman's virginity. At least one of the novels in the sample indicates that, at times, lower-class women were selected as sexual objects by upper-class men when they were practically children; the men waited until they had reached an appropriate age to enjoy the privilege of despoiling their virginity.

In *El derrumbe* (Soler Puig, 1964) Doña Margarita's virginity had been taken by the count at age fifteen after he had raised her and taken care of her family since she was ten years old (p. 25). Later on in the same novel, Lorenzo, the protagonist, attempts a similar strategy with Yolanda, a young lower-class girl, whom he raises and supports with her mother's acquiescence, so that she will become his mistress when she comes of age. However, Yolanda rejects Lorenzo's advances and goes on to become a revolutionary. Taking a virgin was a matter of pride, something a macho could use to show off among other males (p. 97).

Given the importance of virginity at all social levels, and the simultaneous emphasis in the macho ideology on a man's being sexually experienced from adolescence, most sexual encounters of young unmarried males took place in the whorehouse or, in the case of upper- or middle-class males, with some willing (or not so willing) servant. A young man's first visit to a whorehouse is a very common scene in Cuban novels: an image which must have haunted our male novelists because of its impact, and its character of rite of passage. Usually, when a young man was thought to be of age (around fifteen years), he was taken to a whorehouse by an older male figure (frequently his father or an uncle). This was an important male ritual, described in great detail in many Cuban novels and short stories (Ortega, 1957, p. 60; Soler Puig, 1964, p. 73).

Another component of the macho cluster of associated values was the strong rejection of male homosexuality and the virtual denial of the existence of female homosexuality. No less than fourteen references to male homosexuality (including two full-fledged episodes) appear in the sample of novels, while there are only two rather subtle mentions of female homosexuality.

Attitudes toward male homosexuals were usually very negative. To launch an accusation of homosexuality against a political enemy was one of the most terrible insults (Serpa, 1956, p. 94). To call a man a queer was a way of calling him a woman, a direct attack on his masculinity, on his value as macho. It was a way of calling him weak and unworthy of holding power. Rejection of homosexuality led to rejection of anything soft, feminine, in men's fashions; for example, "He didn't like the new fashion of uncreased pants, they seemed to him somewhat effeminate" (Arcocha, 1962, p. 177).

Power was strongly associated with masculinity: a macho did not take orders from a woman; he refused to acknowledge or respect women in positions of power. For example, Lucas, one of the black newspaper sellers whom Romelia indoctrinates as a Communist party activist, refuses to accept Romelia's role as a leader and challenges her in a most direct and *machista* way, by raping her, subjecting her by force to his will. In his words, "I am a man and you are a woman. . . . You are not my boss, you are a woman, and I am hungry for a woman" (Ferrer, 1952, p. 87).

Even minor symbolic threats to his masculinity, coming from an assertive female, upset the macho very much. One typical male prerogative—duty and right—was to light a woman's cigarette. A character in *Los muertos andan solos* (Arcocha, 1962) becomes upset at a violation of this norm. "He felt upset. He had never seen such a thing: a woman offering a light to a man, instead of waiting for him to offer it" (p. 177).

Finally, machos wanted to keep "their" women *in* the house, away from "la calle" (the street) where they could meet other men. Therefore upper- and middle-class men and even workers who could afford it, tried to prevent women from working (Soler Puig, 1963, p. 165). Besides "protecting" women from other men, keeping them at home insured their financial dependence on the male, and ultimately their subservience.

Female Stereotypes: Breakdowns and Rejections

Rejections of the stereotypical role or protest against various aspects of female oppression are very frequent in our sample of novels: Household tasks are described as boring (Labrador Ruiz, 1950, p. 108); women complain about being treated as sexual objects (Arenal, 1967, p. 93); prostitutes occasionally refuse to pay the pimp (Granados, 1967, p. 195); the tasks of motherhood are described as exhausting (Arenal, 1967, p. 18); women complain frequently about boredom (Perera, 1960, p. 111).

Very frequently, strong women who openly reject the traditional female role in words and action appear in the novels. For example, Rosa, the protagonist of *Los muertos andan solos* (Arcocha, 1962) says: "All men are the same. They like to treat us women as if we were trash. To cook their meals, to keep their clothes clean, to take care of the children, to become women of the house. Ah, and above all, women shouldn't have any intelligence or personality, so that men can feel superior to them!" (p. 78).

Middle-class and upper-class women frequently wish or fantasize themselves in different roles. As a very articulate heroine in *Los animales sagrados* (Arenal, 1967, p. 18) phrases it:

Even as a child, she didn't like to play house. Even then, she fancied herself in more important tasks. For a long time, her heroes were Madame Curie and Johnny Weissmuller, the good, strong and silly Tarzan. . . . And afterwards, when she started on more serious reading, the seamen and Alaska gold seekers of Jack London, or the workers, soldiers, and bohemians of Hemingway. And even after, Colette and Simone de Beauvoir and Katherine Mansfield and Carson McCullers. Always strong, far away people, always independent, tortured people. Never housewives. Her mother, who had raised seven children after the father ran away. Or her aunt Emma, waiting fifteen years for a boy friend who never returned from the U.S. Or her sisters, collecting wrinkles, white hairs, and offenses. For all of them, she felt great sympathy but she was not willing, she absolutely never was, to share their destiny.

Women described explicitly as feminists appear in a few novels (Labrador Ruiz, 1950, p. 10; Leante, 1967, p. 89) although not in leading roles. However, characters who deviate clearly and explicitly from the female norm have important roles in many of the novels. In *Lucha de razas* (Boullón, 1957) we find Rosaura described as "a modern type, she smoked, drank, lived alone with an old aunt; . . . in her house she always has meetings with intellectuals; they spoke of everything, without any limitation; she laughed at traditional morality" (p. 17). According to her antistereotypical image, Rosaura *worked*—she was a teacher and Director of Academic Affairs at Felipe's Academy—and she *never married*. The heroine of *Ritmo de juventud* (Patiño Hernández, 1957) is an upper-class female who "contrived the plan of going out to work, to demonstrate, if necessary, that she was capable of earning a living, of being more than a doll, more than a little society girl, an heiress, a princess" (p. 65).

The Strong, Problem-Solving Female

The strong, problem-solving female appears occasionally in the novels, reflecting an undeniable cultural reality. In the lower and middle sectors of society, it was not a rare occurrence to find a woman who was either abandoned by her husband—like, for instance, Sara's mother in *Los animales sagrados* (Arenal, 1967)—or pushed into the role of head of household—such as Estefania's mother in *La sangre hambrienta* (Labrador Ruiz, 1950) by some other combination of factors—and became a strong, active character who managed to earn a living for herself and her children. Other examples are Juana la Isleña and her four cane-cutter daughters in *Los Valedontes* (Iznaga, 1953) and Paco Iznaga's mother in *Una de cal y otra de arena* (Ortega, 1957), who keeps the family alive after her husband loses his job and who is the problem solver and decision maker in the family.

The most extreme deviants from the female norm are frequently criticized and ridiculed in these novels; thus the "mujer hombruna" (masculine woman) in *Los Valedontes* was rejected in the small town (p. 94); the feminist in *La sangre hambrienta* is described as "ugly" and foul-mouthed (p. 10); a highly independent young female in *Una de cal y otra de arena* is accused of being power-hungry and manipulative (p. 120).

Women who defy society's taboos are criticized. For example, there is a strong taboo against unmarried females moving away from the family. Susana, a character in *Los animales sagrados,* who defies the prohibition, is ostracized by her family and subjected to gossip. She recounts her experiences: "When I decided to move away, the whole family devoted itself to watching me day and night, especially my father. By now everybody agrees that I am some sort of a prostitute.

My father does not even come to my house. With my sisters, he gets along fine, they are normal, you know?" (p. 68).

In spite of the threat of punishment for deviations from the norm, many significant nonstereotypical female heroines in the novels are presented in a highly positive light. For example, the only novel written by a woman in the postrevolutionary sample, *Mañana es 26* (Perera, 1960) gives us one of the most fully developed feminine characters in the postrevolutionary Cuban novel. Teresa is an upper-class woman living in Havana on the eve of the Revolution. She is, in a sense, one of the two protagonists of this novel. From the self-centered upper-class woman she was at the beginning, she evolves toward a more committed existence, open to social and political conflicts, willing to become involved and active in the world beyond the confines of the home.

Women play a very vital role in *Ritmo de juventud* (Patiño Hernández, 1957). It is an upper-class woman, Alicia Reyes, who, under the assumed identity of Rosa Espinosa, challenges her prescribed role and looks for a job (thus setting in motion the basic dramatic episode). Lower-class women, although they only appear fleetingly in this novel, are strong, looking for security and satisfaction while simultaneously trying to fend off predatory or potentially predatory men.

Los animales sagrados (Arenal, 1967) centers on the interpersonal conflicts of a disgruntled middle-class white male and the women with whom he tries to communicate. Susana, his mistress, and Sara, his wife, are two extremely interesting female figures who reject in fundamental ways the stereotypical roles assigned to middle-class females. Sara is deeply dissatisfied with the limitations that being a housewife and a mother impose on her: she would like to live an active life, in the world, like her literary heroes and their creators. She sees her life squandered between a husband who only approaches her for sex and her children, who represent another tiring chore, instead of enjoyment. Sara refuses to accept her husband's infidelity and the traditional double standard; she forces him to move out upon learning about his mistress. Susana is an unmarried woman living away from her parents, in search of an elusive meaningful relationship with a man (yet her style of life categorizes her as a semiprostitute to whom males do not even want to talk after a sexual encounter). She is also seeking to erase a series of traumatic experiences in her youth in which she was the victim of class oppression as a scholarship student in a convent school and further humiliated by being accused of making homosexual advances to a rich girl who actually had approached her.

The novel is definitely a "middle-class" novel. Its careful scrutiny of interpersonal relationships and the sophisticated females who so hopelessly deplore their role (still remaining powerless to change it) is definitely class-linked.

Women appear frequently and in significant roles in *Memorias del subdesarrollo* (Desnoes, 1965). Although Sergio's attitudes and behavior toward them remain, in general, quite "machista," his own life is presided over by the women to whom he relates (or does not relate), and a significant complexity and degree of conflict are displayed, revealing cracks in the most traditional role conceptions.

He uses women of the lower classes, or fantasizes about using them. Sergio enters into exploitative relations with them, which he feels free to drop at his convenience. He does not seem to recognize the woman's autonomy. Thus, regarding a middle-class divorcee with whom he had once had an affair, and who has now become a committed revolutionary, Sergio can only explain her revolutionary enthusiasm in terms of a reaction to his rejection (p. 42). On the other hand, he feels exploited by his own wife because he has to support her but especially because she proves resistant to his Pygmalionlike ambition of transforming women into his own image of them (p. 21). Hanna, the daughter of Jewish immigrants who came to Cuba during the Second World War, represents for Sergio the ideal woman, liberated and liberating, who can relate to him as an equal, who could have truly become his companion. Not daring to break with his family and their class-linked expectations (to run a business, make money, and marry the right woman) Sergio misses this opportunity, although he later insists upon finding this lost ideal woman in all the new women he meets.

Changes After the Revolution

The few novels in our sample which deal specifically with postrevolutionary transformations depict significant changes in female status and role, even when they deal only with the first few years after the Revolution. Felipe Montemayor, one of the upper-class protagonists of *En el año de enero* (Soler Puig, 1963), bitterly complains that Fidel Castro has upset women's traditional roles: "The Citizens' happiness is something sacred which rulers must respect, and women contribute a lot to that happiness; you have taken them away from the tasks appropriate to their sex . . . which are precisely the tasks of sex" (p. 38). His distress is caused by the fact that his mistress, formerly devoted to his pleasure, starts to become politicized by watching Castro's speeches on television, then falls in love with a rebel officer, and decides to start working.

A leading character in *El derrumbe* (Soler Puig, 1964) is Yolanda, who became a rebel soldier in the Sierra Maestra: after being very active in the underground, she returns as an army officer, definitely a new female role. Cira, one of the leading characters of *Adire y el tiempo roto* (Granados, 1967), had been a prostitute in Havana at the time of the triumph of the Revolution. She is sent to a rehabilitation center where she learns office skills. After completing her training, she is given a job as a bank employee in a different town, where she can get a fresh start. Thus, *Adire y el tiempo roto* reflects one of the earlier campaigns concerning female status undertaken by the Revolution: abolishing houses of prostitution in major cities and, for once, imprisoning the pimps and not the prostitutes. The prostitutes were sent to rehabilitation centers where they received training in sewing and clerical and other skills.

Conclusions

Females in prerevolutionary Cuba had made marked progress in terms of legal equality, but there were significant differences in practically all other indicators: very limited incorporation into the labor force, overrepresentation in low-income, low-status jobs, and underrepresentation in the high-status occupational categories. The ideal cultural norm placed the woman in the house; strict division of labor and realm of activities (men in "la calle," women in "la casa") seemed to be enforced; virginity had a high social value and a double standard of sexual morality was by and large enforced.

Considerable controversy exists about the changes brought about by the Revolution with respect to the status of blacks and the extent of racial discrimination and prejudice in post-1959 Cuba. Consensus seems to exist on a number of points: institutionalized racism has been wiped out, blacks have benefited from the revolutionary program, which gave priority to meeting the needs of the lower strata of the population, which are disproportionately black. However, prejudice has not been universally eradicated, and while certain black-white differences in education and employment are being narrowed, they will probably not be entirely eliminated for a number of years.

Significant changes in the structure and level of female employment and in the participation of women in collective activities have also been achieved. Changes in the legal system have given new emphasis and dimension to female rights, establishing absolute equality of men and women within the family. Changes in attitudes are more difficult to assess, given the lack of empirical studies. The present picture can best be described as transitional.

An analysis of the various terms employed in the novels to indicate social class position revealed that terms referring to the upper sectors are most numerous, with terms referring to the lower sectors ranking second, and those referring to the middle class a poor third. This suggests the prevalence of a dichotomous conceptualization of the social class structure. However, middle-class location terms are present. Besides, the middle sectors are frequently alluded to without employing a specific term. A trichotomous view of the social class structure is consistent with the data. The picture of the class structure in the novels seems highly complex: it suggests the coexistence in the social consciousness of various conceptions, some of them dichotomous but others reflecting extremely detailed gradations, predominantly in terms of wealth, and still others representing synthetic gradations.

A distinction was drawn between norms, values, or attitudes which seem to be shared by members of all social classes and which are, therefore, considered true cultural themes, and those norms, values, or attitudes which seem to characterize a particular social class. Cultural themes identified in Cuban novels are: a deep concern for the family, and high involvement in family relationships; a high value placed on friendship and the fulfillment of the duties required by its system of reciprocal relationships; a belief in the inevitability of class differences, related to a deeper belief in an unequal distribution of abilities or luck; a generalized cynicism and hopelessness; a widespread insecurity mostly financially based, from which not even the rich are totally exempt; a belief in the impossibility of changing U.S.-Cuban relations; and a very high value placed on cleanliness.

A hypothesis that social class consciousness should increase from pre- to postrevolutionary novels was operationalized as follows: an increase in the overall level of explicitly classified characters was predicted when pre- and postrevolutionary novels are compared. The results were statistically significant in the predicted direction.

The hypothesis that postrevolutionary novels, consistent with an egalitarian ideology, should show an increase in the overall level of lower-class representation also found support in the data, as the average percentage of characters classified as lower class increased from 38.0 percent in the prerevolutionary sample to 47.9 percent in the postrevolutionary sample. The hypothesis that the level of lower-class representation among those characters with important roles should rise in postrevolutionary novels was also supported by the data.

The hypothesis that there should be an increase in black representation among the characters in postrevolutionary novels received significant support, as the average percentage of blacks increased from 11.8 to 19 percent. The hypothesis that there should be an increase in black representation among the characters in leading or important roles failed to be supported, although the difference was in the direction predicted.

The novels show marked differences in the occupational distributions of the four basic sex-race groupings: white males, white females, black males, and black females. An analysis of female occupations in the novels shows a high degree of restriction and stereotyping, and a predominance of lower-status occupations, especially among black females, who are also seen as incorporated into the labor force in greater proportion than white females. Females are seen as under male tutelage, in a state of prolonged childhood and dependency on parents until married, when they become dependent on husband and primarily concerned with the needs of husbands and offspring. The idealized female is seen as a counterpart of the macho ideal and primarily an upper- and middle-class role model. Yet there are frequent indications in the novels of breakdowns and rejections of the female stereotype among upper- and middle-class women. The novels document significant changes in female status and role after the Revolution: the politicization of women, their incorporation into the labor force, and the rehabilitation of highly oppressed female groups such as prostitutes.

On the other hand, the hypothesis that there would be an increase in the number of females among the characters in postrevolutionary novels fails to be supported by the data for females in general, although it was true for black females. Women are seriously underrepresented in the novels when these are compared with census data. The overall ratio of male to female characters for all novels combined was 2.4:1 (while the actual male to female ratio in the population as of 1953 was roughly 1.2:1). The hypothesis that there should be an increase in females among the characters in important or leading roles was also not supported by the data.

The failure to confirm the hypothesis concerning increased female importance and visibility in the novels, while similar hypotheses concerning other oppressed groups (lower-class women, blacks) did obtain significant support from the data, raises an interesting problem. A hypothesis advanced to explain this lack of congruency is based on the lower priority given to female equality vis-à-vis abolition of class differences or racial discrimination during the early years of the Revolution.

NOTES

1. S. Ossowski, *Class Structure in the Social Consciousness* (New York: Free Press, 1963), pp. 6–7.
2. M. C. Albrecht, "The Relationship of Literature and Society," *American Journal of Sociology* 59 (1954), 425–36.
3. See M. C. Albrecht, J. H. Barnett, and M. Griff, eds., *The Sociology of Art and Literature* (New York: Praeger, 1970); H. L. Nostrand, "Literature in the Describing of a Literate Culture," in ibid.
4. G. Bitsztray, "Literary Sociology and Marxist Theory: The Literary Work as a Social Document," *Mosaic* 2 (1972), 47–56.
5. For an analysis of mass mobilization and its role in changing Cuba's political culture, see Finlay, O. Holsti and R. Fagen, *Enemies in Politics* (Chicago: Rand McNally, 1967), pp. 184–231; and R. Fagen, *The Transformation of Political Culture in Cuba* (Stanford, Calif.: Stanford University Press, 1969).
6. Bitsztray, "Literary Sociology and Marxist Theory," p. 49.
7. For a discussion of the possibilities and limitations of the social analysis of literature, see C. Graña, "El análisis social de la literatura: posibilidades y limitaciones," *Revista de Ciencias Sociales* 6 (1962), 215–38. Two significant early attempts at the use of quantification in this area are M. C. Albrecht, "Does Literature Reflect Common Values?" *American Sociological Review* 21 (1956), 722–29; R. Inglis, "An Objective Approach to the Relationship between Fiction and Society," *American Sociological Review* 3 (1938), 526–31. See also A. Pescatello, ed., *Female and Male in Latin America* (Pittsburgh, Pa.: University of Pittsburgh Press, 1973, esp. C. B. Flora, "The Passive Female and Social Change: A Cross Cultural Comparison of Women's Magazine Fiction."
8. F. Peraza, *Bibliografía Cubana,* 1950–1965 (Gainesville: University of Florida Press, 1967); R. N. Abella, "Bibliografía de la novela publicada en Cuba, y en el extranjero por Cubanos, desde 1959 hasta 1965," *Revista Iberoamericana* 30 (1966), 307–11; J. C. Sánchez, "Bibliografía de la novela cubana," *Islas* 3 (September–December 1960), 321–56; Lourdes Casal, "La Novela en Cuba 1959–1967: Una Introducción," *Exilio* 11–13 (1970), 184–217, and "A Bibliography of Cuban Creative Literature: 1958–1971," *Cuban Studies Newsletter* 2 (June 1972), 2–29.
9. In our sample of postrevolutionary novels, only six novels (Arcocha, 1962; Desnoes, 1965; Soler Puig, 1963 and 1964; Perera, 1960; and Granados, 1967) deal with post-1959 events, and even these are limited to the first few years after the triumph of the Revolution. Thus, although some of them deal with the different reactions of various social strata to the Revolution, most of these novels depict prerevolutionary social class structure, or prerevolutionary social class structure in the throes of transition. This fact makes *all* the novels in the sample excellent documents for an analysis of prerevolutionary class structure. On the other hand, postrevolutionary novels, regardless of whether they deal with pre- or postrevolutionary society, should reflect revolutionary values, especially as embodied in the different emphasis given to various social strata and viewpoints.
10. Readings of the novels produced the following: (a) specific information about every character present or described in each novel, summarized on a data sheet; (b) a plot summary of approximately 300 words; (c) a list of all terms explicitly employed in the novels to refer to ethnic or racial groups.

MARIFELI PÉREZ-STABLE

Cuban Women and the Struggle for "Conciencia"

ABSTRACT

Since 1959, women in Cuba have attained a notable presence in their society. Structural constraints and cultural values continue to limit both the actual achievements in reducing inequality between the sexes and the ways in which the struggle for full equality are conceptualized. The absence of a grass-roots women's movement and an autonomous organization, however, has not precluded important inroads in widening the representation of women in leadership positions nor an often dynamic Federation of Cuban Women (FMC). Whether these inroads and dynamism actually constitute (relative) power depends, in part, on how and whether greater resources are allotted to satisfy women's particular material needs. Women's own "conciencia" and bottom-up pressures may well prove to be crucial.

RESUMEN

Desde 1959, las mujeres en Cuba han alcanzado una presencia notable en la sociedad. Las limitaciones estructurales y los valores culturales continúan frenando tanto los logros reales en la reducción de la desigualdad entre los sexos como las maneras en las cuales se conceptualiza la lucha por la igualdad total. Sin embargo, la ausencia de un movimiento femenino de base y de una organización autónoma no ha impedido avances importantes en el aumento de la participación de la mujer en posiciones de liderazgo ni la existencia de una Federación de Mujeres Cubanas (FMC) a menudo dinámica. El que estos avances y dinamismo realmente constituyan poder (relativo) depende, en parte, de si y cómo se destinan mayores recursos a la satisfacción de las necesidades materiales de las mujeres. La propia consciencia femenina y presiones desde abajo de la mujer bien pudieran ser cruciales en este respecto.

Twenty-eight years after the 1959 revolutionary victory, Cuban women have attained a notable presence in their society. Women constitute more than a third of the civilian labor force, have made important advances in traditionally male-dominated occupations, and are slowly assuming leadership positions in the mass organizations, the Communist party (PCC), the Organs of Popular Power (OPP) and the state institutions. The 1986 party congress elevated Vilma Espín, president of the Federation of Cuban Women (FMC), to full membership in the Politbureau. For the first time since the Revolution, a woman is counted among the top policymakers in Cuba.[1]

The analysis of the "woman question" in Cuba is mired in controversy. Official revolutionary discourse on the struggle for women's full equality is steeped in the orthodox Marxist tradition which identifies the exploitation of women with capitalism and, conversely, contends that socialism will create the full conditions for their emancipation. Moreover, the Revolution's primary objectives have been defense, consolidation, and development. The equality of women has almost always been subordinated to these objectives. The integrity of the nation has been the overriding standard by which everything else has been measured. The "woman question" has, therefore, not been raised in reference to the gender problem. And classical Marxism is patently insufficient to address—in theory and in practice—the multifaceted dimensions of the societal and individual processes—in Cuba and elsewhere—that may foster equality between the sexes. Nonetheless, the distinctly inadequate framework in which the role of women is conceived in Cuba should not become a red herring blinding us to the complexities and the achievements of its reality.[2]

A second contentious dimension that plagues the discussion of women in Cuba is the nature of the island's political system. Incontrovertibly, the Cuban Communist party is its dominant, principal institution. Its vanguard structure and leadership are likewise steeped in the classical theoretical legacy and, more saliently, in the practical heritage of twentieth-century socialism. This heritage has, more often than not, expunged the democratic content of the classical legacy from the actual socialist experience. Cuba's revolutionary record bears witness to both the legacy and the heritage. Civil society is weak and the party and the state are stronger (Bengelsdorf, 1985). Consequently, the initiatives to promote women's full equality have tended to originate first in the party leadership for the Federation of Cuban Women and other organizations to broaden and implement and subsequently to direct and orient ordinary women in their daily lives. There is no independent women's movement in Cuba and, generally, neither the party, nor the FMC, nor ordinary women have manifested a strategic understanding of gender issues. However—and this is an absolutely essential stipulation—the party's preeminence and the strength of top-bottom directives should not become a second red herring obscuring the actual and potential bottom-up pressures and initiatives in the vanguard institution's relationship to society.

Cuban Women and the Struggle for "Conciencia" : 53

This essay addresses the problem of women in Cuba with full awareness of the controversy that envelops it. I attempt to grapple with the issues without succumbing to red herrings, but without denying the often intractable barriers they present for disentangling the "woman question." It is divided into four parts: the status of women before the revolution, women and society, women and work, and women and "conciencia."[3]

The Status of Women Before the Revolution

Before 1959, the legal status of Cuban women was, by Latin American standards, secure and complex. In 1917, the 1886 civil code articles that denied women custody over their children upon remarriage were abrogated. Under the new law, women were also granted the right to administer their own property and to appear in court without their husbands' permission. Although controversial in public opinion and strongly opposed by the Catholic church, a divorce law was enacted in 1918.

In the 1920s, a women's congress in Havana influenced the promulgation of new legislation that included the guarantee of female employment in stores selling women's clothes (100 percent) and in stores selling other items like sports and office supplies (50 percent). In the 1930s, Cuban women were enfranchised and protected by an advanced maternity law (Pichardo, 1973). The 1940 constitution incorporated and expanded these post-1917 legislative advances. Its enforcement through complementary legislation followed largely from the militant reformism of the Cuban labor movement in the 1940s. Thus, women's gains before 1959 were *not* to a significant degree attributable to a feminist movement alone.

An educational and labor force profile of Cuban women before 1959 affords us a historical perspective on the struggle for equality and "conciencia" in the Revolution. Except for higher education, women in prerevolutionary Cuba were better educated than men. The 1953 census revealed lower literacy rates for males ten years old and over (74.1 percent) than for women (78.8 percent). More females (72 percent) than males (67 percent) attended grade school; fewer women (23 percent) received no schooling than men (27.6 percent). But, twice as many men (nearly 36,000) received some university education.

The proportion of women in the labor force was 13 percent. Not surprisingly, this employment was largely in low-status, low-paying jobs. One out of every four economically active women was a domestic servant; one out of every six was a professional (84 percent were teachers); one out of every five worked in manufacturing (textile, food and tobacco); one out of every seven was a clerical worker (Grupo Cubano de Investigaciones Económicas, 1963:802–04, 812–14).

Before the Revolution, women had achieved notable legal equality which did not, nonetheless, materialize in high rates of labor force participation, equal presence in higher education, and access to the high-status professions. Post–World War II socioeconomic changes (an innovative import-substitution industrialization program and agricultural diversification), however, were expanding employment opportunities for lower middle-class women, especially in banking, finance, and the state bureaucracy. But the dominant cultural values dictated a barrier between "la calle" (the street), where men belonged, and "la casa" (the home), where women stayed. The 1959 Revolution eminently challenged that barrier. Twenty-eight years later Cuban women—both in Cuba and in the United States under different circumstances—have attained a degree of labor force participation vis-à-vis Cuban men foreign to the old Cuba.[4]

Women and Society

The Federation of Cuban Women has had the primary responsibility for the incorporation of women into Cuban society. During the 1960s, the FMC's main activities centered on the mobilization of women to enter the labor force and to participate in volunteer work, especially in health and education. For example, more than one and a half million women today lend their support to primary school teachers through a network established in 1968. Similarly, nearly 60,000 women are currently activists in health brigades first organized in the late 1960s (Kaufman Purcell, 1970; Azicri, 1979; Casal, 1980). The Federation was also a principal actor in the 1961 literacy campaign, in the establishment of the day-care system, and in the organization of educational programs for former maids, prostitutes, and peasant women (Olesen, 1971; Randall, 1974; Murray, 1979).

The Revolution's institutionalization in the 1970s brought significant changes to the FMC and Cuban women. At the Federation's 1974 congress, Castro asserted: "Women's full equality does not yet exist" (1975:285). A year later, the party congress formulated a strong policy "to propitiate the objective conditions for the increasing incorporation of women to economic, social and political life, to promote in all aspects an ideological work to eliminate all vestiges from the past" (Primer Congreso del Partido Comunista de Cuba 1976:564).

A more militant role for the FMC resulted from the party policy on women's equality: "[The party] also has the duty to pay close attention to all questions that concern women . . . and to defend those interests in the Party and in the state" (Castro, 1980:36). An affirmative action–like policy to promote women to leadership positions ensued.[5]

A cross-cut view of the party, mass organizations, and Popular Power Assemblies reveals a modest representation of women leaders in the mid-1970s.[6] While Cuban women constituted 13 percent of party membership, only 6 percent occupied national cadre positions. Less than 9 percent of the party's central committee (125 full and alternate members) was female; no women sat on the Politbureau and the Secretariat. Women accounted for just 10 percent of the Young Communists' national leadership (29 percent of rank-and-file membership). Women held an even lower proportion (7 percent) in national trade union positions. Even the Committees for the Defense of the Revolution, with 50 percent female membership, had only 19 percent women as national leaders. The 1976 elections to Popular Power assemblies resulted in the following proportion of women delegates: 8 percent at the local level, 14 percent at the provincial level and 21 percent of the National Assembly.

At that time, the PCC's incipient affirmative action policy was reflected in more females in national leadership positions (except for the UJC and the CTC) than among local cadres. This pattern then contradicted the expectation that in socialist countries women are more numerous at the lower levels of party and government (Jancar, 1978).

By 1979–1980, the party's policy had chalked up satisfactory results. Unfortunately, the available information does not permit an exact comparison with the 1975–1976 data, yet an adequate parallel can be drawn. Although the party failed to increase its female membership to equal women's participation in the labor force (32.4 percent in 1980) as it had pledged to do at the 1975 congress, women accounted for 19 percent of its membership in 1980. Out of a 225-member central committee (full and alternate), nearly 13 percent were women. Vilma Espín, the FMC president, was then promoted to alternate status in the Politbureau. Forty percent of Young Communist militants were female. Likewise, more than 40 percent of local trade union leaders were female. While the Popular Power National Assembly reflected a slight increase to 22.6 percent, the proportion of female delegates to local Popular Power assemblies decreased to 7.2 percent. By the end of the 1970s, while the number of women was increasing at both the higher and lower levels of these organizations and institutions, except for Popular Power, they were doing so faster at the lower levels. This emerging pattern may signal the more established trend in other social-

TABLE 1.
Female Membership and Leadership in the Party, Mass Organizations, and Popular Power Institutions in Cuba, 1975–1985 (in percent)

	Cuban Communist Party (PCC)	Communist Youth (UJC)	Cuban Workers' Confederation (CTC)	Committees for the Defense of the Revolution (CDR)	Popular Power
1975–1976					
Female members	13.0	29.0	25.0	50.0	n.a.
Female leaders					
Local	2.9	22.0	24.0	7.0	8.0
Provincial	6.3	7.0	15.0	3.0	14.0
National	5.5	10.0	7.0	19.0	21.0
1979–1980					
Female members	19.1	40.1	n.a.	50.0	n.a.
Female leaders					
Local	16.5	n.a.	39.4	41.0	7.2
Provincial	15.0	n.a.	17.9	31.0	17.4
National	9.0	14.3	17.1	30.0	22.6
Central Committee	13.0	26.4	n.a.	n.a.	n.a.
1984–1985					
Female members	21.9	41.0	48.9	n.a.	n.a.
Female leaders					
Local	23.5	47.6	44.6	47.2	11.5
Provincial	16.9	28.9	37.5	15.7	21.4
National	13.8	19.5	31.8	17.7	22.6
Central Committee	16.0	27.1	n.a.	2.0	n.a.

Sources: Primer Congreso del Partido Comunista de Cuba (1976:585); *Bohemia*, November 16, 1976, p. 48; September 17, 1985, p. 82; Second Congress of the Communist Party of Cuba (1981:78, 415–21); Federation of Cuban Women (1979:37); "Memoria del IV Congreso de la UJC" (1982:7); Castro (1986:88, 92); Radaelli (1985); Espín (1985:52; 1986: 65–66); *Memorias: XV Congreso de la CTC* (1984:268–69); *Granma*,

ist countries and challenge the party and the FMC to a more diligent pursuit of the full equality of women at all levels.

By 1984–1985, women continued to make inroads, even if unevenly. As noted above, the main accomplishment was the promotion of Vilma Espín to full membership in the PCC Politbureau: she is the only woman in the fourteen-person body. Two other women were included as Politbureau alternates (two out of ten). None was among the ten-member Secretariat. Women constituted 16 percent of the 225 full and alternate members of the Central Committee and 13.8 percent of national PCC cadres as compared to 13 percent and 9 percent, respectively, in 1980. Female party membership increased slightly to 21.9 percent—still significantly below the labor force participation rate (37.3 percent).[7] The women's share in Popular Power increased to 11.5 percent and 21.4 percent, respectively, at the local and provincial levels but remained stagnant at the national level.[8] Similarly, the available data seem to indicate, again with the exception of Popular Power, an entrenchment of the 1979–1980 trends: slight overall improvements, but greater representation at lower levels.

The relative success of affirmative action toward women reflects both the party's commitment and the FMC's pursuit of equality. Castro recognized the Federation's efforts at the 1980 party congress: "The Federation of Cuban Women has made a valuable contribution placing women in leadership posts, working diligently to remove the obstacles that prevent this" (1981:23). These obstacles have been identified as material and cultural in nature: educationally, as was the case before the Revolution, Cuban women do not differ significantly from men. Table 2 summarizes educational levels in Cuba in 1970 and 1981.

Moreover, educational trends among Cuban women point to an even greater leveling in the potential leadership recruitment pool. Unlike other socialist countries where certain careers seem to point toward a political future, Cuba has yet to manifest such a pattern. Economics and engineering, careers that could have weight significant in the selection of administrative cadres, have a 55 and 27 percent female enrollment, respectively. Moreover, women constitute 81 percent of philosophy majors—a politically selective career that opens doors to cadre positions in the party and its schools (Larguía and Dumoulín, 1983:30). Overall female enrollment in higher education in 1985 was 52.7 percent, up from 40.6 percent in 1979 (Radaelli, 1985:17; Espín, 1980:21).

Since 1984, however, medical school enrollment has been subjected to a 52:48 ratio of women to men. Without this quota, women would outnumber men 3 to 2. Civilian medical aid is a crucial component of Cuban foreign policy. Quotas were necessary, Castro argued, for two

TABLE 2.
Distribution of Cuban Males and Females Six Years and Older by Educational Level, 1970 and 1981 (in percent)

	1970		1981	
	Males	Females	Males	Females
Primary school	80.5	81.1	57.2	61.1
Secondary school	14.7	13.9	26.7	24.1
High school	.4	2.0	6.8	5.9
University	1.7	1.2	4.8[a]	3.5[a]
Nonspecified level	2.7	1.8	4.5	5.4
Total	100.0	100.0	100.0	100.0

Sources: Primer Congreso del Partido Comunista de Cuba (1976:588); *Censo de población . . . de Cuba* (1983:151–52).

Note: The author estimated the distribution by adding three different population groups in each additional level: those currently enrolled at that level, those who completed the corresponding level, and those who did not complete such a level. The nonspecified category is actually a residue for which no information is given [Editor].

a. A breakdown by sex for university students was not available for 1981. The 1981 census registered 3.2 percent of the population (total) at the university level. On the conservative assumption that the proportions of males and females are the same in 1981 as for 1971, I have estimated 1981 figures.

reasons: women would encounter greater family and personal obstacles in fulfilling international tours for extended periods and the recipient countries have not undergone the ongoing change in cultural values with respect to women that Cuba is experiencing (*Bohemia,* March 2, 1984:53; Castro, 1985:4). This disturbing development underscores the quandary of the woman question in Cuba: the role of women in Cuba is often subordinated to national goals that in turn may be predicated on sexist values. What Cuban women think about the quota policy in view of how Cuba's foreign policy needs have been conceived is simply unknown.

In the mid-1970s, the party conducted a survey among 302 men and 333 women in Matanzas Province that underscores the cultural and material obstacles to the promotion of women to leadership positions. The survey sought to tap the reasons for the small number of women elected as Popular Power delegates. When asked why women did not occupy leadership positions, nearly 60 percent answered that women were responsible for taking care of home, children, and husband. When women were asked about their willingness to serve if elected, 54 percent said that they could not because of family responsibilities. When both men and women were asked why fewer than 10 percent of the candidates had been women, one-third again pointed to household and child-care obligations. Finally, a question was asked about the personal characteristics expected of a delegate; 45 percent responded: "moral, serious, decent" for women and only 20 percent alluded to the same virtues for men (Primer Congreso del Partido Comunista de Cuba, 1976:583–84).

The 1976–1979 decrease in female local Popular Power delegates from 8 to 7.2 percent disturbed both the party leadership and the FMC: "We feel that there are still prejudices and false conceptions about women in our population and that the overload of work that weighs many women down is an obstacle to promotion" (Espín, 1980:24). Fidel Castro expressed a similar concern:

But isn't there some prejudice too? Isn't there some prejudice, even among women who go to the polls and vote prejudiced? I'm not saying that women must be voted for just because they are women . . . but no one should not vote for a woman because she happens to be a woman . . . I think that the percentage of women elected in the Popular Power elections, in the grass-roots elections, is really low. (Castro, 1980:37)

It would be interesting to determine the statistical profile of women who are politically active: if the average woman who works, also studies (43.2 percent of working women are enrolled in adult education courses), is a party and/or trade union activist and spends over four hours a day on domestic chores, she certainly would have neither the time nor the disposition to serve as a delegate even if elected (García Alonso, 1978:44; Castro, 1981:23; Radaelli, 1985:17; Espín, 1985:31). Nonetheless, by 1984, women constituted 11.5 percent of all delegates to local Popular Power assemblies (*Bohemia,* April 27, 1984:48). In October 1986, 17.1 percent of local delegates elected were women (*Granma,* October 28, 1986:1). This not unimpressive increase may well be a testimony to the ten-year-old struggle by the party and the FMC to augment women's presence in Popular Power and a more activist stance by Cuban women. In the future, however, the female leadership profile in the other organizations and institutions must be carefully scrutinized, for a tradeoff may well occur.

Padula and Smith (1985) rightfully note that women's undeniable social and economic advances since 1959 have not been translated into the actual exercise of power. Cuban women today account for somewhat more than 25 percent of leadership positions (computed from table 1). Aguirre (1976) documented an average of about 6 percent for 1968–1974. However, occupying public office at whatever level is not necessarily the equivalent of power. The institutions and organizations in which women hold these offices must be analyzed in view of the

Cuban system. Policy outputs must be weighed in relation to women's presence and policies that address the material interests of women. In the next section, I argue that the FMC was successful in lobbying for a revision of employment policies toward women.

Women and Work

During the 1960s, Cuban women slowly increased their share of the labor force. By 1968, the prerevolutionary 13 percent level had been barely surpassed (15.8 percent) (Mesa-Lago, 1981:118). In 1968, the Ministry of Labor passed two resolutions dealing with women's employment: Resolution 47 reserved jobs preferentially for women, and Resolution 48 banned women from more than 400 jobs which allegedly could be prejudicial to their health. The 1970 mass mobilizations for the 10-million-ton sugar harvest spurred a campaign to encourage women to join the urban labor force to allow men to go to the countryside. By 1970, women represented 18.5 percent of the labor force (Centro de Estudios Demográficos, 1976:176). Then, the female labor force was quite unstable: for every woman who became a worker, three returned to "la casa."[9]

The 1970s witnessed an interesting development with respect to female employment. Early in the decade, the revolutionary leadership launched a campaign against persistent inequalities between men and women. The expansion of the female labor force was seen as fundamental to overcoming these inequalities. However, in 1975, the government adopted an economic management and planning system that resulted in a partial rationalization of the labor force: Cuba entered the 1980s with a labor surplus. A tension evidently existed between female employment expansion and the imperative to increase efficiency and productivity through the elimination of underemployment. In the mid-1970s, women accounted for nearly 26 percent of the labor force (JUCEPLAN, 1975:56). For a while, it looked as if that percentage would remain stable or decrease.

The 1974 FMC congress voiced a criticism of the 1968 Labor Ministry resolution (Res. 48) which prohibited women from holding certain jobs:

At the XIII Workers' Congress we expressed our opinion that the Ministry of Labor's resolution 48 prohibiting certain jobs for women should be submitted to scrutiny since we believe that the term prohibition implies discrimination . . . therefore we suggest that women should be told of the conditions and risks of those jobs and allow them to decide whether or not to perform them. (*Memorias: II Congreso . . . FMC* 1975:38)

Two years later, the labor ministry passed Resolution 40, which barred women from nearly 300 job categories. Its selection was allegedly based on the health hazards the jobs presented for women.[10] Given the unemployment problem, however, it may well be surmised that the resolution aimed to address this issue. Prohibiting women from qualifying for 300 job categories (some were then occupied by women and the resolution prescribed their transfer) created employment for surplus male workers. Women without jobs do not constitute the same urgent, social problem that unemployed men do, or so seemed the implicit message of the resolution. Behind-the-scenes debate and lobbying followed the 1976 resolution. In 1977, in fact, Vilma Espín told me that the FMC was seeking its modification. Bengelsdorf (1985) reported that the original 300-job list has been whittled down to about 25. Espín, moreover, recently reasserted the 1974 FMC position vis-à-vis job prohibitions for women: "The establishment of prohibitions for women in general is indeed negative because they constitute a violation of the principle of equality. . . . These prohibitions are only acceptable when a pregnant woman or her unborn child might be affected" (Espín, 1986:39)

By 1981, women had increased their participation in the labor force to 31.3 percent, a proportion the party then committed itself to maintain, but not necessarily expand (*Censo de población y viviendas de 1981*). Between 1976 and 1980, 40 percent of the women who entered the labor force did so as technical, skilled, or professional personnel.[11] Occupational qualifications have apparently and partially deferred gender-related job restrictions. At the 1980 FMC congress, Castro alluded to this debate: "I know that other questions have been discussed here related, for example, to some jobs which are not authorized for women" (Castro, 1980:36). He also made an implicit reference to the unemployment problem, but nevertheless observed the following with respect to women workers: "I think we must be very careful in that certain situations do not lead us to retrace our steps in what we have gained for women, which is a lot. We must consolidate it and progress more, if possible" (ibid). Similarly, Vilma Espín noted: "The further incorporation of women will depend primarily on their skills and training, and will come about slowly in accordance with the country's economic development" (1980:20). Castro concluded:

I was saying that we had to be careful not to fall back on what we have achieved so far, for we have had to work very hard and struggle very hard against incomprehension and prejudice to bring about a climate of equality.... And of course, if we fall back with respect to jobs, if we fall back in the economic field, we will start going back on everything else we have gained. (1980:36)

The FMC has established employment control commissions in coordination with the labor unions and Popular Power provincial assemblies to analyze job opportunities for women and supervise hiring practices under the post-1975 management and planning system (Espín, 1980). Female workers are sometimes considered a hindrance to enterprise "profitability": women are more likely than men to stay home to care for a sick child or elderly family member or be late because of children and family responsibilities.[12] Also, managers may be reluctant to promote qualified women for similar reasons: women may not be able to assume greater responsibility on the job due to the double burden of "la calle" and "la casa" (*Bohemia,* November 16, 1984:39). Women managers are probably more sensitive to the problems of women workers, but they account for less than 23 percent of management posts, most of which are in junior positions (Radaelli, 1985:16). The 1984 labor congress turned down a proposal to allow earlier retirement for women (at fifty instead of fifty-five years) as detrimental to gains in female employment: managers would hesitate to hire workers who could retire at an even younger age (Veiga, 1984:8–9). By 1985, nonetheless, women accounted for 37.3 percent of the labor force[13] and had attained a notable degree of stability (Castro, 1986:78). For every hundred women entering the labor force, fewer than four dropped out.[14] Nazzari (1983) quite accurately points out that the implementation of the economic management and planning system would increase both the costs of female employment and the tendency to discriminate against women workers. That, in fact, working women have not borne that burden to the extent anticipated in the late seventies may perhaps be attributed both to their determination to stay on the job and to the activities of the FMC on their behalf.[15]

The structure of female employment is, however, a different matter. Women's work was fundamentally altered in the 1960s as paid domestic work virtually disappeared. Table 3 summarizes structural changes in female employment during the 1970s and early 1980s. While Cuban women continue to work in jobs that are extensions of their traditional roles (nursing, clerical work, textiles, primary school teaching), advances have been attained in industry, construction, and transportation. Moreover, these advances are likely due to technical and professional women who represent 55.4 percent of such qualified personnel. Female educational trends and official policy to link technically qualified workers to production may portend a gradual reach of women workers beyond their traditional spheres.[16]

A support services infrastructure is a necessary and vital prerequisite for women's labor force participation. Survey data mentioned above clearly underline the fact that women's work overload limits their political activism. The ongoing battle against prejudice, while significant, cannot soon be expected to result in a sufficiently widespread and profound transformation of "conciencia" to alleviate this overload. A minimal material infrastructure to ease women's double burden is in place, but the late 1970s economic recession slowed down resources for its continued rapid growth. The day-care center program, for example, did not expand to the 150,000-children capacity projected in 1975. By 1980, day care was provided for about 90,000 children (Castro, 1975:285; Espín, 1980:23). In 1985, the FMC congress indicated that 96,000 mothers had their children in day care, a figure that may or may not reflect an increase in the number of children attending since 1980 (*Granma*, March 26, 1985:3). Notwithstanding, female employment, as noted above, has continued its upward trend.

Cuba's present economic situation constrains a rapid expansion of the social infrastructure supportive of women's labor force participation. The late 1970s and early 1980s evidenced this infrastructure's slower growth. Yet, by 1986, women accounted for something under two-fifths of the economically active population. The revolutionary leadership's commitment to maintain female employment will sooner or later require greater resources for women workers' support services. The extent to which these resources are in fact allotted will be decisive for working women and indicative of the FMC's successful articulation

TABLE 3.
Females in the Cuban Labor Force, 1970, 1979, 1981 (in percent)

	1970	1979	1981
Agriculture and cattle raising	5.0	14.8	13.2
Industry	19.1	24.8	28.4
Construction	2.0	11.9	9.9
Transportation	2.9	13.4	15.5
Communications	44.9	42.0	45.8
Commerce	36.1	43.0	43.0
Social services	48.7	63.4	69.4

Sources: JUCEPLAN (1975:17); Federation of Cuban Women (1980: 11–12); *Anuario Estadístico de Cuba* (1982:115, 121).

Note: It is not clear whether the table describes the labor force or state civilian employment [Editor].

of their interests. Undoubtedly, women's pressures from below and their grass-roots understanding of these interests could well be catalysts for a more assertive FMC.

Women and "Conciencia"

"Feminine, not feminist," responded Vilma Espín to a question concerning the FMC in a 1974 interview (Steffens, 1974:22). Her response succinctly embodies the contradictory trends in the development of a more egalitarian "conciencia" between men and women in Cuba. The 1975 family code establishes that both partners in marriage have equal rights and duties in child care and household chores to enable both to pursue their jobs (Ministry of Justice, 1975:20). The 1976 constitution addresses equality between the sexes on broader terms than both the 1940 constitution or the 1959 fundamental law.[17] Article 43 reads: "Women have the same rights as men in the economic, political and social fields as well as in the family" and commits the state "to create all the conditions which help to make real the principle of equality" (*Constitution of the Republic of Cuba,* 1975:26). The 1975 party congress's thesis on the full equality of women boldly rejects the sexual double standard: "It is imperative that everyone be aware that what is sanctionable for one is sanctionable for the other also. There cannot be one morality for women and another one for men" (Primer Congreso del Partido Comunista de Cuba, 1976:26). Recently, Vilma Espín expressed a more "feminist" outlook on women's equality, including sexual equality:

Often women who have extramarital relations are more severely judged than men who systematically engage in adultery. Evaluations, promotions, sanctions and membership in political organizations must be based on the same prerequisites in all spheres for both men and women. In most cases, the so-called moral issues fall exclusively within a couple's intimate purview and not within that of organizations and institutions. (Espín, 1986:58)

Some people, perhaps mostly men, were alarmed at the revolution's challenge to tradition: "Some were frightened when the discussion of the Family Code project was launched. . . . We don't see why anyone should be frightened, because what should really frighten us as revolutionaries is that we have to recognize that women still do not have absolute equality in Cuban society" (Castro, 1975:283).

The importance of the family and the image of women as mothers, however, are attitudes that persist with force in Cuban society. Article 34 of the constitution reads: "The state protects the family, motherhood and matrimony"; Article 36, though, grants equal legal rights to all children, whether born in wedlock or not (*Constitution of the Republic of Cuba*, 1975:21). The family code notwithstanding, child care is perceived as women's responsibility: "Children need careful and loving attention, their physical and psychological needs require great tenderness and warmth to be expressed" (*Granma*, March 18, 1979:7). The speaker is a woman Central Committee member. In 1984, however, Vilma Espín commented that child care and household chores should be shared by men and women. She emphasized the implication of "sharing": "If we use the term 'help' we are accepting that these are women's responsibilities and such is not the case. We say 'share' because they are a family responsibility" (*Bohemia*, November 16, 1984:40). In a 1986 article, Espín characterized this sharing as a principle and a directive of the party applicable to all, not just young people. Espín also bluntly condemned those men who consider household and child-care responsibilities to be "inherently" women's duties and states that these men are exploiting and discriminating against women. Women's rights to leisure time and to participate in other activities beyond home and work, she argues, are violated if men abstain from sharing domestic chores (Espín, 1986:59–62).

Conclusion

In the early 1970s, Cuba's largely male leadership focused on the status of women. They promoted a climate of equality through measures such as the family code and the thesis of the 1975 party congress on women's equality. Women's full incorporation into Cuban society required their joining the labor force. However, in the mid-1970s, economic imperatives rationalized underemployment and an employment problem appeared. The Labor Ministry's 1976 resolution represented an attempt to deal with the unemployment problem by limiting women's job opportunities.

The FMC and the party leadership concurred in asserting the priority of women's equality even in the face of unemployment. However, the indispensable infrastructure to support working women has not grown, as was predicted in 1975. An important measure of the actual significance of women in leadership positions throughout Cuban society may be the extent to which future resources are channeled for the services women need in order to engage in the labor force and political activities. While important and ideological campaigns that underscore women's equality cannot—in and of themselves—sustain a transformation of "conciencia," the fact that women in Cuba, in spite of material constraints, have made the advances that they have in labor force participation and leadership posts is indeed a tribute to their determination to break the barriers between "la casa" and "la calle." Whether they continue these advances hinges on their rank-and-file pressure, the FMC's efficacy in articulating their interests, and the party's responsiveness.

More than 37 percent of Cuba's workers are women.[18] Working women moreover also relate to the trade unions, the party, enterprise management, and other organizations at the point of production. The present decade is likely to furnish evidence to gauge the compatibility of the climate of equality of the 1970s with the exigencies of discipline, productivity, and efficiency of the 1980s. Nothwithstanding the insufficient conceptualization of the "woman question" in Cuba and the vanguard party problematic, Cuban women may well be forging their own consciousness of their contributions to Cuba and their needs amid their society's continuing social transformation. Such a "conciencia"—rooted in their actual experiences—could be a factor in crafting egalitarian gender relations as a goal guiding their behavior and in strengthening civil society in relation to the party and the state.

NOTES

1. That Vilma Espín is a full member of the Politbureau and two other women are alternate members are indications of the Cuban leadership's continued awareness of the role of women throughout Cuban society, including at the pinnacle of power. That it took twenty-seven years for a woman to enter the inner sanctum of the Revolution's top policy-making body is indicative of the quagmire in which the "woman question" is trapped in Cuba. Both cultural and structural factors undoubtedly impinge upon women's subordinate position. However, the issue of who enters the top echelons in Cuba, how they are selected, whether they remain or are removed is quite complex, has varied over time and has responded principally to the exigencies of revolutionary survival and consolidation. For example, in 1965, in the anti-Batista struggle, defense of the Revolution was probably the single most important criterion for leadership. By 1975, the second central committee reflected the broader unity—both real and symbolic—that the 1970 crisis had imposed on Cuban leaders. During the 1970s, the Revolution began to articulate the imperative—again, both real and symbolic—of addressing "special interests," i.e., the need to increase the party's working-class composition and to wage an ideological campaign for the full equality of women. In 1980, the Second Party Congress convened under the shadow of the Polish Solidarity Movement and the Mariel exodus. The links that a ruling Communist party forges with the "masses" was of preeminent concern. Espín—along with the general secretaries of the other mass organizations—then entered alternate membership in the Politbureau. By 1986, the problems of "representativeness" and leadership transition affected the composition of the highest party bodies. It could be argued that it took twelve years for a woman to become a full

Cuban Women and the Struggle for "Conciencia" : 67

member of the Politbureau; only in 1974 was the "woman question" raised in more forceful terms. Yet, whether a woman's journey to the Cuban Politbureau took twenty-seven or twelve years, it is crucial to underscore the uneven, zig-zag development of revolutionary change. In 1923 Leon Trotsky noted: "The curve of revolutionary development is a very complicated line" (Trotsky, 1973). His simple observation should be seriously considered by contemporary analysts of revolutionary change.

2. See Murray, 1979; Bengelsdorf, 1985; and Molyneaux, who forcefully argues that an understanding of how women struggle for and benefit from social change must start by "recognizing difference rather than assuming homogeneity" (1986). As such, "women's interests" may be a meaningless term, one that should instead be differentiated by class, race, or ethnicity. Molyneaux proposes two other categories: *strategic gender interests,* derived from the analytical understanding of women's subordination and of alternatives to this condition, and *practical gender interests,* arising from women's concrete position in the sexual division of labor. The second category seems more suggestive in the Cuban context. The refinement of concepts and data to apply to contemporary Cuba a differentiated analysis of women's interests needs to be tackled at a later date. Meanwhile, the crude concept of "women's interests" will be used throughout this essay.

3. I use "conciencia" to mean the social and individual (male and female) awareness of the material and cultural exigencies required to mitigate inequalities between the sexes, at home and in society.

4. Prieto, 1984; Cuban women make up a much higher proportion of the U.S. labor force (54 percent) than women in Cuba (31 percent). But to be meaningful, these figures require a comparison of the two societies, since cultural and structural factors interact; however, analysis of these factors is beyond the scope of this article.

5. The 1975 party congress adopted a thesis on the full equality of women in Cuban society which established an "affirmative action" policy toward women. This policy is explicit throughout the thesis, notably when it states that the party had "to establish an appropriate policy of promotion, from the base to higher levels, with the concrete object of achieving a presence for women commensurate with their actual participation and possibilities" (Primer Congreso del Partido Comunista de Cuba, 1976:590). As this essay demonstrates, that policy's record has been mixed. The Federation has repeatedly expressed its intention to implement the 1975 resolution. At the 1980 FMC congress, Espín noted that the Federation had to intensify its "ideological work" to dilute prejudices preventing women from assuming leadership positions, and "along with those of the political and mass organizations, to obtain a female representation in the state commensurate with women's participation and experience in the revolution" (Espín, 1980:24). At the 1985 FMC congress, she observed that when the "affirmative action" policy is properly pursued, women are promoted to leadership posts, and cited the example of the National Bank of Cuba, with nearly 44 percent women in cadre positions (Espín, 1985:47), whereas in 1968-1974 there were only 5 percent (Aguirre, 1976:33). See also Espín, 1986.

6. Aguirre (1976:29-34) gives a breakdown of women in leadership positions, 1968-1974, as compiled by the Central Intelligence Agency's *Directory of Personalities of the Cuban Government, Official Organizations and Mass Organizations.* Of nearly 28,000 positions (not including the FMC) in which sex could be identified, under 2,000 (approximately 6 percent) were held by women. The party, the Young Communists, the CDRs, and the CTC were between 3 and 6 percent female. While there may have been changes since the later 1970s, the above breakdown provides a valuable point of reference.

7. As I have found in other analyses of party composition, 1976-1985, the slight increase

in women party militants is puzzling. For example, party policy notwithstanding, production workers *declined* from nearly 41 percent in 1980 to a little over 37 percent in 1985. In contrast, administrative personnel increased from 4 to 7 percent, and professional/technical workers from 14 to 16 percent. Given that women are well represented in both sectors, their modest increase is perplexing. Note that the PCC grew slowly in 1980-1985 (1.2x), compared to the 1975-1980 period (2x) *and* also experienced a large turnover—nearly 40 percent of members in 1985 had been in the party five years or less. How women and workers are *not* promoted to the party rank and file, contrary to explicit policy, is a crucial question that needs further analysis (see Pérez-Stable, forthcoming).

8. One may question the significance of the presence of women in a National Assembly that meets briefly twice a year. However, the issue is not the representation of women but the weight of the Assembly in the Cuban political system. In 1978 Domínguez focused on the symbolic rubber-stamp role of the Assembly, but in 1982 characterized it as a somewhat more dynamic institution. See also Bengelsdorf (1985), who explores the role of Popular Power at all levels in the Cuban Revolution's efforts to revitalize the democratic elements of the socialist project.

9. Espín, 1985:31. Labor force participation rates (women in the labor force as proportion of the female population of working age) were 17.8 percent in 1953, 17.7 percent in 1970, and 31.0 percent in 1982. Figures for 1953 and 1970 are for women over 14 years; for 1982, over 15 years (Centro de Estudios Demográficos, 1976:181 and *Anuario Estadístico,* 1982:64, 119). Regarding the stagnation of women's labor force participation rate between 1953 and 1970, Lewis, Lewis, and Rigdon (1977:xvii) comment, "To many women from the slums, 'liberation' did not imply independence from home and children and incorporation in the labor force and mass organizations. 'Liberation' meant *release* from outside work, taking care of their own homes, and having time to spend time with their children."

10. Res. 40 superseded Res. 48 (see *Granma,* 1 June 1976; Espín, 1985:36-37; 1986:39). Both resolutions determine female employment according to both cultural and structural factors. However: (1) In the late 1960s the Cuban economy suffered a labor shortage partly because of its mobilizational strategies for agriculture. Res. 47 explicitly states that men should vacate specified jobs in favor of women so that men could go to rural areas. Res. 48, in perhaps more exclusively ideological terms, discusses women's biological limitations for holding certain jobs. (2) Since the 1973 CTC and the 1974 FMC congresses challenged both resolutions because of their discriminatory content and the absence of a labor shortage (*Memorias: XIII Congreso de la CTC,* 1974: 52; *Memorias, II Congreso . . . FMC,* 1975:173-74), it was not unreasonable to expect the abolition of both. (3) Res. 48 was supplanted by Res. 40 in 1976, more than two years after the CTC and FTC congresses called for their abolition. While it reduced the number of jobs closed to women from 400 to 300, the 1976 resolution perpetuated the sex-typed stratification using a biological rationale. Meanwhile, economic rationalization had begun to yield a labor surplus. It is reasonable to conclude that Res. 40 continued the discriminatory job categories because of the unemployment problem. (In 1977, a national labor union leader privately agreed with me.) (4) The often convoluted history of these resolutions underscores that the revolutionary commitment to female employment has put economic development goals first and women's emancipation second; the ideal has often been subverted by sexist notions of biological determinism. Res. 40, 47, and 48 have apparently been superseded by the State Committee on Labor and the Social Security res. 511, which deals largely with women's preferential access to nearly 500,000 jobs (Espín, 1985:36-38).

11. Espín, 1980:20-21. Percentages of women employed at the skilled (9 years'

study), technical (12 years' study), and professional (university degree) levels are as follows (Larguía and Dumoulín, 1983:21–22):

	Skilled	Technical	Professional
Geology, mining, and metallurgy	13.9	20.7	28.5
Sugar, chemical, and food industries	43.7	50.7	41.0
Electronics, computing, and communications	28.3	22.1	18.0
Construction	15.3	28.8	28.1
Energy sector	20.7	13.4	11.9
Agriculture	14.6	24.2	27.8

12. Article 219 of the 1984 Labor Code allows women unpaid leave of absence for caring for sick children up to age sixteen. No similar provision is considered for men (*Código de Trabajo*, 1985:57). The 1985 FMC congress witnessed a lively debate about the importance of having men stay overnight at the hospital with a sick child (Castro, 1985).

13. This figure probably refers to state civilian employment, which historically shows a higher female participation rate than the labor force in general, because of the exclusion of both private agriculture and the armed forces [Editor].

14. Espín, 1985:31. Provincial and local Popular Power Assemblies directly administer a number of local industries (such as textiles, furniture, household goods). Since the mid-1970s, these industries have increased their annual production from approximately 25–30 million pesos to around 250–300 million in 1982. These industries have been instrumental in opening up jobs for women. In 1982, local industries also contracted home work to more than 20,000 women, who produced goods valued at nearly 80 million pesos. However, contract work at home should be carefully watched by both the FMC and the CTC. While the government passed a regulatory resolution, such work lends itself to low pay and long hours in isolation, without the aid of unions or other mass organizations. Local industries employed more than 45,000 women in 1984 (Espín, 1985:32; *Bohemia* [1984], March 16:23; April 27:28–31; June 22:28–31; August 3:32–33).

15. Espín (1986:42–43) lists incidents in which managers have resorted to "legal pretexts" to lay off women in favor of male workers. Alleged reasons included: absence due to family sickness, physical deficiency (as in construction), adultery, pregnancy, single motherhood, and technical deficiency. A version of this article was published in *Bohemia*, October 17, 1986.

16. Average yearly wages in the following sectors of the Cuban economy in 1981, and the percentage of women in each, are as follows (*Anuario Estadístico de Cuba*, 1982:114, 121, 188):

	Pesos	% Women
Community and personal services	1,814	28.3
Commerce	1,817	43.0
Education	1,943	62.9
Public health and social welfare	1,955	69.4
Communications	1,960	45.8
Finance and insurance	2,118	65.5
Industry	2,138	28.4
Science and technology	2,251	55.1

The statistical yearbooks do not disaggregate data that would provide a sense of occupational wage differentials by sex. Obviously, teachers and nurses account for a substantial proportion of technical and professional women. Yet, important inroads are evident, for example, in the 20–23 percent female technical personnel at two modern industrial plants in Santa Clara and Moa (Espín, 1985:33). Nazzari (1983) also concludes that there is no significant gap in the national average wages of men and women.

17. The articles on the family in the 1940 constitution, the 1959 fundamental law, and the 1976 constitution bear a striking resemblance. However, the last also includes an article on women's equality and the state's commitment to promote and support it (de la Cuesta and Alum, 1974:251–52, 411–12; *Constitution of the Republic of Cuba,* 1976:28–29, 34).

18. These figures probably refer to state civilian employment [Editor].

REFERENCES

Aguirre, Benigno E. 1976. "Women in the Cuban Bureaucracies: 1968–1974." *Journal of Comparative Family Studies* 7, 23–40.
Anuario Estadístico de Cuba. 1982. Havana: Comité Estatal de Estadísticas.
Azicri, Max. 1979. "Political Participation and Social Equality in Cuba." *SECOLAS Annals* 10, 66–80.
Bengelsdorf, Carollee. 1985. "Between Vision and Reality: Democracy in Socialist Theory and Practice: The Cuban Experience." Unpublished.
─────. 1985. "On the Problem of Studying Women in Cuba." *Race and Class* 2, 35–50.
Bohemia, various issues.
Casal, Lourdes. 1980. "Revolution and 'Conciencia': Women in Cuba." In *Women, War and Revolution,* ed. Clara Berkin and Clara M. Lovett. New York: Holmes & Meier.
Castro, Fidel. 1975. "Discurso del comandante en jefe Fidel Castro en el acto de clausura." *Memoria: II Congreso Nacional de la Federación de Mujeres Cubanas.* Havana: Editorial Orbe.
─────. 1980. "Speech delivered by Commander in Chief Fidel Castro at the Closing Session of the Federation's Third Congress." *Boletín FMC.* Havana.
─────. 1981. *Main Report: Second Congress of the Communist Party of Cuba.* New York: Center for Cuban Studies.
─────. 1985. "Speech Delivered by Commander in Chief Fidel Castro at the Closing Session of the Federation's Fourth Congress." *Granma Weekly Review,* March 24.
─────. 1986. *Informe Central: Tercer Congreso del Partido Comunista de Cuba.* Havana: Editora Política.
Censo de población y viviendas de 1981, República de Cuba. 1983. Havana: Comité Estatal de Estadísticas.
Centro de Estudios Demográficos. 1976. *La población de Cuba.* Havana: Editorial de Ciencias Sociales.
Código de Trabajo. 1985. Departamento de Asuntos Laborales y Sociales. Havana: CTC Nacional.
Constitution of the Republic of Cuba. 1985. Havana: Instituto del Libro.
Cuesta, Leonel de la, and Rolando Alum. 1974. *Constituciones cubanas desde 1812 hasta nuestros días.* New York: Ediciones Exilio.

Domínguez, Jorge I. 1978. *Cuba: Order and Revolution.* Cambridge, Mass.: Harvard University Press.
———. 1982. "Revolutionary Politics: The New Demands for Orderliness." In *Cuba: Internal and International Affairs,* ed. Domínguez. Beverly Hills, Calif.: Sage Publications.
Espín, Vilma. 1980. "Central Report Rendered by Comrade Vilma Espín, President of the Federation of Cuban Women at the Federation's Third Congress." *Boletín FMC.* Havana.
———. 1985. *Informe Central: FMC IV Congreso.*
———. 1986. "La batalla por el ejercicio pleno de la igualdad de la mujer: acción de los comunistas." *Cuba Socialista* 6, 27–68.
Federation of Cuban Women. 1980. *Cuban Women: 1975–1979.* Havana:FMC.
García Alonso, Maritza. 1978. "Presupuesto de tiempo de la mujer cubana: un estudio nacional, abril de 1975." *Demanda* 1, 33–58.
Granma, various issues.
Granma Weekly Review, various issues.
Grupo Cubano de Investigaciones Económicas. 1963. *Estudio sobre Cuba.* Miami: University of Miami Press.
Jancar, Barbara Wolfe. 1978. *Women Under Communism.* Baltimore: Johns Hopkins University Press.
JUCEPLAN. 1975. *Aspectos demográficos de la fuerza laboral femenina en Cuba.* Havana: Dirreción de Estadística de Población en Cuba.
Juventud Rebelde, various issues.
Kaufman Purcell, Susan. 1970. "Modernizing Women for a Modern Society: The Cuban Case." In *Female and Male in Latin America,* ed. Ann Pescatello. Pittsburgh, Pa.: University of Pittsburgh Press.
Larguía, Isabel, and John Dumoulín. 1983. "La mujer en el desarrollo: Estrategias y experiencias de la revolución cubana." X Congreso Latinoamericano de Sociología, Managua, Nicaragua.
Lewis, Oscar, Ruth M. Lewis, and Susan M. Rigdon. 1977. *Four Women: Living the Revolution.* Urbana: University of Illinois Press.
Mesa-Lago, Carmelo. 1981. *The Economy of Socialist Cuba: A Two-Decade Appraisal.* Albuquerque: University of New Mexico Press.
"Memoria del IV Congreso de la UJC." 1982. *Juventud Rebelde,* July.
Memorias: II Congreso Nacional de la Federación de Mujeres Cubanas. 1975. Havana: Editorial Orbe.
Memorias: XIII Congreso de la CTC. 1974. Havana: CTC Nacional.
Memorias: XV Congreso de la CTC. 1984. Havana: Editorial de Ciencias Sociales.
Ministry of Justice. 1975. *Family Code.* Havana: Instituto del Libro.
Molyneaux, Maxine. 1986. "Mobilization Without Emancipation? Women's Interests, State and Revolution." In *Transition and Development: Problems of Third World Socialism,* ed. Richard R. Fagen, Carmen Diana Deere, and José Luis Coraggio. New York: Monthly Review Press.
Murray, Nicola. 1979. "Socialism and Feminism: Women and the Cuban Revolution, Pts. 1 and 2." *Feminist Review* 2, 57–73; 3, 99–108.
Nazzari, Muriel. 1983. "The 'Woman Question' in Cuba: An Analysis of Material Constraints on Its Solution." *Signs: A Journal of Women in Culture and Society* 2, 246–63.
Olesen, Virginia. 1971. "Context and Posture: Notes on Socio-Cultural Aspects of Women's Roles and Family Policy in Contemporary Cuba." *Journal of Marriage and the Family* 3, 548–60.

Padula, Alfred, and Lois Smith. 1985. "Women in Socialist Cuba." In *Cuba: Twenty-Five Years of Revolution,* ed. Sandor Halebsky and John M. Kirk. New York: Praeger, pp. 79–92.

Pérez-Stable, Marifeli. "The Politics of Socialism: Cuban Workers and the Revolution." In *The Cuban Reader: Myths and Realities,* ed. Philip Brenner, William Leogrande, and Donna Rich. Grove Press, forthcoming.

Pichardo, Hortensia. 1973. *Documentos para la historia de Cuba 2.* Havana: Instituto del Libro.

Prieto, Yolanda. 1984. "Reinterpreting an Immigration Success Story: Cuban Women, Work and Change in a New Jersey Community." Ph.D diss., Rutgers University.

Primer Congreso del Partido Comunista de Cuba. 1976. *Tesis y resoluciones.* Havana: Departamento de Orientación Revolucionaria.

Radaelli, Ana María. 1985. "For the Full Equality of Women." *Cuba International,* July, 13–17.

Randall, Margaret. 1974. *Cuban Women Now: Interviews with Cuban Women.* Toronto: The Woman's Press.

Second Congress of the Communist Party of Cuba. 1981. *Documents and Speeches.* Havana: Political Publishers.

Steffens, Heidi. 1974. "FMC: Feminine, not Feminist." *Cuba Review* 4, 22–24.

Trotsky, Leon. 1973. *Problems of Everyday Life.* New York: Monad Press.

Veiga, Roberto, 1984. "Informe central." *Trabajadores.* February 27.

YOLANDA PRIETO

Cuban Women in the U.S. Labor Force: Perspectives on the Nature of Change

ABSTRACT

This article looks at the factors responsible for the high rate of labor force participation among Cuban women in the United States by studying a sample of 107 Cuban-born women in Hudson County, New Jersey. It is perplexing that so many Cuban women in the United States work, given the strong disapproval of female work outside the home in prerevolutionary Cuba. This study suggests that one of the strongest reasons behind the high labor force participation of Cuban women in the sample is the predominantly middle-class origin and/or ideology of Cuban immigrants. The upward mobility of the Cuban family in the United States seems to justify the massive entrance of women into the labor force.

RESUMEN

Este artículo examina los factores reponsables por la alta tasa de participación laboral de las mujeres cubanas en los EE.UU. mediante el estudio de una muestra de 107 mujeres nacidas en Cuba en el Condado de Hudson, New Jersey. Resulta sorprendente que tantas mujeres cubanas trabajen en los EE.UU. dada la fuerte desaprobación hacia el trabajo femenino fuera del hogar que existía en la Cuba pre-revolucionaria. Este estudio sugiere que una de las razones primordiales que explican la alta participación laboral de las mujeres cubanas en la muestra es el origen predominantemente de clase media y/o la ideología de los inmigrantes cubanos. La movilidad ascendente de la familia cubana en los EE.UU. parece justificar la entrada masiva de mujeres en la fuerza laboral.

The challenge to the traditional place of women in Cuban society was one among the many changes brought about by the 1959 Revolution. The attempt to transform structures and deeply rooted attitudes that had kept women at the bottom of the social ladder generated enthusiasm but also a great deal of anxiety among males and females who had accepted "the woman's destiny" as something natural or inevitable.

One of the ways in which the new government began to promote the integration of women into society was to make their massive entrance into the labor force a goal. In prerevolutionary Cuba there was a strong disapproval of women working outside the home. The ideal place for women was "la casa" (the home), as opposed to "la calle" (the street). This distinction had moral connotations: good women would stay home, where they belonged, and avoid the street, where they would be exposed to the dangers of male sexuality. Thus, working outside the home was seen to be risky and done only if absolutely necessary. However, staying at home was possible only for those women, generally from the middle and upper classes, whose fathers or husbands could provide sufficiently for the family. The majority of working women were poor and needed their jobs for economic survival. Many were domestics, some worked in other service occupations, and a small percentage had industrial jobs. But in general, the total percentage of women in the labor force in 1956–57 (when the last prerevolutionary census was taken) was rather low (14.2 percent).[1]

The dramatic changes in the role of women as a result of the Revolution has been one of the numerous reasons that many families left Cuba after 1959. The "destruction of the family" was, according to Cuban men interviewed in a study conducted in Chicago in 1969, an outcome of the revolutionary government's policies concerning women (Fox, 1970: 279). These men pointed out that women not only worked outside the home, but also performed rough work in paid and unpaid agricultural labor and participated in the armed forces and in revolutionary committees. This confirmed their fears that socialism had a deleterious effect on women and the family.

In light of this historical experience, it is interesting that those who left Cuba after the Revolution, once believers that the natural place for women is the home, have significantly changed their behavior. While in 1970 the percentage of women in the labor force in Cuba was 18.3, the 1970 U.S. Census showed that the proportion of Cuban women in the U.S. labor force was almost three times as large as that of their counterparts in Cuba (55.1 percent) (Junta Central de Planificación, 1975; U.S. Bureau of the Census, 1973). In 1980, Cuban women exhibited the highest rate of labor force participation of all females in the three major Hispanic groups in the United States: 55.4 percent, compared with 49 percent Mexican-American and 40 percent Puerto Rican (U.S. Bureau of the Census, 1983).

What are the reasons behind this significant behavioral change on the part of Cubans in the U.S. concerning women and work? Is it economic need due to migration? Is it contact with an advanced, industrial society, where a great number of women have always worked? Is it the availability of jobs where Cubans have settled? Is economic mobility a valued family goal that justifies the massive entrance of women into the labor force?

This article will attempt to shed some light on these questions by examining the results of a study conducted in Hudson County, New Jersey, the second largest concentration of Cubans in the United States. The sample consisted of 107 Cuban-born women. Data on labor force participation and on attitudes about work outside the home were gathered primarily through structured and in-depth interviews with the respondents.

From Cuba to the United States: Economic Achievement and Middle-Class Ideology

The post-1959 Cuban migration to the United States, at least until the 1980 Mariel boatlift, was not representative of the Cuban population. As is well known, Cubans leaving the island were predominantly white, professional or semiprofessional, and mainly from urban areas. Consequently, the Cuban migration of the 1960s has been defined as a middle-class phenomenon by many authors, the media, and the general public. However, this is not quite accurate; even before Mariel, Cubans migrating to the United States represented a mixed population. Persons of working-class origin were also leaving the country, due in part to Cuba's difficult economic situation, especially in the late 1960s (Portes, 1969; Amaro and Portes, 1972; Prohias and Casal, 1974; Portes, Clark, and Bach, 1977).

The predominantly middle-class origin of the Cuban emigrés to the United States has been said to assist the group in becoming economically integrated into U.S. society. Moreover, Cubans' middle-class ideology, in particular their work ethic, is believed to be responsible for the economic success experienced by the group in a relatively short time.[2]

Studies about Cubans in the United States have interpreted their relatively successful economic integration into U.S. society precisely along the lines of Cuban "middle-classness." Even though studies vary in emphasizing different characteristics of the migrants and the communities they have established, their interpretations of Cubans' economic success are ultimately related to the predominant social class of origin of the group under scrutiny. Thus, many studies stress the importance of transferable abilities that Cubans brought with them when they came to the United States, such as occupational skills and education. Some focus on the development of strong enclave immigrant economies. Others call attention to specific characteristics of Cuban households, such as low fertility rates, the economic contribution of most family members, and a high level of female labor force participation (Portes, 1969; Amaro and Portes, 1972; Prohias and Casal, 1974; Portes, Clark and Bach, 1977; Portes and Wilson, 1980; Perez, 1986; Rogg, 1974; Rogg and Santana-Cooney, 1980).

The role of class ideology or belief systems has not been sufficiently examined in studies of Cubans' economic integration in the United States. This is understandable because "ideology" is much harder to define, operationalize, and ultimately "prove." However, to examine such belief systems becomes important if we want to understand more fully the dynamics that shape and differentiate the behavior of various groups in a complex society such as that of the United States.

At the theoretical level, there has always been an interest in the relationship between one's location in the social structure, belief system, and economic behavior. For example, classical sociological theory provides a starting point for this discussion. Karl Marx and Max Weber attributed an important role to ideas in influencing people's economic actions. Of course, neither implied a mechanical connection between ideas, individual or group action, and class location in society. Beliefs, according to Marx and Weber, are socially determined and differ from one group to another. Though working from very different perspectives, these thinkers concur remarkably when studying the motivation and the logic in the ideas and behavior of the middle strata of society. Thus, if we believe that some of their theoretical propositions can be applied to the here and now, we could refer to Marx's "class interest of the petite bourgeoisie" or to Weber's "work ethic as the ascetic trait of the middle class" as essentially describing the same phenomenon: individual or group action guided by a world view that emphasizes economic achievement.

It is precisely this relationship between socioeconomic or social class of origin, the ideology or belief system of that particular class or group, and economic behavior, that I am concerned with in this article. If we accept that middle-class individuals predominate among Cuban migrants, it would be logical to assume that their values correspond with the dominant achievement-oriented ideology of the U.S. middle class. Even when considering that not all Cubans in the United States come from the middle class (and most who did lost that status when migrating anyway), a generalized image develops about Cubans that the general public and the migrants themselves share, and which is to a great extent real. This image embodies middle-class characteristics (a respect for hard work, ambition, and abiding by the law) and persists regardless of former or present class position. Precisely because this middle-class image is maintained and reproduced in society even after one's original structural position has disappeared (that is, a middle-class position in Cuba), I believe that ideology plays an important role in influencing the behavior of these immigrants—especially economic behavior. The strong work ethic of Cubans, product of a previous middle-class position and ideology, generates a high degree of economic activity and, for many, economic success in the new country. The contribution of Cuban women to this economic success is vital. It is mainly in this context that the high incorporation of Cuban women into the labor force in the United States is analyzed in this essay.

Cuban Women in the United States: A Case Study

Cubans have settled primarily in Florida, but there are other areas of concentration in the United States. New Jersey contains a large Cuban settlement with about 10 percent of the total 806,223 Cubans listed in the 1980 U.S. census. In New Jersey, Cubans live mainly in Hudson County, a 46.4-square-mile area located within minutes of New York City. The county seat is Jersey City. Cubans reside primarily in Union City and West New York, where they constitute 32 percent and 39 percent of the population, respectively.

Since Cuban women have an even higher rate of labor force participation in New Jersey than they do nationally (59.4 percent, compared with 55.4 percent nationally), this site provides a particularly appropriate context in which to ask our initial research question.

The Labor Market in Hudson County

Traditionally, the largest single source of employment in Hudson County has been manufacturing, of which the apparel and textile industries are extremely important. These industries are labor-intensive, requiring many workers. Immigrants, especially minorities and women, have provided a steady supply of labor. But even though manufacturing continues to be the most important source of employment in this area, its decline since 1960 has been staggering. Between 1970 and 1980 Hudson County lost a total of 42,315 jobs in the manufacturing sector (Hudson County Planning Board, 1974; U.S. Department of Commerce, 1982). Yet the apparel industry has not been the hardest hit. In Hudson County, despite the employment decline in manufacturing over the past decade, small and competitive firms (some of them owned by Cubans and other immigrants) still provide jobs for women and minorities. For example, in 1980, 82 percent of the economically active population of Hudson County of Spanish origin was employed in manufacturing (U.S. Bureau of the Census, 1982). This fact may help explain the high rate of incorporation of Cuban women into the area's work force. These local, smaller firms are able to remain in business partly because of the mainly female pool of immigrant labor that has traditionally been available in Hudson County.

Methodology

In order to investigate why so many Cuban women work, I drew a sample of Cuban-born women in the Jersey City Standard Metropolitan Statistical Area (equivalent to Hudson County). Data collection took place between July 1979 and May 1981. Random and nonrandom techniques were used in the selection. The random and nonrandom components of the sample were drawn in two different stages. Because I lacked a sampling frame that included all Cuban women in Hudson County, my alternative was to approximate a multistage cluster sample, employing census tracts.

Using the 1970 census figures, I assigned a percentage of interviews per tract proportionate to the percentage of Cubans living in each tract. Once I determined the number of interviews per tract, I assigned the same number of blocks as designated interviews for the tract. Twenty-two tracts were included in the study out of a total of twenty-seven. The final number of cases selected was 107. Respondents had to be at least thirty years old so they would be able to compare their experiences in Cuba and in the United States.

During the data collection period, a new wave of refugees came to the United States from Cuba through the port of Mariel. Some of these new refugees came to the study area. This event gave me an opportunity to find out if the newcomers were significantly different from the earlier Cubans, and to evaluate the impact of their presence on the basic research questions. The randomized interviews represent 26 percent of the total sample; 74 percent had already been interviewed. There were still six census tracts, a total of twenty-eight blocks, to complete. I decided to randomize the rest of the sample to see whether the new wave was changing the general patterns of the Cuban community of the area. I drew a randomized multistage cluster sample by listing each household of the remaining twenty-eight blocks and randomly selecting the interviews assigned per block.[3] The final numbers of new immigrants from Mariel selected and interviewed was five, that is, 4.7 percent of the total (107). In general the new cases were not too different from the rest of the community. All of them except one were relatives of families in Union City and West New York; they had been expecting to leave Cuba for years and seized the first opportunity to do so.

An initial run using cross-tabulation analysis was performed on every variable by random and nonrandom sample. No significant statistical difference was found between the two on any of the variables. Thus, these two subsamples were collapsed and treated equally as one single random sample.

I collected data primarily through interviews using a structured questionnaire. In addition, I interviewed in depth a smaller subsample using recording tapes. These interviews were open-ended. Broad questions were asked and generally the women talked freely.

The structured interviews lasted about one and a half hours each. The taped interviews were much longer; some of them ran from three to four hours. The refusal rate was very low (4.7 percent), and with the exception of one woman, the excuse given was lack of time.

In the following pages I will describe some of the salient characteristics of the sample of Cuban women in Hudson County and explore how these characteristics relate to labor force participation. My conclusions suggest that the attitudes about women, work, and the family expressed by the respondents are related to their former class positions and/or ideology.

Selected Characteristics of the Hudson County Sample and Labor Force Participation

Women in the Hudson County sample had an even higher rate of participation in the labor force (68.2 percent) than other women in the

TABLE 1
Female Labor Force Participation Among Selected Hispanic Groups in the United States, 1980 (in percent)

	Total Female Population	Mexican-Americans	Puerto Ricans	Cubans	Total Spanish-Speaking
United States	49.9	49.0	40.1	55.4	49.3
New Jersey	50.6	52.1	43.1	59.4	50.6
Hudson County, N.J.	49.2	—	—	—	52.2
Hudson County sample[a]	—	—	—	68.2	—

Sources: U.S. Bureau of the Census, *U.S. Summary, 1980* (1983), and *New Jersey, 1980* (1983).
 a. Drawn from the present study, conducted July 1979–May 1981.

area and higher than Cuban women in New Jersey and the nation (see table 1). Women interviewed in the Hudson County sample (median age, 49.7 years) were considerably older than Cuban and other Hispanic and non-Hispanic females nationally. This was partially due to the sample selection procedure, which established a minimum age of thirty.

A great majority, 73.8 percent, were married. Having a husband has traditionally meant having someone to depend on economically, but this was not the case here. As can be seen in table 2, 70 percent of the married women in the sample participated in the labor force. This is a higher percentage than women in the category that included divorced, separated, and widowed women. The explanation is that some of these women were beyond working age, while others were unmarried heads of households taking care of young children. In general, however, a significant proportion of the women in each category worked for pay.

Children, especially if they are young, have traditionally kept women from joining the work force. The mean number of children among women in the sample was 2.0, while the mean number of persons per household was 3.2. In 50.5 percent of the cases, the children were living with their parents. Thirty-one percent of the women interviewed reported that some of the children were living at home and some lived elsewhere. Generally, those living elsewhere were married. In fewer cases there were children away at school. Most college-attending children of the women in the sample commuted to a nearby campus.

TABLE 2
Marital Status and Labor Force Participation of 107 Cuban Women in Hudson County, N.J., 1979–81

	Single		Married		Divorced, Separated, Widowed		Total	
	%	N	%	N	%	N	%	N
Working women	83.3	5	70.1	56	54.5	12	68.2	73
Women who do only housework	0.0	0	21.5	17	36.4	8	23.4	25
Retired women	16.7	1	6.3	5	4.5	1	6.5	7
Women seeking, but unable to find work	0.0	0	1.3	1	4.5	1	1.9	2
Total	100.0	6	100.0	79	100.0	22	100.0	107

Sources: See table 1.
Note: Chi square = 6.18; significance = 0.4; degrees of freedom = 6. Sample drawn from the present study, conducted July 1979–May 1981.

The percentage of women with children under age six in the sample was low, 3.7 percent. (Remember that respondents had to be at least thirty years old). Even so, we found a difference between workers and nonworkers by number and age of children. Only 3.3 percent of the workers had children under six, while 6.3 percent of the nonworkers were in this category. Similarly, 21.3 percent of the workers have no children at all, while all of the nonworkers had children. Child care responsibilities, especially for young children, explained why some women did not participate in the work force.

Table 3 shows that almost half (48.1 percent) the women interviewed in this sample had worked for pay in Cuba before coming to the United States. The fact that so many women in the sample had worked in Cuba reflects at least two things. First, the assumption that few Cuban women did not work outside the home (or for pay) may have been more a myth than a reality, especially in the decade preceding the Revolution. It is quite possible that many salaried women were not counted by the census as part of the labor force. Some of the occupations that sample members reported (such as working as a seamstress) could have been carried out at home.

Second, the majority of women in the Hudson County sample came to the United States during the late 1960s and early 1970s. During those years one of the goals of the revolutionary government had been to incorporate more women into production. Opportunities for women, therefore, were opening up in Cuba that did not exist earlier. Work outside the home was becoming more acceptable. Many of the women in the sample who worked in Cuba did so because jobs were

TABLE 3
Labor Force Participation of 106 Cuban Women in Cuba and the United States

	Cuba Did Not Work %	Cuba Did Not Work N	Cuba Worked %	Cuba Worked N	United States %	United States N
Working women	70.9	39	66.7	34	68.8	73
Women who do only housework	23.6	13	23.5	12	23.6	25
Retired women	5.5	3	5.9	3	5.7	6
Women seeking, but unable to find work	0.0	0	3.9	2	1.9	2
Total	51.9	55	48.1	51	100.0	106

Sources: See table 1.
Note: Totals differ slightly from table 2 because of one missing case. Sample drawn from the present study, conducted in Hudson County, N.J., July 1979–May 1981.

available and they could earn money without incurring disapproval. Their joining the work force was independent of their later decision to leave the country.

As seen in Table 3, having worked or not having worked in Cuba does not have an impact on labor force participation here. The distribution of women according to their economic activity in Cuba is almost identical among those who opted to work in the United States and those who did not.

As previous studies have indicated, the Cuban community of Hudson County, unlike the Cuban population nationally, contains a significant proportion of persons from rural and semirural areas and small towns in Cuba (Rogg, 1974). They have not achieved the educational levels of the rest of the country. For example, while 44 percent of Cubans in the United States are high school graduates, only 12.4 percent of the respondents in our sample had attained that level. There was little variation between the educational level of married women and that of their husbands.

The large majority of the working women in the sample were in blue-collar occupations in the apparel and textile industries. This fact is not surprising, given the lower educational level of the sample and the predominance of blue-collar, especially manufacturing, employment in this area. As shown in table 4, more women in the sample were concentrated in the blue-collar occupations (generally as operatives) than their husbands. The older age of Cuban women in the Hudson County sample and their poor knowledge of English may account for their high concentration in factory work. By contrast, 14.3 percent of men were in the service category, compared with only 4.1 percent of the women.

Also interesting was the difference in the professional, technical, and managerial category, where 8.1 percent of the women were concentrated, as opposed to only 1.4 percent of the men. Yet more men than women owned businesses. Since the difference in educational levels between males and females was not significant, the fact that there were more women professionals indicates that it was easier for some educated Cuban women to enter traditionally acceptable professions for women, such as teaching or social work. For example, of the women interviewed who had been lawyers in Cuba, most were working in social service agencies in Jersey City or New York. Educated men, on the other hand, may have concentrated their efforts in business.

Cubans suffered a significant loss of occupational status after coming to the United States (Moncarz 1969; Rogg 1974). But they appear to have adapted their old values and aspirations to their new circumstances even when their new social location was not the same. To

TABLE 4
Occupations of Employed Cuban Women in Hudson County, N.J., and Husbands, 1979–81 (in percent)

	Total Women[a]	Husbands
Owning a business	6.8[b]	12.9
Professional, technical, managerial work	8.1	1.4
White-collar work	10.8	11.4
Blue-collar work	67.6	51.4
Service work	4.1	14.3
Self-employment	1.4	1.5
Other	1.2	7.1

Sources: See table 1.
Note: Sample drawn from the present study, conducted July 1979–May 1981.
   a. Includes both married and unmarried women; 5 of the total working women were single; 12 were separated, divorced, or widowed (see table 2).
   b. Many women reported owning businesses with their husbands.

determine the degree of occupational mobility experienced by the sample, we compared occupational status in Cuba and the United States. Broad occupational categories were used: blue-collar and service work were considered low-status occupations; white-collar work and being self-employed, a middle status; and owning a business or practicing a profession, high status. Data for husbands as heads of households in Cuba and in the United States were used for this purpose, since not all women in the sample had occupations in Cuba. Table 5 compares the occupational status levels of husbands in Cuba and in the United States.

Although there is a significant association between occupational status in Cuba and in the United States (because a sufficient number of people maintained the same occupations), there is also a pattern of downward mobility. For example, 47.2 percent of white-collar and self-employed workers in Cuba became blue-collar or service workers in the United States, and 52.6 percent of those owning businesses or in the professions in Cuba moved down to the white-collar category in the United States. Conversely, a high percentage (68.2 percent) of those having blue-collar or service jobs in Cuba remained in the same category after emigration. Among those in the blue-collar and service categories in Cuba, 22 percent moved up to white-collar jobs in the United States, and 9.1 percent became business owners or professionals.

The majority of women who worked for pay in Cuba and also went to work in the United States experienced downward mobility. Fifty-six percent of those who worked in Cuba and held white-collar jobs in their country moved down to blue-collar occupations in the United

TABLE 5
Husbands' Occupations in Cuba and in the United States (in percent)

	\multicolumn{6}{c}{Cuba}		
	Blue-Collar Work and Service Work[a]		White-Collar Work and Self-Employment		Owning a Business and Professional Work		United	States
	%	N	%	N	%	N	%	N
Blue-collar and service work	68.2	15	47.2	17	10.5	2	44.2	34
White-collar work and self-employment	22.7	5	44.4	16	52.6	10	40.3	31
Owning a business	9.1	2	8.3	3	36.8	7	15.6	12
Total	28.6	22	46.8	36	24.6	19	100.0	77

Sources: See table 1.
Note: Sample drawn from the present study, conducted July 1979–May 1981. Chi square = 17.70; significance = .01; degrees of freedom = 4.
a. Does not include professional services.

States. This movement obviously reflects the difficulties that most working women had in maintaining the same occupation after emigration. Language problems were the main impediment to staying in the same occupational field. Women in white-collar, professional, and business occupations in the United States had held similar positions in Cuba. This pattern indicates that those women in Cuba in the professions and with higher levels of education and knowledge of English could transfer their skills more easily to the United States.

Why Do so Many Cuban Women Work?

This discussion can only refer to Cuban women and work in the Hudson County sample. However, the answers of these respondents may suggest general patterns in the behavior of Cuban women in the United States. We asked the women in the sample their main reason for working. Eighty-three percent said to help the family financially; 5 percent said to pay for their children's education. Others gave more personal reasons, such as becoming economically independent (9.5 percent) and self-realization (2.7 percent).

The answers confirmed what many studies about immigrant women in the United States have found: working outside the home is a response to the economic needs of the family. Wage labor was viewed by Cuban women as an extension of their family obligations and as an important contribution to the family economy. In general, women's economic contribution represented about 40 percent of the total family income.[4]

The central importance of family in explaining why so many Cuban women work outside the home is reflected in the way they spend their salaries. When given a series of categories to indicate how they spent their money, 70.1 percent mentioned food first. Paying the rent or mortgage was another top priority for 53 percent. For 32.4 percent, utilities were among the three most important expenditures. Education of the children was one of the top priorities for 15 percent of the women.[5]

In the opinion of many of the respondents, having small children at home was the most powerful reason why a woman should not work: 57.5 percent said they should not work when children are young. On the other hand, 36.8 percent responded that having small children was no impediment to work, although some qualified this statement by saying that there was no reason a mother should not work if children are cared for by a trustworthy person, preferably a relative. Only 3.8 percent said women with children should never work, 0.9 percent responded that women with children should not work if their husbands objected, and the same proportion stated that women with children should never work unless there was a great need in the family.

Employment outside the home was seen as necessary to supplement the needs of the family. However, one central element here is that most Cuban women in the sample clearly expressed that they worked to help the family regain what it had lost in Cuba as a result of the Revolution, and for that end, any type of work became acceptable. Thus, female employment outside the home is seen as vital not only for survival, but also for the upward mobility of the family.

An elementary school teacher in the Hudson County sample illustrates the above points:

I always worked in Cuba because I enjoyed my career. Maybe it was because I always saw my mother work (she was a teacher) and it became so natural. Here, I do the same kind of work I used to do in Cuba and I like it. I am an elementary school teacher. Even though my husband has a business now I want to continue working. I think it would be inconsiderate on my part to stay home while he works. Life is very expensive and we Cubans are used to living comfortably. . . . No wonder most Cuban women have jobs here. Cuban women have been forced to help their families recuperate in only a few years the standard of living they had achieved in Cuba before communism took over.
—Married white woman, forty years old, middle-class with university education in Cuba, from Las Villas.

The reasons for this strong emphasis on participating in the labor force are intimately connected to the specific characteristics of the Cuban migration. Cubans have a strong work ethic. This is in part geared toward substituting for the social and economic rewards that the family lost in the homeland (even if this work ethic can satisfy only material wants at first). Therefore, factors pertaining to the specific nature of the Cuban migration to the United States and the reception offered the group in this country have to be taken into account. The high level of participation of Cuban women in the U.S. work force is one way in which the family can achieve faster economic success and substitute for the lost economic and social rewards enjoyed in Cuba.

Cuban "refugees" of the 1960s, like those from other socialist countries, were determined to succeed in U.S. society and brought skills that allowed success in many cases and reinforced their drives. Thus, the high incorporation of Cuban women into the U.S. labor force has to be seen in the context of a migrant group that wants to regain a middle-class life and its symbols: owning a home, sending the children to college, and saving for the future. These material achievements may not be the equivalent of obtaining a middle-class status in U.S. society—Cubans are a Hispanic minority in the United States—but it paves the way for the mobility of the family (especially of the children) to that status in the future. This goal justifies the massive entrance of women into the labor force and their acceptance of manual, blue-collar work.

These generalizations apply to the workers who left in the late 1960s and early 1970s as well as to former middle-class Cubans. Former working-class women in the sample were from families aspiring to middle-class status before the Revolution. In their view, coming to the United States was the only way in which their aspirations could be realized.

A formerly working-class woman talked about her family's reasons for leaving Cuba in the early seventies and about why she thinks Cubans work so hard in the United States:

Why did we leave Cuba? Well, because we didn't like that system ["no nos gustaba aquello"]. The reason was political. In Cuba there was no place to better yourself. The Revolution brought many people down instead of helping them to improve themselves. That is why Cubans work so hard here, because they are used to always struggling to have something and to secure a better future for their children. They did that in Cuba, too, no matter how poor they were.

> —Married white woman, forty-three years old, working-class with some secondary education in Cuba, from Havana.

Being a "burden" to the U.S. government, to relatives, or to society in general was a concern for many interviewees. A former secondary school teacher reflected on the reasons why Cubans work so hard and how this is seen by other groups:

Cuban women work out of necessity unless they have a profession they like. The husband's salary is not sufficient. In Cuba, it was enough if the man worked. You could even have servants. But here, life is different. If there are children in the family, both husband and wife have to work to provide these children with a good education. I think the main reason for working is economic need. Many people say that Cubans work hard because they want to have two cars and many other things. I think that is not totally true. Many other people are envious of us because we work hard. Even the Americans sometimes! For example, my daughter has the highest point average in her class, and many kids (especially American kids) resent the fact that she is Cuban and number one. But the reason why we are successful is because we work hard and are responsible. . . . When we came to this country we had a lot of debts. We went to Spain first, and our relatives here had to send the plane tickets for us to come here, plus money to live on during the months we had to wait in Spain. When we got here we wanted to work doing *anything* to pay our relatives back. So we didn't work to buy luxuries then but to support ourselves and pay our debts. Only when we finished paying them did we start thinking about buying things. It is not right to be a burden to this government or to people who have helped you, even if they are your relatives.
—Married white woman, forty-eight years old, middle-class with secondary education in Cuba, from Las Villas.

As the above quotes suggest, a strong factor behind the high level of labor force participation among Cuban women is their predominantly middle-class origins or aspirations and a middle-class ideology of upward mobility. Although these findings apply only to the sample studied here, similar reasons may explain the equally high level of labor force participation of Cuban women nationally and in the Cuban concentrations in the United States. (For data, see Wilber, Jaco, Hagan, and del Fierro, 1976, vol. 3; Ferree, 1978; Diaz, 1981).

Thus, we see that the characteristics of Cuban immigrants explain in part their heightened economic activity. But these characteristics would not mean much if there were no labor market for these human resources. The correspondence between the needs of industries for workers and the high motivation of Cubans to work explains the high levels of Cuban women in the work force in Hudson County, New Jersey.

Conclusion

This article attempts to explain the high level of labor force participation of Cuban women by analyzing a sample of Cuban-born women in Hudson County, New Jersey. Given the negative attitudes existing in prerevolutionary Cuba about women working outside the home, it becomes important to understand this paradoxical behavioral change among Cubans who left the island, among other things, to escape radical changes affecting the traditional role of women and the family.

Although unusual characteristics of the sample—such as there being fewer children, and children of older age than is the case with other Hispanic groups—account for higher female labor force activity, the strongest factor behind the intense economic activity of Cuban women (as for Cubans in general) is the combination of middle-class values or aspirations, a rejection of the socialist revolution taking place in their homeland, and positive attitudes about the U.S. economic and political system. These strong beliefs, common among refugees from socialist countries, are manifested in a powerful work ethic and aspirations for social mobility. Primarily to compensate for the lost rewards in their home country, this group justifies the massive entrance of women into paid production.

These conclusions raise other questions, however. Do Cuban women in the United States feel that they are more "liberated" now because they work outside the home? Moreover, is female labor force participation in general an indicator of female emancipation? This last question has been indeed posed by feminist scholars studying women and work. Like Cuban women, immigrant and other women in the United States and elsewhere have seen work outside the home as a way to help the family and not as a means to sexual liberation.

However, the process of participating in the labor force appears to confer an independent identity (perhaps only an economic one at first) on women, whether or not they are conscious of an identity change. For example, despite the fact that the overwhelming majority of women interviewed maintained that the principal reason for work was to help the family economically, 64.4 percent said that they would work even if their families did not need the money. A much lower percentage (35.6 percent) stated that they would prefer to stay home under those circumstances.

Many women workers in the sample admitted feeling more independent as a result of having a job. The process of participating in the labor force may make Cuban women more cautious of the significance of work in their lives, beyond that of meeting the needs of their families. It is to be hoped that incorporation of Cuban women into the U.S. labor force will pave the way for their increased participation in other public spheres in the Cuban community and in American society at large.

NOTES

This article, from my Ph.D. dissertation, is part of a larger research project supported by the Ford Foundation. It is adapted from two earlier articles: "Women, Work and Change: The Case of Cuban Women in the U.S.," Latin American Monograph Series 9, Northwestern Pennsylvania Institute for Latin American Studies, Mercyhurst College [Erie, Pa.], 1979; "Cuban Women and Work in the United States: A New Jersey Case Study," in *International Migration: The Female Experience,* ed. Rita J. Simon and Caroline Brettell (Totowa, N.J.: Rowman and Allanheld, 1986).

1. Consejo Nacional de Economía, 1958. In the late 1940s and early 1950s, increasing numbers of lower middle-class and upper-class women joined the labor force, the former group mainly because of changes in the Cuban economy (Kaufman-Purcell, 1970:260–61). Economic expansion, U.S. investments in utilities, communications, oil refining, and tourism generated white-collar work opportunities, particularly for educated lower middle-class women.

According to census figures, between 1943 and 1953, the number of female typists and stenographers increased from 1,253 to 5,420; the percentage of female elementary teachers increased from 77.5 to 84.3, and that of female professors increased from 53.6 to 67.8. Many women also became service workers (waitresses and janitors), undoubtedly because of the growth of tourism. More women also became domestics, as more families could afford their services.

2. "Middle-class" here denotes professional, semiprofessional, and entrepreneurial categories, in which a certain level of education is needed and aspirations to economic success are implied.

3. I could not use a random selection process because of the impossibility, given limited time, resources, and research assistants, of listing every household in every block in order to construct a sampling frame.

4. Median income in the sample was $6,336. Median total family income, out of six income categories, was between $13,000 and $15,999.

5. Even though most women interviewed stressed the importance of education to upward mobility, few cited their most important reason for working as to provide for their children's education. This discrepancy is explained by the fact that some women gave "education of the children" as a motive for working, while others included that motive in the response "helping the family financially." Indeed, financial self-sufficiency was encouraged in children. In most cases, because of the older age of the sample, children had already finished college; and many had received financial aid and/or had worked to pay for their education.

REFERENCES

Amaro, Nelson, and Alejandro Portes. 1972. "Situación de los grupos cubanos en Estados Unidos." *Aportes* 3.
Consejo Nacional de Economía. 1958. *El empleo, el subempleo y el desempleo en Cuba.* Havana: CNE.

Diaz, Guarione, ed. 1981. *Evaluation and Identification of Policy Issues in the Cuban Community.* Miami: Cuban National Planning Council.
Domínguez, Virginia. 1977. "The Nature of Change: Cuban Women in the United States." Presented at the Conference on Women and Change, Boston University, May 6–7.
Ferree, Myra Marx. 1979. "Employment Without Liberation: Cuban Women in the United States." *Social Sciences Quarterly* 60 (June).
Fox, Geoffrey E. 1970. "Honor, Shame and Women's Liberation in Cuba." In *Female and Male in Latin America,* ed. Anne Pescatello. Pittsburgh, Pa.: University of Pittsburgh Press.
Hudson County [N.J.] Planning Board. 1972. "Distribution of Cuban Population. Map No. 8." *Hudson County Population Study.* Jersey City, N.J.: County of Hudson.
———. 1974. *Economic Base Study.* Jersey City, N.J.: County of Hudson.
Junta Central de Planificación. 1975. *Censo de población y viviendas, 1970.* Havana: Editorial Orbe.
Junta Nacional del Censo. 1945. *Censo de 1943.* Havana: P. Fernández y Cía., S. en C.
Kaufman-Purcell, Susan. 1970. "Modernizing Women for a Modern Society: The Cuban Case." In *Female and Male in Latin America,* ed. Anne Pescatello. Pittsburgh, Pa.: University of Pittsburgh Press.
Marx, Karl, and Frederick Engels. 1974. *The German Ideology.* New York: International Publishers.
Moncarz, Raul. 1969. *A Study of the Effect of Environmental Change on Human Capital Among Selected Skilled Cubans.* Washington, D.C.: Clearinghouse for Federal Scientific and Technical Information, U.S. Department of Commerce, National Bureau of Standards.
Oficina Nacional de los Censos Demográfico y Electoral. 1955. *Censos de población, viviendas y electoral. Informe General, 1953.* Havana: P. Fernández y Cía, S. en C.
Pérez, Lisandro. 1986. "Immigrant Economic Adjustment and Family Organization: The Cuban Success Story Reexamined." *International Migration Review* 20 (Spring).
Portes, Alejandro, Juan M. Clark, and Robert L. Bach. 1977. "The New Wave: A Statistical Profile of Recent Cuban Exiles to the United States." *Cuban Studies* 7 (January).
Prohías, Rafael, and Lourdes Casal. 1974. *The Cuban Minority in the United States: Preliminary Report on Need Identification and Program Evaluation.* Boca Raton: Florida Atlantic University.
Rogg, Eleanor M. 1974. *The Assimilation of Cuban Exiles: The Role of Community and Class.* New York: Aberdeen Press.
Rogg, Eleanor M., and Rosemary Sanatana Cooney. 1980. *Adaptation and Adjustment of Cubans: West New York, New Jersey.* Hispanic Research Center Monograph No. 5, Fordham University.
U.S. Bureau of the Census. 1973. *Final Report, 1970.* Washington, D.C.: GPO.
———. 1983. *Characteristics of the Population, General Social and Economic Characteristics, U.S. Summary, 1980.* Washington, D.C.: GPO.
———. 1983. *General Social and Economic Characteristics, New Jersey, 1980.* Washington, D.C.: GPO.
U.S. Department of Commerce. 1982. *County Business Patterns, 1980.* Washington, D.C.: GPO.
Weber, Max. 1958. *The Protestant Ethic and the Spirit of Capitalism.* New York: Charles Scribner's Sons.
Wilber, George, D. E. Jaco, R. J. Hagan, and Al del Fierro. 1976. *Minorities in the Labor Market.* Vol. 1: *Spanish Americans and Indians in the Labor Market.* Vol. 3:

Metropolitan and Regional Inequalities Among Minorities in the Labor Market. Lexington: University of Kentucky Press.

Wilson, Kenneth L., and Alejandro Portes. 1980. "Immigrant Enclaves: An analysis of the Labor Market Experience of Cubans in Miami." *American Journal of Sociology* 86, no. 2.

Yans-McLaughlin, Virginia. 1971. "Patterns of Work and Family Organization: Buffalo's Italians." *Journal of Social History* 2 (Autumn).

AFRO-CUBANISM

JORGE CASTELLANOS
ISABEL CASTELLANOS

The Geographic, Ethnologic, and Linguistic Roots of Cuban Blacks

ABSTRACT

Black slaves were introduced in Cuba from a vast region in western Africa and from Mozambique, on the eastern coast. This article explains the origin of certain general denominators, such as "lucumí," "arará," "carabalí," "mina," "gangá," and "congo." We define five areas of provenience and identify particular groups within each area, employing geographic, ethnologic, and linguistic criteria.

RESUMEN

Los esclavos negros fueron introducidos en Cuba desde la vasta región de Africa del oeste y desde Mozambique, en la costa este. Este artículo explica el origen de ciertos denominadores generales tales como *lucumí, arará, carabalí, mina, gangá* y *congo*. En el presente trabajo definimos cinco áreas de origen e identificamos grupos particulares dentro de cada área mediante el uso de criterios geográficos, etnológicos y lingüísticos.

The first blacks arrived in Cuba with the conquistadores who took possession of the island in the second decade of the sixteenth century.[1] As soon as the Spaniards settled in Cuba, the demographic disaster that ensued almost wiped out the entire Indian population creating a critical dearth of manual laborers. The colonists sought a solution to this problem through an increasing importation of black slaves. Since then, directly or indirectly, legally or illegally, African slaves were systematically introduced in Cuba. This active slave trade brought into the island a minimum of 850,000 Africans, most of them in the nineteenth century.[2] Thus, from the very beginning, blacks have played a decisive role in the development of Cuban economy, social life, and culture. The purpose of this article is to trace the areas of provenience of the Cuban blacks, considerably enlarging the number of peoples and tribes mentioned in the pioneering works on this subject by Fernando Ortiz, Philip Curtin, and Leví Marrero, adding also a linguistic dimension to classification on the basis of mere geography and ethnologic tradition.[3] This task is far from easy. Cuban slaves referred to themselves and were called by their masters in a number of ways, sometimes by their tribal or clan names, sometimes by regional or political denominations. These terms, when transcribed into Spanish, often became unrecognizable. Nevertheless, many of these names, suggesting general areas of origin, were preserved in Cuba, and we will begin by discussing them. The most important are Lucumí, Mandinga, Arará, Mina, Gangá, Carabalí, and Congo.

Lucumí

The origin of the term *Lucumí* has been the subject of a great deal of speculation. Lydia Cabrera says: "Lucumí is the name given in Cuba to the Yorubas, who occupy the western part of southern Nigeria, with the provinces of Abeokuta, Lagos, Yebú, Ondo."[4] In one of William Bascom's early works we find: "In Cuba, the Yoruba speaking people are known as Lukumi (Lucumi). . . . In some very early maps of West Africa, the kingdom of Ulkamy is placed to the north and northwest of Benin, but I have not been able to find any place or people in this part of Nigeria who are today known by a name like Lukumi."[5] Bascom seems to have abandoned later the hypothesis that the term Lucumí designated a political group or a geographical region in Africa when he says: "In Cuba the descendants of Yoruba slaves are known as Lucumí, a name probably derived from a Yoruba greeting, oluku mi, meaning 'my friend.' "[6]

Yet Olfert Dapper, in his *Description de l'Afrique* (1686), talks about the kingdom of Ulcami or Ulcuma, a country situated between Arder and Benin, toward the northeast.[7] One of the characteristics of this kingdom is that it sold a great number of slaves—either war prisoners or criminals—to the Dutch and the Portuguese to be sent to the New World. Dapper also mentions the neighboring kingdom of Benin, where their god (*sic*) is called "Orisa" (the Yorubas called their gods "orisha") and where annual festivities honoring the sea were held. Both these kingdoms were located in the territory occupied by the ethnic group we know today as Yoruba. Dapper provides two maps: in the first one, a map of Africa, next to Benin we find a region designated as "Ulcuma"; in the second one, called "Nigritarum Regio," this same region appears as "Ulkumi."

In 1734, Captain William Snelgrave mentions a country he calls "Lucamee" lying toward the northeast of the kingdom of Ardra.[8] In his book he also provides a map of the same region, where we find the kingdom of Ulcuma or Ulcami.⁹ None of these works mentions the term *Yoruba*, originally used to refer only to the Oyo and then employed by missionaries in the nineteenth century to designate all the tribes of that general region and their common language.¹⁰ It seems, therefore, that in remote times there was a kingdom in Africa called Ulcami, Ulcumi, or Lucamee from which the word *Lucumí* originated.

Many Cuban slaves, when asked about their origin, named the political unit to which they belonged instead of mentioning their tribe, and called themselves Lucumí. In Cuba this word was used in a very general sense to refer not only to the Yoruba proper, but also to what Murdock calls the Yoruba Cluster, which includes the Egba, Oyo, Ife, and the Ijebu.¹¹ Thus, for instance, slaves used to call themselves Lucumí-egbado, Lucumí-oyo, Lucumí-iyebu, etc. Also, some neighboring tribes not included in the Yoruba Cluster seem to have been called Lucumí.¹²

Mandinga

In Cuba, *Mandinga* was a general term that included not only the Mandinga or Malinke proper (a group that inhabited the upper Niger, and the Senegal and Gambia valleys) but also other neighboring peoples like the Bambara and the Diola or Yola. Strongly influenced by the Arabs, they came to Cuba primarily in the early centuries of the colonization, bringing with them their Moslem beliefs. Roger Bastide claims that the cult of Allah was indubitably established on the island. "Yet, ultimately, as in Brazil, the adherents of Islam joined the Yoruba group, and Allah, thereafter, became identified with Olorun or even with Obatalá, the sky-god whose name was oddly truncated into Obbat-Allah."¹³

Arará

In the Cuban historical sources, such as the official government records of the registration of mutual help societies ("sociedades de socorros mutuos") founded by former slaves, numerous types of Arará appear, such as Arará-cuévano, Arará-sabalú, and Arará-magino.¹⁴ It is known today that the Arará, Aradas, or Ardas were Dahomeans. As quoted above, Dapper mentions the kingdom of Arder, southwest of Ulcami or Ulcuma.¹⁵ In his map "Nigritarum Regio" and in the one provided by Snelgrave, Ardra is located east of the Volta River in the Dahomean territory occupied by the Ewe and the Fon, according to Murdock.¹⁶ Ortiz says that in Cuba the Arará were sometimes confused with the Lucumí (see note 12). Something similar happened in Brazil, where the Dahomean people eventually modeled their own subculture on that of the more influential Yorubas.[17] The fact that slaves were often identified by not only tribal, ethnic, or linguistic terms but also geographical and political denominations is illustrated by the previously cited name Arará-sabalú. We have already seen what Arará means. Sabalú is a city located in the north of the old kingdom of Dahomey, approximately ninety miles north of Allada and close to the Weme River.[18]

Mina

The slaves in Cuba were sometimes called after the specific place from which they were shipped. The name *Mina* probably designated a small group associated with the Popo (Ewe Cluster) as well as the slaves brought from the trade station of San Jorge da Mina, established by the Portuguese in the Fanti territory of the Gold Coast.[19]

Gangá

The true nature of the Gangá—a denomination used not only in Cuba, but in Mexico and Puerto Rico as well—is one of the most intriguing questions of Cuban ethnology. José María de la Torre in 1854, Henri Dumont in 1866, Esteban Pichardo in 1875, and Fernando Ortiz in 1906 and 1916, give abundant proof of the presence of Gangá in colonial Cuba.[20] De la Torre and Dumont place their orgin in the Grain Coast—northwest of Cape Palmas—and the slopes of the surrounding mountains, in close contact with the nearby Mandinga. G. Aguirre Beltrán and Manuel Alvarez Nazario, referring to the Gangá in Mexico and the Cangá in Puerto Rico, indicate that they came from early colonial days to the end of the eighteenth century from the coast and immediate interior region of Sierra Leone and the territory today included in northern Liberia. According to Aguirre Beltrán, Gangá is just a contraction of Gangará, a name used by the Arabs and certain African tribes to refer to the Mende and other members of the southern Malinke sector of the Mandinga family who were settled in the area just mentioned.[21]

The name Gangá has not been found in the African ethnological maps. The Cuban Gangá, however, used to add an identifying label to their so-called national name, calling themselves Gangá-cramo, Gangá-fay, Gangá-conó, Gangá-quisí, etc. With the help of those labels, the localizations of these early Gangá groups becomes a relatively easy task, as shown in the following chart:[22]

CUBAN NAME	AFRICAN NAME
Gangá-quisí	KISSI
Gangá-gola	GOLA
Gangá-fay	VAI?
Gangá-conó	KONO
Gangá-cramo	KRAN
Gangá-tomu	TOMA

The Kissi, Gola, Vai, Kono, Kran, Toma, and the Mende, with which they were intimately related, form a cluster of peoples located exactly where the nineteenth-century scholars indicated: southern Sierra Leone and northern Liberia.

Apparently there is no difficulty in identifying these slaves. However, Lydia Cabrera refers to the Gangá-arriero as a "nation" or tribe that spoke like the Congo (Bantu) and places them among the Congo. Also, in the booklet that accompanies Cabrera's recordings of Afro-Cuban religious music we find a series of Gangá-Ñongobá chants called "mambos" by the family of Gangá ancestry who interprets them.[23] "Mambos" is the name given to Congo ritual songs. Further study of the labels added to the Gangá generic name in Cuba reported by Cabrera, Ortiz, and other sources leads to a surprising result, as shown in the following chart:[24]

CUBAN NAME	AFRICAN NAME
Gangá-gorá	ANGAS (subgroup: Goram)
Gangá-fay	ANGAS? (subgroup: Pai)
Gangá-bandoré*	NDORO
Gangá-insuru	ANGAS (subgroup: Sura)
Gangá-yoni	TIV (subgroup: Iyon)
Gangá-cundo	KUNDU
Gangá-ñongobá*	PUKU (subgroup: Nyong)

*See note 36.

Carabalí

A substantial number of slaves arrived in Cuba from the Bight of Biafra region. These slaves, who were called Carabalí, came from an area that includes southeastern Nigeria (Calabar) and western Cameroon. The term *Carabalí* originates from Calabari, "people of the Calabar." In Cuba they are also known as Brícamos.[25]

A more detailed examination of the ethnic groups in this area can be found below, in our classification of the areas of provenience. Secret societies were very prominent among the Carabalí, and it is from them that the famous Abakuá Secret Society, the Ñáñigos, originates.[26] The Carabalí are culturally and linguistically heterogeneous. They can be classified into two main groups: the Ekoi, Ibibio, Mbembe, and Yako tribes belong to what Murdock calls the Bantoid Cluster who, according to Greenberg's classification, speak languages of the Benue Congo subfamily. The Ibo and the Ijaw, on the other hand, belong to the Central Cluster and speak languages of the Kwa subfamily.[27] Sandoval, referring to Colombian slaves, says: "The particular Caravalies are countless and do not understand one another, nor do they speak languages mutually intelligible with pure Caravali."[28]

The Carabalí can be considered, geographically and culturally, as an intermediate hinge between the areas that gave rise to the two main Afro-Cuban cultural clusters: the Lucumí (Yoruba) and the Congo (Bantu). The Angas, Ndoro, Tiv, Kundu, and Puku form a cluster of peoples located north of the Bight of Biafra, in the Southern Nigerian Plateau. According to George Murdock, all these peoples, with the exception of the Angas, are Bantoid, or as the Cuban terminology goes: Congo.[29]

Obviously, there are two separate clusters of African peoples known as Gangá in Cuba. For the sake of convenience they may be called Gangá I and Gangá II. The Gangá I (related to the Mandinga culture and located in Sierra Leone and Liberia) were abundantly represented in the Cuban slave trade in the first three colonial centuries. The Gangá II (for the most part culturally and linguistically Bantoid and located mainly in the Nigerian Plateau) came in substantial numbers in the nineteenth century. Henri Dumont, who practiced medicine in many Cuban sugar mills in the first half of the nineteenth century gives testimony of the almost total absence of the Mandinga in the Cuban plantations at that time, and added: "It is a long time since [they] have been transported into Cuba."[30]

History easily explains this change in trade direction. After the British abolished the slave trade in 1807, they took over Sierra Leone in January 1808 and established in Freetown a naval base that became their African center for the pursuit of the transatlantic trade. It is only logical that their closest neighbors to the north, east, and south (the Mandinga and the Gangá I) were particularly well protected against the slave traders. When the Gangá II group started to arrive in ever increasing numbers during the nineteenth century, many of them, as mentioned above, belonged to the Angas people. Very probably this fact explains why they (and their neighbors) were called Gangá, a denomination perfectly established in Cuba to designate Africans who, after all, came from the general vicinity of the Gulf of Guinea.

Congo

In Cuba, the name Congo was applied not only to the ethnic group known as Kongo and its numerous subgroups, but like Lucumí and Carabalí was a general term used to designate peoples coming from a much wider cultural area. The Cuban Congos are originally from a region that we have named Lower Guinea—Congo North and Angola—or, more specifically, from the area between southern Cameroon and the southernmost border of Angola. All of these peoples speak Bantu languages belonging to the Bantoid group, Benue-Congo subfamily. This is why in Cuba the terms *Congo* and *Bantu*, when referring to culture, have become interchangeable. Even the Macuá of eastern Africa (Mozambique) are sometimes called in Cuba Congo macuá. Culturally, the most influential of these groups was the Kongo (or Bakongo) proper. Thompson explains: "Kongo people, several million strong, live in modern Bas-Zaire and neighboring Cabinda, Congo-Brazzaville, and Angola. The present division of their territory into these modern political entities masks the fact that the area was once united, under the suzerainty of the ancient kingdom of Kongo, as one of the most important civilizations ever to emerge in Africa."[31] The Congos were very numerous in Cuba and left a cultural and religious heritage second only to that of the Yorubas.

This exploration of the most important names given in Cuba to the African slaves, together with an examination of existing statistics on the slave trade, enables us to delineate five precise geographical areas as the sources of enforced African migration to the island:

1. *Northwestern sub-Sahara area:* including Senegambia, Guinea, Sierra Leone, and Liberia, from the Senegal River to Cape Palmas.

2. *Upper Guinea area:* from Cape Palmas to the eastern border of the Niger Delta, including the Ivory Coast, the Gold Coast (Ghana), Togo, the Republic of Benin (Dahomey), and southern Nigeria.

3. *Bight of Biafra area:* Calabar and northwestern Cameroon.

4. *Lower Guinea area:* including Gabon, Congo-Brazzaville, Cabinda, western Zaire, and Angola.

5. *Mozambique area:* in the southeastern coast of the African continent.

A vast ethnic, linguistic, and cultural diversity predominated in the five sub-Saharan regions from which the Cuban slaves originated.

What follows is an effort to integrate in an outline: (1) the geographic provenience of the Cuban slaves, (2) the tribal names and other general denominations given to the slaves as they appear in Cuban sources, like the works of José A. Saco, Fernando Ortiz, María Teresa de Rojas, Esteban Pichardo, Felix Erénchun, Jacobo de la Pezuela, Cirilo Villaverde, Henri Dumont, Leví Marrero, and Lydia Cabrera, (3) the names of African ethnic groups as found in Murdock, and (4) the linguistic affiliations of these groups following primarily Greenberg's classification of African languages.[32]

Each of the five geographic areas has been subdivided according to linguistic criteria. Since the slaves brought to Cuba, with the exception of the Hausa and the Angas, spoke languages belonging to the Niger-Congo family of the Congo-Kordofanian linguistic stock, we will not state these in each case. When we consider the Hausa and the Angas, however, the family and linguistic stock will be provided. We have listed in capitals—following Murdock's spelling—the names of the African ethnic groups that were brought to Cuba. Opposite each we have placed the names by which these groups and their subgroups were known in Cuba, according to the sources mentioned above.

1. Northwestern Sub-Sahara (general area of origin of the Mandinga and the Gangá I)

West Atlantic Subfamily

WOLOF	Jelofe, Iolof, Jolofo
FULANI	Fula, Fulbe[33]
BIJOGO?	Biohó
DIOLA, YOLA	Iola
BANYUN	Casanga (Kassanga: subgroup of the BANYUN)[34]
PEPEL	Bran (Bram: subgroup of the PEPEL)[35]
KISSI	Gangá-quisí
VAI?	Gangá-pai
GOLA	Gola, Gangá-gola
NALU	Nalú
BIAFADA, BIAFAR	Biafara

Mande Subfamily

MALINKE, MANDINGO	Mandinga
MENDE	Mende, Mande
BAMBARA	Bambara
SUSU, SOSO	Musoso[36]
KONO	Gangá-conó

NGERE	Ingre[37]
TOMA	Tomu (classified as Gangá by Ortiz)
Voltaic (Gur) Subfamily	
BOBO	Mobwá (Bwa: subgroup of the BOBO)[38]
Kwa Subfamily (Kru Branch)	
KRA, KRAN	Gangá-cramo
SAPO	Sapo, Zapé

2. Upper Guinea (general area of origin of the Lucumí and the Arará)

Kwa Subfamily

Ewe Branch

EWE	Ewe
GA	Agaa[39]
FON	Arará-magino (Mahi: subgroup of the FON)[40]
GUN	Gun
POPO	Popó, Mina-Popó, Mina (Mina: subgroup of the POPO)[41]

Akan Branch

ASHANTI	Achante, Mina-ashante
FANTI	Fanti

Yoruba Branch

YORUBA	Lucumí, Oyó, Lucumí-Oyó (Oyo: subgroup of the YORUBA)[42]
EGBA	Egguado, Egbado, Lucumí-egbado, Ketu (Ketu: subgroup of the EGBA)[43]
IFE	Fee, Yesa, Yeza, Lucumí-yesa (Ijesha: subgroup of the IFE)[44]
EKITI	Ekiti
IJEBU	Iyebu, Yebú, Lucumí-yebú

Nupe Branch

NUPE	Nupe, Akpa, Tacuá[45]

Chad Family: Afro-Asiatic (Hamito-Semitic) Linguistic Stock

HAUSA	Hausa

West Atlantic Subfamily

SOKOTO?	Fula, Fulbe[46]

Voltaic Subfamily

BARGU	Baribá (subgroup of the BARGU)[47]

3. Bight of Biafra (Calabar; general area of origin of the Carabalí and the Gangá II)

KWA subfamily

 Ibo Branch
  IBO   Ibo[48]

 Ijo Branch
  IJAW, IJO   Iyo, Brasi, Bras (Bras: subgroup of the IJAW)[49]
           Carabalí (Kalabary: subgroup of the IJAW)[50]

Benue-Congo Subfamily

 Cross-River Group
  IBIBIO   Bibí, Ibibis, Ibibios, Efik (Apapas Chiquitos), Ekete (Efik and Eket: subgroups of the IBIBIO)[51]
  EKOI   Ekoi, Apapas grandes, Hatan (Atam: subgroup of the EKOI[52]
  YAKO   Uyanga (subgroup of the YAKO)[53]
           Ekuri (subgroup of the YAKO)[54]
           Ikumora (Ekumuru or Ikumunu: subgroups of the YAKO)[55]

 Jukunoid Group
  MBEMBE   Mbembe, Nbembe, Mambembe

 Bantoid Group
  KOSSI   Mumboma, Mumbona, Embo (Mbo: subgroup of the KOSSI;[56] classified as Congo by Cabrera)
  TIV   Gangá-yoni (Iyon: subgroup of the TIV)[57]
  KUNDU   Cundo (classified as Gangá by Ortiz)
  PUKU   Ñongobá, Gangá-ñongobá (Nyong: subgroup of the PUKU;[58] classified as Gangá by Pichardo and Cabrera)
  BATEKE   Bateke (classified as Congo by Cabrera)
  NDORO   Bandoré, Gangá-bandoré

Chad Family: Afro-Asiatic (Hamito-Semitic) Linguistic Stock
  ANGAS   Gangá, Gangá-insuru, Gangá-gorá, Ganga-fay? (Sura, Goram, and Pai: subgroups of the ANGAS)[59]

4. Lower Guinea (Congo North and Angola; general area of origin of the Congos; all speak languages of the Benue-Congo Subfamily, Bantoid Group)

NGUMBA?	Angunga[60]
FANG	Engüei (Mwei: subgroup of the FANG)[61]
BANGI	Mobangué
LUMBO	Munyacara, Munyaca, Ba-Yaca (Yaka, Bayaka: subgroups of the LUMBO)[62]
BUNDA, BABUNDA	Babundo
VILI	Cabinda, Cabenda, Kabinda (Kabinda: subgroup of the VILI)[63] Loango (subgroup of the VILI)[64]
MISANGA	Nisanga
YOMBE, MAJOMBE	Mayombe
SUNDI	Musundí, Musunde
KONGO, BAKONGO	Congo, Bakongo, Mpangu (Mpangu: subgroup of the KONGO)[65]
MBALA, BAMBALA	Mumbala, Bambala
KIMBUNDU	Loanda, Muluanda, Mbaka, Mondongo, Ngola, Angola, Mundembu (Loanda, Mbaka, Ndongo, Ngola, Ndembu: subgroups of the KIMBUNDU)[66]
KUMBE	Kumba
MAKA	Bikas (Bikay: subgroup of the MAKA)[67]
SANGA	Bombó (subgroup of the SANGA)[68]
SORONGO	Musulongo (Musurongo: subgroup of the SORONGO)[69]
BANGALA, BANGELA	Banguela, Banjela, Benguela
LUNDA	Lundé Butuá
LUPOLO	Esola (Esela: subgroup of the LUPOLO)[70]
LUIMBE	Nbanda (Mbande: subgroup of the LUIMBE)[71]
SONGO	Songo
SELE	Embuila (Mbui: subgroup of the SELE)[72]
KISAMA	Quisama, Kisiamo
SUKU	Ksamba, Kisamba (Samba: subgroup of the SUKU)[73]

5. Mozambique (all speak languages of the Benue-Congo Subfamily, Bantoid Group; in Cuba are considered Congos)

| NDAMBA | Mundamba |
| MAKUA | Macuá |

The correlation of the names by which the slaves were known in Cuba with the ethnological map of Africa proves that the vast majority of black slaves came to Cuba from a belt running parallel to the western coast of sub-Saharan Africa, approximately from the Senegal River to the Cunene River or, in modern political terms, from the south of Mauritania to the south of Angola. Apart from this belt, the only other area of provenience is found in southeastern Africa, in Mozambique.[74]

An examination of the cultural situation within that belt at the time of the slave trade leads to the conclusion that the slaves did not bring to Cuba a unified and homogeneous culture for the simple reason that such a monolithic entity did not exist. The Africans that were brought into Cuba came from ethnic groups that had developed many different social, political, and economic institutions over the years. They differed in customs, religious beliefs, languages, and artistic styles. The same cultural diversity has been noted about the newcomers in other countries of Latin America, for example, by Bastide in Brazil, Pavy and Escalante in Colombia, Alvarez Nazario in Puerto Rico, and Aguirre Beltrán in Mexico.

The recognition of this reality should not obscure the fact that a powerful current of identification ran underneath this obvious cultural diversity. Although their forms outwardly differed, the basic cultural framework of the societies established in the belt was remarkably similar. These peoples had arrived at somewhat different levels of technological development, but they were all agriculturists or, at least, advanced horticulturists. They belonged to thousands of different tribes and clans, but they all lived within somewhat similar kinship systems, with intricate codes governing relations among numerous categories of kin. They spoke hundreds of different languages but, as we have seen, almost all their languages belonged to the same family of the Congo-Kordofanian linguistic stock. They had a rich variety of religious cults, with diverse pantheons, mythologies, and liturgical systems, but they all practiced a model of religious life characterized by several common elements. These are: (1) belief in a supreme and only God, (2) belief in a pantheon of intermediary divinities, (3) ancestor worship, and (4) belief in the power of the dead, who were perceived as capable of communicating with the living and affecting their destiny.[75] The examples could be multiplied ad infinitum. Diversity within a fundamental unity: that was the rule for culture in the slave trade belt.

Awareness of this constant tension between continuity and discontinuity, between homogeneity and heterogeneity, should guide contemporary anthropological research in Cuba, avoiding the simplistic—but very common—approach to Afro-hispanic acculturation from the point of view of the interaction between two well-defined cultural entities: the "European" and the "African." It is not the intention of this article to dwell upon the relations between culture and origins—a subject that obviously demands the extension of a book[76]—but simply to provide specific and detailed points of departure to the search for West African influences on Cuban culture and institutions. This is particularly valid in the field of religion, where the rich diversity and intermingling found in Afro-Cuban "reglas" (or cults) is only understandable in the light of the constant dialectical struggle between the differentiated backgrounds of specific peoples and tribes and the generalized West African "heritage" shared by all the slaves introduced in the island. The same would be true for any analysis of song styles, storytelling techniques and themes, the use of proverbs, and many other aspects of Afro-Cuban folklore.

NOTES

1. In 1515 the Cuban governor Diego Velázquez informed King Ferdinand that many black slaves had been taken from Santo Domingo to Cuba (Academia de la Historia de Cuba, *Papeles existentes en el Archivo General de Indias relativos a Cuba y muy particularmente a La Habana*, vol. 7 [Havana, 1931], p. 7). See also Ruth Pike, "Sevillian Society in the Sixteenth Century: Slaves and Freedmen," *Hispanic American Historical Review* 47 (1967), 345. Probably the first black slaves had come with Velázquez himself and most of them were "ladinos," originally brought from Spain (Leví Marrero, *Cuba: Economía y Sociedad*, vol. 1 Río Piedras, P.R.: Editorial San Juan, 1972], p. 80).

2. The first scientific estimate of the number of Cuban slaves imported from Africa was made by Philip Curtin in *The Atlantic Slave Trade: A Census* (Madison: University of Wisconsin Press, 1969), pp. xviii, 31–43. Curtin made good use of Hubert Aimes, *A History of Slavery in Cuba* (New York: Putnam, 1907). Curtin's original figures have been readjusted by D. R. Murray, "Statistics on the Slave Trade to Cuba, 1790–1867," *Journal of Latin American Studies* 3 (1971), 131–49; also by David Eltis, "Exports of Slaves from Africa, 1821–1843," *Journal of Economic History* 2 (1977), 409–33; and more recently by James A. Rawley, *The Trans-Atlantic Slave Trade* (New York: Norton, 1981), p. 75. Manuel Moreno Fraginals has raised the number of importations to 1,012,386 slaves ("Africa in Cuba: A Quantitative Analysis of the African Population in the Island of Cuba," in *Comparative Perspectives on Slavery in the New World Plantation Societies*, ed. Vera Rubin and Arthur Tuden [New York: N.Y. Academy of Sciences, 1977], pp. 189–91). Rawley considers Moreno's estimate "startling." It may be so, but the truth is that every revision of the Cuban slave trade figures after Curtin's 1969 census has pushed the estimate upward. The massive character of the importation must be

taken into consideration to explain the enormous extension of the areas of provenience and the ethnological, linguistic, and cultural diversity involved in the traffic.

3. Fernando Ortiz, *Los Negros Esclavos* (Havana: Editorial Revista Bimestre Cubana, 1916), pp. 24–51; Curtin, *The Atlantic Slave Trade*, pp. 243–47; Leví Marrero, *Cuba: Economía y Sociedad*, vol. 2 (Madrid: Editorial Playor, 1974), pp. 362–63.

4. Lydia Cabrera, *Yemayá y Ochún* (Miami: Ediciones C.R., 1974), p. 20. Translations ours for all Cabrera references.

5. William Bascom, "The Yoruba in Cuba," *Nigeria Magazine* 37 (1951), 10.

6. William Bascom, *Shangó in the New World* (Austin: University of Texas Press, 1972), p. 13.

7. Olfert Dapper, *Description de l'Afrique* (Amsterdam: Wolfgang, Wesberger, Boom and Van Somereu, 1686), p. 307.

8. William Snelgrave, *A New Account of Some Parts of the Guinea and the Slave Trade* (London: James and Paul Knapton, 1734), p. 89.

9. Ortiz, *Los Negros Esclavos*, and Gonzalo Aguirre Beltrán, *La Población Negra de México* (Mexico City: Ediciones Fuente Cultural, 1946); both also mention Dapper's and Snelgrave's maps.

10. Peter C. Lloyd, "The Yoruba of Nigeria," in *Peoples of Africa*, ed. James L. Gibbs, Jr. (New York: Rinehart and Winston, 1965), p. 551.

11. George P. Murdock, *Africa: Its People and Their Culture History* (New York: McGraw-Hill, 1959), pp. 244–45.

12. For example, the Arará and the Ibo were frequently included among the Lucumí (Ortiz, *Los Negros Esclavos*, pp. 26, 38). The Yoruba are also known as Lucumí in Colombia (cf. Aquiles Escalante, *El Negro en Colombia* [Bogotá, 1964]) and in Mexico (cf. Aguirre Beltrán, *La Población Negra de México*). In Haiti and Brazil they are known as Nago, because, according to Aguirre Beltrán (ibid., pp. 132–33), that was how they were called by their neighbors the Fon. However, in Murdock (*Africa*, p. 245), we find a group called Nago or Anago, which is a subgroup of the Egba (Yoruba Cluster). In Cuba, the Yoruba language was known as Anagó (cf. Lydia Cabrera, *Anagó: Vocabulario Lucumí* [Miami: Ediciones C.R., 1970]).

13. Roger Bastide, *African Civilizations in the New World* (New York: Harper and Row, 1971), p. 105.

14. Ortiz, *Los Negros Esclavos*, pp. 27–28.

15. Dapper, *Description de l'Afrique*, p. 307.

16. Murdock, *Africa*, pp. 252–53.

17. Bastide, *African Civilizations*, p. 133.

18. Harry A. Gailey, *History of Africa: From Earliest Times to 1800* (New York: Holt, Rinehart and Winston, 1970), p. 101.

19. Ortiz, *Los Negros Esclavos*, p. 43. For the Colombian Mina, see Paul D. Pavy, "The Provenience of Colombian Negroes," *Journal of Negro History* 52 (1967), 51.

20. José María de la Torre, *Compendio de Geografía Física, Política, Estadística y Comparada de la Isla de Cuba* (Havana, 1854), p. 53. Henri Dumont, "Antropología y Patología Comparada de los Negros Esclavos," *Revista Bimestre Cubana* 10 (1915), 164, 170; 11 (1916), 264–68. Esteban Pichardo, *Diccionario Provincial Casi Razonado de Voces y Frases Cubanas* (Havana, 1875), p. 159; Ortiz, *Los Negros Esclavos*, pp. 35–37, 165n., and *passim*. (Dumont wrote his book in 1866, but it was not published until it appeared in 1915 in serialized form in the *Revista Bimestre Cubana*.)

21. Aguirre Beltrán, *La Población Negra de México*, pp. 116, 120; Manuel Alvarez Nazario, *El Elemento Afronegroide en el Español de Puerto Rico* (San Juan, P.R.: Instituto de Cultura Puertorriqueña, 1961), pp. 56–57.

22. From Murdock, *Africa*, pp. 260–61.
23. Cabrera, *Anagó*, p. 141. See also *Música de los Cultos Africanos en Cuba* (Havana, n.d.).
24. From Murdock, *Africa*, pp. 94, 274–75.
25. Lydia Cabrera, *La Sociedad Secreta Abakuá* (Miami: Ediciones C.R., 1970), p. 63.
26. This secret society has been exhaustively studied by Lydia Cabrera in ibid. and in *Anaforuana: Ritual y Símbolos de la Iniciación en la Sociedad Secreta Abakuá* (Madrid: Ediciones R., 1975). Cf. also Harold Courlander, "Abakuá Meeting in Guanabacoa," *Journal of Negro History* 29 (1944), 461–70.
27. The Yoruba language also belongs to the Kwa subfamily.
28. Quoted in Pavy, "The Provenience of Colombian Negroes," p. 50. Sandoval in 1627 did not make clear what he understood by "pure caravali."
29. Murdock, *Africa*, pp. 89–99. On p. 91 Murdock states, "Although for the sake of convenience the peoples of the province are classified below according to language, it should be emphasized that in this region cultural and linguistic differences reveal an extremely low degree of correlation." Our classification of some of the groups into Gangá I and Gangá II is ambiguous in two cases: the Gangá-fay could be either the Vai (Gangá I) or the Pai (Gangá II); also the Gangá-gola and the Gangá-gora could be the same group.
30. Dumont, "Antropología," pp. 266–68.
31. Robert F. Thompson, *The Four Moments of the Sun* (Washington, D.C.: National Gallery of Arts, 1981), p. 27.
32. Joseph Greenberg, *The Languages of Africa* (Bloomington: Indiana University Press, 1963).
33. The Fulani were "scattered throughout the western Sudan, from Senegal in the West to the Cameroon and French Equatorial Africa in the East" (Murdock, *Africa*, p. 412). To the Fulani belonged, among others, the Adamawa, Bauchi, Fouta Toro, Kita, Liptako, Masina, Sakoto, etc. It is very difficult to determine to which of these groups the Cuban Fula or Fulbe belonged.
34. Ibid., p. 265.
35. Ibid.
36. The affixes (prefixes and suffixes) *mu, mo, ba,* mean "people" or "nation." Thus, for example, *Musoso* means roughly "the Soso people."
37. Ortiz (*Los Negros Esclavos,* p. 38) mentions them, but says they are Carabalí.
38. Murdock, *Africa*, p. 79.
39. The Agaa are Lucumí and neighbors of the Mina, according to an informant of Lydia Cabrera (*La Sociedad Secreta Abakuá*, p. 71).
40. Murdock, *Africa*, p. 253.
41. Ibid.
42. Ibid., p. 245.
43. Ibid.
44. Ibid.
45. The Nupe were called Akpa by the Lucumí (Ortiz, *Los Negros Esclavos*, p. 47). Bascom also refers to the Nupe (Takpa) people of Cuba ("The Yoruba in Cuba," p. 19).
46. See note 33.
47. Murdock, *Africa*, p. 80.
48. In Cuba the Ibo were confused sometimes with the Lucumí and sometimes with the Carabalí (Ortiz, *Los Negros Esclavos*, p. 38; see also Cabrera, *La Sociedad Secreta Abakuá*, p. 71).
49. Murdock, *Africa*, p. 244.

50. Ibid.
51. Ibid., p. 243.
52. Ibid.
53. Ibid.
54. Ibid.
55. Ibid.
56. Ibid., p. 274.
57. Ibid., p. 92.
58. Ibid., p. 275.
59. Ibid., p. 92.
60. The Angunga were called Congos Reales (Royal Congos) in Cuba (Ortiz, *Los Negros Esclavos*, p. 25).
61. Murdock, *Africa*, p. 280.
62. Ibid., p. 275.
63. Ibid, p. 292.
64. Ibid.
65. Ibid.
66. Ibid.
67. Ibid., p. 280.
68. Ibid., p. 292.
69. Ibid.
70. Ibid.
72. Ibid., p. 293.
72. Ibid., p. 292.
73. Ibid., p. 293.
74. The number of slaves who came to Cuba from Mozambique must be much less than the 29.5 percent of the total suggested by Curtin (*The Atlantic Slave Trade*, p. 247) for the nineteenth century. In this case Curtin was working with incomplete statistical samples.
75. Cf., among others, E. Bolaji Idowu, *Olodumare: God in Yoruba Belief* (New York: Praeger, 1963); Geoffrey Parrinder, *West African Religion* (London: Epworth Press, 1961); John S. Mbiti, *African Religions and Philosophy* (Garden City, N.Y.: Doubleday, 1970). Concerning Cuba: Fernando Ortiz, *Hampa Afrocubana: Los Negros Brujos* (Madrid: Librería de Fernando Fe, 1906), and, besides the works by Lydia Cabrera already mentioned, see her classic *El Monte* (Miami: Ediciones C.R., 1971); *Yemayá y Ochún* (Miami: Ediciones CR., 1974), "Babalú-Ayé, San Lázaro," in *Enciclopedia de Cuba*, vol. 6, pp. 268–82; *La Regla Kimbisa del Santo Cristo del Buen Viaje* (Miami: Ediciones C.R., 1977), *Reglas de Congo, Palo Monte, Mayombe* (Miami: Ediciones C.R., 1979); *Vocabulario Congo: el Bantú que se Habla en Cuba* (Miami: Ediciones C.R., 1984). Sidney W. Mintz and Richard Price (*An Anthropological Approach to the Afro-American Past: A Caribbean Perspective* [Philadelphia: Institute for the Study of Human Issues, 1976], p. 5) add two interesting examples of the diversity-identification mechanism: the Yoruba "deify" their twins, while their neighbors the Igbo destroy them at birth. Yet both people respond to the same set of principles having to do with the religious significance of unusual birth. Also, "witchcraft" may play an important role in the social life of a tribe and be absent in another, but both social groups may still subscribe to the rule that social conflict leads to illness and misfortune through "supernatural" processes of which "witchcraft" is only one element.
76. The authors have in preparation a book on the origins and development of Afro-Cuban culture.

EDWARD J. MULLEN

Los negros brujos: *A Reexamination of the Text*

ABSTRACT

The early work of the Cuban ethnographer, Fernando Ortiz, has received little critical attention in spite of the fact that it is often associated with the emergence of Afro-Cubanism. Presented here is a reading of *Los negros brujos* that details its interrelationships with the world of popular culture and myth in early twentieth-century Cuba. While most readings of this work have focused on the cultural/historical dimensions of the text, here it is argued that in spite of its outward appearance as a scientific treatise replete with copious notes, charts, and drawings, it is a text that shows a basic complexity not altogether dissimilar to that exhibited by the documentary or nonfictional narrative in contemporary Latin American literature and can be best analyzed by a combination of traditional and postmodernist critical methodologies. Thus an initial inquiry into the facts of the book's publication, sources, and major themes help to place it in a meaningful context, while more recent modes of analysis show how Ortiz consciously exploited the resources of literary narrative to both heighten certain features of style and make meaningful connections with other types of writing.

RESUMEN

Los primeros trabajos del etnógrafo cubano, Fernando Ortiz, han recibido poca atención crítica aún cuando los mismos están a menudo asociados con el surgimiento del afro-cubanismo. Este artículo presenta una lectura de *Los negros brujos* que detalla sus interrelaciones con el mundo de la cultura popular y el mito en la Cuba de principios del siglo veinte. Mientras muchas lecturas de este trabajo se han concentrado en las dimensiones culturales/históricas del texto, aquí se argumenta que a pesar de su aparencia externa como un tratado científico completo que consta de notas abundantes, gráficos, y dibujos, éste es un texto que muestra una complejidad básica que en cierto modo se asemeja a la exhibida por la narrativa documental y nonficcional de la literatura latinoamericana contemporánea y que por lo tanto puede analizarse mejor mediante una combinación de metodologías críticas tradicionales y postmodernistas. De esta manera, una investigación inicial sobre los hechos de la publicación, fuentes y temas fundamentales del libro ayudan a colocar el mismo en un contexto significativo, mientras que modos de análisis más recientes muestran como Ortiz explotó conscientemente los recursos de la literatura narrativa a fin de resaltar ciertos elementos de estilo así como de hacer conexiones significativas con otros tipos de escritos.

Although it is axiomatic in any discussion of the genesis of Afro-Cubanism to refer to the pioneering work of the Cuban "pensador," Fernando Ortiz Fernández (1881–1969), and in particular to his *Los negros brujos* (1906) and *Los negros esclavos* (1916), scarcely any critical attention has been focused on these books. Yet they bear a paradigmatic relationship to the movement as a whole and occupy a central position in the development of the Cuban essay.[1] While Ortiz is today perhaps better known for his *Contrapunto cubano del tabaco y el azúcar* (1940), a cultural and economic study of Cuba in which he coined the term *transculturación*—a construct now subsumed into the general critical vocabulary of most scholars of Afro-Cubanism—he seems to have been written out of the script of contemporary academic criticism. In spite of the fact that major scholars rather consistently refer to his work as "trail-blazing" and "pioneering," he has never been the object of a complete book, and with the exception of a recent important essay by Gustavo Pérez Firmat only one brief article has been written about him in English.[2]

Precisely because Ortiz was neither a literary figure in the formal sense nor a professional musicologist, anthropologist, or historian (although he wrote books and essays in all these fields), his work has been gratuitously parceled out to a number of subject specialists and rarely given full attention by scholars in any of these disciplines.

In his fundamental study, *Race and Colour in Caribbean Literature*, G. R. Coulthard was among the first to point to the importance of Ortiz's role in the dissemination of literary "negrismo":

> It seems certain that these works of Ortiz helped attract the attention of Cuban intellectuals to the rich vein of Negro folklore in Cuba and to open new perspectives on the artistic and literary potentialities of Cuban popular art in general. And it was precisely the atmosphere of Afro-Cuban dancing, singing and superstition that appeared as the main constituents in literature when, to use a phrase of Ortiz: "In 1928 the drums begin to beat in Cuban poetry."[3]

In fact, glancing at the comments that appear in a wide variety of books and journals, one quickly gets the impression that those who write about Ortiz have in fact never read his early books, or, if they have, they are not sure what Ortiz was. F. S. Stimon calls him an anthropologist,[4] Félix Lazo an essayist,[5] Odilio Urfé labels him a cultural anthropologist,[6] while René Depestre classifies him broadly as a

Los negros brujos: *A Reexamination of the Text* : 113

scientist.[7] Gastón Baquero attacked him as a racist,[8] while Eric Williams called him "the Caribbean white man at his best."[9] In other cases, his dates of birth and death are listed incorrectly, as are routinely the dates of his so-called major books. These inconsistencies represent more than a random set of errors, I believe, but are instead a good example of how a critical text has in fact rewritten an authorial text. In short, readers know about Ortiz not from reading him but from reading *about* him. In a case somewhat analogous to that of Nicolás Guillén, whose reputation is now so hallowed and whose life so mythologized that anything he wrote in early life is bound to command the importance of his later works, the early work of Ortiz has now been subsumed under the critical label of his later work in which he presented a considerably altered view of Cuba's black population. It was, however, Ortiz's early work that was to supply writers such as Alejo Carpentier, Ramón Guirao, and Lino Novás Calvo, among others, with the raw materials for their initial literary explorations of Afro-Cuban life. Therefore, it is precisely this early stage that needs a critical reexamination.[10]

Roberto González Echeverría, in an important book on Alejo Carpentier, spoke in the following terms of the importance of Ortiz's earlier works:

Fernando Ortiz's important role in the birth of Afro-Cubanism cannot be disputed, but stands in need of revision. A lawyer by training, Ortiz became interested in African culture for what it could reveal about crime in Cuba. In his early writing he is predominantly a criminologist, as the full title of his first book (1906) indicates: *Hampa afro-cubana: los negros brujos (apuntes para un estudio de etnología criminal)* [*Afro-Cuban Underworld: Black Sorcerers (Notes for a Study of Criminal Ethnology)*]. Prefaced by Cesare Lombroso, of whom Ortiz declares himself to be an admiring disciple, the book is a detailed study of witchcraft among Cuban blacks, undertaken with the avowed intention of understanding the phenomenon better in order to eliminate it quicker.... During his early period, Ortiz had much in common with Sarmiento; just as Indians represented for the Argentine an obstacle in his program of civilization, so did the blacks appear then to Ortiz as a regressive force. His work is important for the Afro-Cuban movement because it underlines the salient aspects of African culture in Cuba and constitutes the first systematic written account of its myths and beliefs.[11]

Thus standing midway between the work of the nineteenth-century Cuban liberal intellectuals such as Domingo del Monte, José Antonio Saco, Félix Tanco y Bosmeniel, Anselmo Suárez y Romero, Cirilo Villaverde, José Jacinto Milanés, José Antonio Echeverría, etc., and the full flowering of the Afro-Cuban movement embodied in the work of Nicolás Guillén in the early twenties, Ortiz's early explorations of Cuba's African heritage not only represent a curious bridge in Cuban intellectual history but also comprise a text that deserves comment and analysis on its own grounds.[12]

From its haunting title onward, *Los negros brujos* proves on close examination to be more than a curious medley of facts on African religious cults in Cuba (the way in which the text is normally read) but reveals itself also as a document of multiple levels of meaning that mediates, through a combination of fictive and historical methodologies, between Cuba's past and future. By seeking to rediscover those cultural elements that could be viewed as genuinely Cuban, Ortiz joined the effort of other Latin American writers such as Manuel Ugarte, Alcides Arguedas, Carlos Bunge, and Francisco García Calderón, who, armed with the ideological apparatus of the social organicists, sought to diagnose the cultural ills of a backward Latin America. On yet another level, the work of Ortiz, who was among the first to trace the cultural legacy of Cuba backward in a linear fashion to Africa, followed a line of inquiry begun by the Italian criminologist Cesare Lombroso (1835–1905), which was continued by Franz Boas (1858–1942), and which culminated in the more popular theories of Margaret Mead (1901–1978). All of these found important models in primitive societies for the study of contemporary social problems. Ortiz's work can also be compared to the work of modern anthropologists in the sense that he was applying new methodologies to make sense out of data that otherwise would have had no coherence.

While most readings of *Los negros brujos* have focused on the cultural-historical dimensions of the text, it can be argued that in spite of its outward appearance as a scientific treatise replete with copious notes, charts, and drawings, it is a text that shows a basic complexity not altogether dissimilar to that exhibited by the documentary or nonfictional narrative in contemporary Latin American literature and is best analyzed by a combination of traditional and postmodernist critical methodologies. Thus an initial inquiry into the the facts of the book's publication, sources, and major themes help to place it in a meaningful context, while more recent modes of analysis can show how Ortiz consciously exploited the resources of literary narrative to both heighten certain features of style and make meaningful connections with other types of writing.

The Publishing Axis

Los negros brujos was first published in Madrid in 1906 (Librería de Fernando Fé) with the following title: *Hampa afro-cubana: Los negros*

Los negros brujos: *A Reexamination of the Text* : 115

brujos (Apuntes para un estudio de etnología criminal.[13] Text and notes occupy some 432 pages. In addition, there is an epigraph by José María Heredia, a "carta-prólogo" by Cesare Lombroso, and a four-page note by Ortiz entitled "Advertencias preliminares." The text is broadly divided into two parts, the first consisting of the following chapters: "La mala vida cubana," "Los negros en Cuba," and "Los negros en Cuba (continuación)." The second is divided as follows: "La brujería," "La brujería (continuación)," "Los brujos," "Difusión de la brujería," "Extracto de las noticias publicadas por la prensa de la Habana referentes a varios casos de brujería," and "Porvenir de la brujería." The text is buttressed by some 812 notes, forty-eight sketches by an Italian lawyer, Gustavo Rosso, one reproduction of an untitled "lámina de la época," and six photographs of condemned criminals. A second edition in 1917 resulted in a considerable reduction of both the text (chapters 2 and 3 were omitted entirely) and notes.

Ortiz's initial plan to write a series of studies on Cuba's black population can be ultimately traced to his student days in Madrid, where he became interested in theories of criminal behavior. Writing some thirty-three years later in *Estudios Afrocubanos,* he spoke of the genesis of the book: "Mi libro *Los negros brujos* fué publicado en 1906, habiendo sido redactado por mí desde 1902 a 1905, de cuyos años tres los pasé en Italia y sólo uno en La Habana, donde inicié mis investigaciones directas. Es cierto que yo, como poco antes había hecho el Dr. Nino Rodrígues en el Brasil, fuí al estudio etnográfico de Cuba desde el campo de la antropología criminal en el cual tenía yo mis más fervientes aficiones."[14]

It is important to realize that when Ortiz began writing the materials that would be ultimately incorporated in *Los negros brujos,* he had little or no direct knowledge of his subject. What he knew about Cuba's black population had been largely gleaned—as he later confessed—from reading *Los criminales de Cuba y José Trujillo* (Barcelona: F. Giró, 1882) and from his observations of artifacts in the Museo de Ultramar. This may help to explain the scientific exoticism of this first book, with its haunting photographs and curious sketches of objects related to voodoo, which appear more like museum pieces than integral parts of a book.[15]

It is remarkable that a work such as *Los negros brujos,* which was to become the point of departure for an extensive exploration of "Cubanidad" (a search for the Cuban national essence), was written by a man who spent the better part of his early life outside of Cuba, and thus could hardly be considered "typically" Cuban. It was perhaps this early expatriation from his native land (to use the critical formulation suggested by Andrew Gurr)[16] that led to a peculiar self-consciousness toward Cuba and heightened Ortiz's awareness of certain features of Cuban language and culture that would have otherwise passed unnoticed.

The Thematic Axis

If we assume that generic boundaries have meaningful implications for the way in which texts are read and how readers respond to them, then the problem of definition becomes central to any kind of textual analysis. Although Ortiz himself defines the book as a study in the emerging science of criminal ethnography—"El presente libro es una modesta contribución a empresa científica de tanta monta"[17]—a closer examination of the text and a study of the facts of publication reveal that *Los negros brujos* is not an organic book at all, but rather a collection of essays.[18] It is important to note that some were published contemporaneously with the appearance of the *Los negros brujos*[19] and treat in varying degrees the following subjects: the science of Positivism, theories of race and criminal behavior, the practice of witchcraft in Cuba, linguistic and cultural transmissions from Africa, and philosophical observations on the possibilities for amelioration of the conditions of life in Cuba.

Thus while the table of contents of the book itself (most probably an editorial, not an authorial, decision) seems to imply the continuous development of a single theme, *Los negros brujos* can be separated into three distinct thematic units: (1) an essay on the racial and psychological features of the Cuban population in which Ortiz elaborates his thesis that the study of criminal behavior in Cuba is a particularly propitious topic for the emerging science of criminal ethnology, (2) a series of related essays on the origins of Cuba's black population and study of their superstitions, and (3) a closing essay that is largely a call for legal reforms and social hygiene.

Since both the opening and closing essays frame Ortiz's book and are responsible for most of its intellectual content, they deserve more detailed comment both from the perspective of what they say and the specific linguistic protocols with which Ortiz presents his arguments. "La mala vida cubana" (pp. 2–15), which was published separately,[20] is in its simplest terms an inquiry into those factors that have produced Cuba's criminal low life. Ortiz fundamentally viewed behavior as a correlative of race. Thus the Spaniards who came to Cuba from southern Spain were seen as impulsive and violent, while their counterparts from Castile were hard-working, intelligent, and noble. This basic racial dichotomy was to produce according to Ortiz the basic stratification in the dominant white ruling class. The importation during the nineteenth century of black slaves and Chinese and Indian workers completed the ethnic mosaic of the island and led ultimately to the formation of Cuba's peculiar form of low life. Echoing the ideology of Cuba's late nineteenth-century intellectuals, Ortiz viewed Spain's colonial policies as essentially destructive and as one of the motivating forces behind the curious cross-contamination of the island's psychologically inferior racial groups: "Al llegar los negros entraban todos en la mala vida cubana, no como caídos de un plano superior de moralidad, sino como ineptos, por el momento al menos, para trepar hasta él" (p. 17).

It is important to understand that Ortiz, who (as we have indicated earlier) had no personal contact with blacks, had shaped his notions of racial hierarchies from his readings in criminology. Thus he believed that Cuba's blacks were morally primitive, that is, that they came from a less developed civilization. Hence, their basic attributes—lust, superstition, fear—were not genetically inherent but were rather a direct result of the relatively primitive stage in which their civilization found itself in relation to other cultures.

Ortiz's concluding chapter, "Porvenir de la brujería," located some 382 pages from the opening essay, offers a summary and synthesis of the author's views regarding the island's future. It is linked on both a conceptual and a metaphoric plane with his initial ideas. Ortiz believed that any future hope for the improvement of Cuba's intellectual, moral, and social climate rested with the de-Africanization ("deculturación" in the terminology of Moreno Fraginals)[21] of its black population. Here Ortiz followed a line of reasoning that can be ultimately traced back to the Cuban intellectuals of the generation of 1830 who were concerned over the demographic preponderance of blacks on the island and its economic and moral consequences: "La brujería en fin es un obstáculo a la civilización, principalmente de la población de color, ya por ser la expresión más bárbara del sentimiento religioso desprovisto del elemento moral que en algunas épocas y países alcanza una especie de simbiosis de aquél" (p. 394).

Although Ortiz's attitudes toward race would change over the years, culminating in the publication of *El engaño de las razas* (Havana: Páginas, 1945), a book in which he denies the very validity of the term "race," the images he projected in *Los negros brujos* would have an important impact upon the cultivators of the stylized images of blacks that were produced during the 1920s. Ortiz's attitudes toward race are to a large extent a product of his Positivist heritage—which merits some attention.

If the dominant literary vogue of the period during which Ortiz wrote *Los negros brujos* was Modernism, the controlling philosophy for the production of expository prose was Positivism.[22] Derived principally from the mid-nineteenth-century writings of Auguste Comte, John Stuart Mill, and Herbert Spencer, Positivism was based on the reductive methodologies of the emerging natural sciences and sought to explain all phenomena in the light of empirical data. It was soon co-opted by the architects of the emerging social sciences (criminology, sociology, anthropology), who began a systematic inventory of human behavior in light of the prevailing medical notions of the day.

Within the context of Latin American literary and intellectual thought of the early twentieth century, an important expression of Positivism's empirical approach to society was a strong interest in race and theories of race. The thesis that race was an integral determinant of culture and civilization had been elaborated by Arthur de Gobineau in *Essai sur l'inegalité des races humaines* as early as 1884. The most influential book on late nineteenth-century thought in Latin America, however, appears to have been that of the French social psychologist Gustave Le Bon, whose *Lois psychologiques de l'évolution des peuples* (1894) was widely read in Latin America. Le Bon firmly believed in the concept of racial hierarchies and warned that miscegenation would lead to racial inferiority.[23] It is important to realize that contemporaneous with the development of these theories of race and class were medical discoveries concerning pathogenesis—the origination and development of disease. The fact that microorganisms caused human disease was not discovered until the late 1800s when the work of Louis Pasteur and Robert Koch became widely known. This new scientific information was quickly subsumed into the language system, and the metaphor of pathogenesis achieved a status somewhat similar to the use of technical language in contemporary discourse.

Thus while on an intellectual level one can view the organization of *Los negros brujos* as little more than a synthesis of late nineteenth-century modes of analysis with roots in Positivism—an exercise in impressionistic historiography—Ortiz used a central metaphor drawn from the emerging science of microbiology to shape his data. If we accept Hayden White's thesis that all discourse is by its very nature rhetorically textualizing,[24] the type of discourse that Ortiz employs is strongly characterized by the metaphor of pathogenesis. This likeness or analogy between the world of medicine and society in general became the connective tissue that linked and to some extent dramatized the significance of the data he had gathered. Cuba as a social construct was sick and could only be salvaged through an elimination of all foci of infection. Thus Ortiz writes in his opening chapter: "Los tipos de su mala vida han de parecerse, como los de su *vida buena,* (pues así como la enfermedad se desarrolla según las condiciones fisiológicas del individuo en quien hace presa, así el hampa es un reflejo de la sociedad en que vegeta)" (p. 2). And again: "En este campo gris, para expresarlo gráficamente, vegetan con preferencia los parásitos de la mala vida cubana. . . . De ahí que los carácteres de la mala vida en Cuba sean particularmente complejos en proporción a las varias cloacas que en ella vierten sus patógenos detritus" (p. 15).

The final chapter is characterized by an even greater use of this basic image, which again takes as metaphoric vehicle materials from microbiology: "La brujería es . . . el caldo de cultivo adecuado para el desarrollo del microbio criminoso" (p. 224). "En estas consideraciones que anteceden debe basarse toda obra de higienización social contra la brujería y de aniquilamiento de sus parásitos" (p. 231).

One of the results of Ortiz's curious amalgamation of racial, medical, and criminal theories was a consistent tendency to underscore the primitive, sensuous nature of Cuba's black population. His attitudes toward race were perfectly consistent with the ideological patterns of his time and project one of the ideological paradoxes of Western civilization: primitive peoples are perceived to be more directly in touch with nature, their feelings, and the erotic enchantment of a world untouched by the corrosive alienation and inhibitions of modernity, but are also lost in irrational fears, taboos, and anxieties that can only be dispelled by the rationalizing effects of civilization. *Los negros brujos* seems to capture at times these disjunctive images in one visual frame. The following description of a ritual dance, itself drawn from secondary sources, illustrates the point well:

El baile comienza con un canturreo monótono en que se corea un estribillo del brujo. No transcurre mucho tiempo, una vez empezado el baile, sin que la excitación erótica se manifieste en toda la crudeza africana. Los movimientos lascivos del baile están sometidos al son de los tambores y a menudo se oye la voz de un negro gritando ¡iebbe! ó ¡iebba! . . . No es raro que los negros sudurosos se despojen de la camisa, mostrando sus bustos lustruosos y sus bronceados brazos que ciñen con febril abrazo el cuerpo de la bailadora (p. 205).

It is curious that from the writings of Christopher Columbus to the work of D. H. Lawrence in the 1920s the imaginative concept of the American Indian in European literature has been one of primitive excellence,[25] while that of the black—constructed largely through a parallel literature of discovery—has been one of negative primitivism, a threat to the established order. This negative vision presented as a threat to established sexual and moral societal codes permeates the text of *Los negros brujos* and resembles closely some of the earliest texts of the Afro-Cuban vogue such as Ramón Guirao's "Bailadora de la rumba" and José Zacarías Tallet's "La rumba" (both published in 1928), which evoke images of unbridled sensuousness.

The Literary Axis

While *Los negros brujos* has been traditionally read (or misread) as a cultural-historical document of some significance in the development of Afro-Cubanism, what critical consideration it has received to date has focused on its relationship to historical truth, its accuracy, its inclusiveness. Little consideration has been given to its status as a literary text. A careful reading will reveal, however, that *Los negros brujos* is a text that stands between the literally truthful on the one hand and the purely imaginative on the other. If we operate from the assumption that *Los negros brujos* is not an organic book but a related series of essays, then it is legitimate to ask what strategies Ortiz employed to gain his desired explanatory effect. The recent studies of Hayden White, William Siebenschuh, and Suzanne Gerhart[26] indicate the increasing interest shown by scholars in approaching historical or nonfictional texts with the methodologies usually reserved for the privileged texts of the literary canon. The current debate over the boundary between fiction and nonfictional texts suggests that it may be productive to apply to a given genre methodologies usually thought to be the exclusive domain of another.

An excellent example of this tendency to revise traditional notions of generic boundaries is Gustavo Pérez Firmat's recent study of one of Fernando Ortiz's other earlier works, *Un catauro de cubanismos* (Havana: n.p., 1923). Here Pérez Firmat studies Ortiz's *Catauro* (an early compendium of "Cubanismos") not as a work of philology but rather as a fiction whose subtext is Cuba's intellectual independence vis-à-vis its European, colonial (read: Spanish) models. The critic writes:

But for my argument Ortiz's eccentricity is beside the point. Or rather, it is precisely the point, since I regard the *Catauro* as a work of philological fabulation, a "logofiction" that obeys a logic and incarnates a consistency different from those of scientific inquiry. I approach the *Catauro* as one would approach a novel—and perhaps as one should approach works of criticism as well: with an eye for the motif rather than for the syllogism, for texture rather than for truth. The accuracy of Ortiz's etymologies interests me less than the role they play in the book's plot, and I use the term "plot" advisedly, for in its mixture of the political and the literary the word traces precisely the contours of the

Los negros brujos: *A Reexamination of the Text* : 121

book. The *Catauro* is a philological fiction with a political theme. One important motif in this theme is the excision of Cuban Spanish from its peninsular matrix, what Ortiz terms the "avoidance" of peninsular etymologies.[27]

Much like *Un catauro de cubanismos,* and perhaps in anticipation of it, *Los negros brujos* displays at a very early stage in Ortiz's writing career a propensity to approach factual data from a fictional perspective. Some of these fictional indicia, which link the diverse components of the text, can be apprehended at a level of formal strategies. Susan Sniader Lanser's recent work on point of view in prose fiction,[28] based largely on reader response theory, offers a particularly productive mode of examining these modalities. While Lanser's book is a study of texts that are primarily fictive, her comments on the importance of the text-as-object (such as the primacy of titles, epigraphs, prefaces)[29] offer a way of looking at a particularly complex work such as *Los negros brujos,* which because it appeals to so many disciplines at once (criminology, sociology, linguistics, formal history, folklore, etc.) seems to slip out of our critical grasp. As Lanser points out, structures such as titles, prefaces, and epigraphs convey a voice and a perspective—a point of view that enables the reader to construct an image of the author and to deduce the text's genre.[30]

Both editions of *Los negros brujos* are prefaced with an important epigraph drawn from the Cuban-born French poet José María de Heredia's "La Magicienne," which was published in *Les Trophées* (1893). This poet, second cousin to José María Heredia (1803–1839), died in 1905, one year before the publication of *Los negros brujos.* The epigraph reads: "Partout je sens, j'aspire, à moi-même odieux, / Les noirs enchantements et les sinistres charmes / Dont m'enveloppe encore la colère des Dieux."

This text not only in an obvious way accentuates the mysterious-exotic qualities that Ortiz's so-called treatise would emphasize, but also establishes an intertextual relationship between Ortiz's text and an entire tradition of romanticized images of primitive peoples. It should be remembered that earlier the Cuban José María de Heredia's "El Teocali de Cholula" had evoked images of Mexico's past in the same terms used by European romantics to imagistically create a medieval past about which they had read but obviously never experienced.[31] On yet another level, the lines drawn from "La Magicienne" (a poem probably known by well-educated Cubans, given Heredia's enormous popularity) refer to the legend of the Eumolpidai, a mysterious ancient priestly sect, and thus function as an introduction to the thematic content of the book and underscore its imaginative fictive dimension.[32]

Of considerable importance, too, is the role of the extrafictional voice, to borrow a term from Lanser,[33] in Ortiz's prologue suggestively titled "Adventencias preliminares." Here Ortiz stresses the tentative nature of his material, marking out to some degree its generic boundaries:

> He titulado *apuntes* al presente estudio, no por falsa modestia, sino porque, efectivamente, no es sino una recopilación de ellos. La dificultad de las investigaciones positivas en el ambiente del hampa; las relativamente escasas fuentes de estudio, la vastísima complejidad del tema, y mi ausencia de Cuba durante estos últimos tiempos, han impedido que mi estudio fuese más completo y acabado. (p. xiv)

Also in a fashion similar to the prologues of certain nineteenth-century novels, he provides readers with a combined warning and invitation, a promise to titillate based on an assumption of prudery:

> Así como algunos erotómanos hallan en la contemplación de las figuras ilustrativas de los científicos tratados de anatomía descriptiva un incentivo para sus aberraciones sexuales, y algunas personas de impresionabilidad aguda no pueden soportar la descripción de ciertas enfermedades, así hay individuos que buscan en los libros acerca de la mala vida, una fuente de nuevos excitantes para sus vicios, y otros que no resisten su lectura sin sentirse asqueados ante la gangrena puesta en ellos al descubierto. (p. xiv)

This constant stress on the *tentative* nature of his materials,[34] on their inherent *fictionality*,[35] together with the use of strategies often associated with fictional works, such as the anonymous confidant, and the wholesale incorporation of a wide range of discourse, call to mind the nonfiction or documentary narrative that is enjoying considerable visibility in contemporary Latin American literature. Ortiz to some degree anticipated this phenomenon but operated from the opposite direction: instead of incorporating historical materials within a fictive frame, he utilized the strategies of fiction within a historical, quasi-scientific frame. Thus in addition to the extrafictional voice of Ortiz as historical author, the supplier of factual data, *Los negros brujos* incorporates a great number of voices, each supplying its own perspective on the material presented and each imbued with a different level of diegetic authority. These include: direct quotations from a variety of source books, indirect quotations in which material has been paraphrased or rewritten, intercalations of folk material (prayers, sayings), references to archival material (police reports), recreated dramatic dialogue, and intercalations of newspaper reports. While these various discourses have been woven together by the historical author to form the whole we know as this *text,* each voice has a certain perspective and a relationship to putative fact, and their arrangement, disposition, and focus ultimately alter the way in which these discourses are read.

For example, Ortiz, who constructed much of his text from a wide variety of secondary sources, often inserts these secondary texts at the same level of narration as that of the historical author. The curious (haphazard) arrangement of punctuation he uses to set off these inserted texts and the location of references in the middle of the page produce blocks of multileveled narrative not altogether dissimilar from what one would expect to find in a novel.

Another way to visualize the fictional nature of *Los negros brujos* is to consider its stated purpose vis-à-vis its mode of articulation. Thus, while on the one hand Ortiz's project is rooted theoretically in Positivist methodologies that imply rationality, order, and objectivity, the discourse that attempts this enterprise is consistently cast in a language that belies its purpose and calls into doubt the validity of its theoretical assumptions. Thus like the nineteenth-century author who frequently intrudes into his own narrative world, Ortiz often directly addresses the reader: "En otro lugar más oportuno de este libro insistiré con detalles acerca de esta hipótesis, excuso por tanto extenderme aquí en una digresión" (p. 85). At other times he calls into question his own ideas: "Me han sido descritos instrumentos de tortura dignos de la Santa Inquisición pero no he podido comprobar su existencia, que en todo caso debió ser muy limitada" (p. 40). The form of *Los negros brujos*—both organizational and linguistic—its ability to integrate diverse discursive modes into one frame, calls to mind Henry James's dictum that the novel is "the most independent, most elastic, and most prodigious of literary forms."[36]

It becomes clear that Ortiz used two fundamental strategies to fuse in book form what otherwise would have had the appearance of random thoughts: the classic patterning modalities of nineteenth-century fiction and an intertextuality with popular forms, specifically media fable. There is a point of conjunction between form and meaning in Ortiz's text that can be seen in the form of an erotic-ethnic myth which Fernando Ortiz chose to express with a specific kind of discourse. As Leslie Fielder has noted with regard to North American literature, forms of popular literature have enabled writers to probe aspects of the national consciousness closed to the classic literary texts of "high culture."[37] Thus, while *Los negros brujos* can be read as a factual study of criminal behavior among a subculture of blacks in lower-class urban and rural Cuba, it is also a book in which Ortiz projects a shared myth with his readers, one deeply rooted in Western tradition and one which had found particular resonance in Hispanic literature: the horror of miscegenation and black rape. *Los negros brujos* has as its unifying literary core, its "plot" so to speak, an archetypal story: the murder and dismemberment of a white child by blacks.

Ortiz's deliberate choice of a sensational murder story with racial overtones to serve as the fictive underpinning of what purports to be a serious study is a telling example of the importance played by the generic codes of popular writing in the elaboration of *Los negros brujos*. While the sources for much of the book are scientific treatises, dictionaries of African languages, travel books, and early histories of Cuba, the point of origin for the Niña Zoila episode was recent Cuban history, and Ortiz's sources were versions of the story which had been reported in the popular press. This case, involving the abduction of a young girl in the province of Matanzas whose heart was removed from her body in order to prepare an *embó* (a curative potion) used to assist a black woman in conceiving a child, received wide media attention. The Cuban ethnologist Rómulo Lachatañeré later spoke of the event in these terms: "El caso que produjo más sensación fué el ocurrido en el mes de diciembre de 1904, condenándose a muerte al brujo Bocú y sus 'cómplices,' acusados de dar muerte a la niña Zoila. Bocú y sus compañeros fueron linchados por una multitud enfurecida. Esto ocurrió en la provincia de Matanzas."[38]

It should be remembered that since the Haitian Revolution (1793–1804), which brought a flood of exiles to Cuba with terrible stories of rape, murder, and looting, the fear of a similar revolt of blacks in Cuba was a constant theme in a wide variety of literary and cultural discourses. This antiblack paranoia was so pervasive during late nineteenth-century Cuba that it is reasonable to assume that it had a significance for Ortiz's audience similar to nightmare images of black-white rape and brutality that were captured in pulp fiction around the time of the Civil War in the United States.

Ortiz's narration of the story of the Niña Zoila is based on a classic structural pattern of nineteenth-century fiction. Consequently, the references to this murder story, read in conjunction with the point of view established by the extrafictional voice, insistently foreshadow the events that are to unfold. Thus a brief allusion to the practice of witchcraft early in the text (p. 168) serves to prefigure its more detailed presentation approximately midway in the book (pp. 234–35), which in turn is followed by a resolution and summary of events at the end of the text. In short, Ortiz effectively uses a distinct type of discourse, one—to use the terminology of Mas'ud Zavarzadeh—that is

Los negros brujos: A Reexamination of the Text : 125

"bireferential," simultaneously pointing to the external world of factual events (such as the murder, the trial) and to its *own* text.[39] In short, the Niña Zoila episode restates, albeit more subjectively, the factual information Ortiz has previously presented in a different frame, using a popular voice (that is, the print medium), a voice that allowed Ortiz to satisfy the public (commercial) demands of his book while still remaining theoretically within the limitations of fact. It should be remembered that *Los negros brujos* (most certainly its first edition) was a discourse directed more toward an audience in Madrid than readers in Cuba, and as such Ortiz attempted to deal with fact through media fable.

Apart from the element of plot lent to Ortiz's discourse by the Niña Zoila episode, he also used many intercalations of journalistic prose in other parts of his book. However, if one examines the long chapter "Extracto de las noticias publicadas por la prensa de la Habana referentes a varios casos de brujería" (pp. 343–82), it becomes clear that we are not dealing with exact reproductions of newspaper clippings or documentation similar to what modern writers like Julio Cortázar have done in *El Libro de Manuel* (1973) or Reynaldo González in *La Fiesta de los tiburones* (1978), but with texts that have the physical appearance of "data" but which have been considerably shaped and rewritten by Ortiz. Thus the sixty-five extracts from the press (arranged chronologically from September 1902 until September 1905) contain letters, dramatically recreated dialogues, straight reportage, retold stories, and frequent interventions by Ortiz himself, who at times comments on the legal aspects of the reported cases to shore up his fundamental thesis that cult practices are at the root of Cuba's problems with crime.

The following example illustrates well the tone and emotional perspective that characterize the majority of these "theoretical documents":

1902
Septiembre

TACO TACO.

En este pueblo hubo un verdadero escándalo, pues se hizo correr la especie de que la señorita de aquella localidad, M. C., estaba hechizada, y que a fin de devolverle la salud, iba a ser operada por los *brujos*. A la joven se le extrajeron ranas, alfileres y un gato prieto. . . . sin rabo y sin orejas, que fué quemado allí, en presencia de todos. Entonces se dijo, y hasta se publicó en *La Discusión,* que el *gato prieto* era nieto y a la vez hijo del señor F. C., padre de la hechizada.

Según referencias, para desembrujar a la infeliz mujer, ésta fué desnudada completamente y tendida en el suelo junto a una hoguera ante un centenar de personas. Tras unos conjuros el brujo provocó el aborto a fuerza de golpes y pisotones. (p. 345)

Ortiz's wholesale incorporation of a large body of journalistic pieces is telling, since that strategy allows him to explore the subconscious of contemporary Cuban reality through the use of yellow journalism—a form that in turn is modeled on the "novela de folletín" but which is paradoxically presented via a format that ostensibly tells the truth.

The contiguity of Ortiz's discourse with the sensationalism of the popular print media calls attention to an earlier text that no doubt served for much of *Los negros brujos* as both an organizational model and the thematic matrix: *Los criminales de Cuba y el inspector Trujillo: Narración de los servicios, prestados en el cuerpo de policía de La Habana.* Edited by Carlos Urrutía y Blanco (1750–1825), a Spanish general and politician, this curious amalgam of information on nineteenth-century Havana, a kind of colonial almanac, is ostensibly a biography of José Trujillo y Monagas, a colonial police officer in Havana. In addition to presenting his biography, the book contains one of the earliest essays on the secret African cult of the "ñáñigos," reproductions of secret cult insignia, a brief lexicon of Afro-Cuban words, and extensive case histories of criminals drawn from the pages of the colonial press: *La Voz de Cuba, La Discusión, La Correspondencia de Cuba.* Urrutía's colonialist reading of Cuban society not only presented a similar attitude toward Cuba's black population but also anticipated some of the strategies seen at play in Ortiz's text. Thus Urrutía strengthens his claim to truth by the use of framing devices, by claiming to the reader that what he writes has basis in fact and by intercalating documents into the text.

I would argue that much like *Un catauro de cubanismos, Los negros brujos* is a text much more concerned with the evolution of Cuban culture, with coming to grips with one of the fundamental problematics of New World culture, than with a study of criminal behavior per se. Whereas in his construction of the *Catauro* Ortiz was clearly more concerned with the problems of language (anticipating the later formulations of Juan Marinello in this regard), *Los negros brujos* is a classic example of a Caribbean portrayal of African traditions that betrays, however inadvertently, its roots in popular myth and culture.

While many contemporary writers and critics claim that the circumstances of contemporary reality (rapid urbanization, a collapse of the socioeconomic infrastructure, terrorism, etc.) have forced writers to adopt new strategies of self-expression, they may not realize that early twentieth-century Cuba had much the same effect on Fernando Ortiz.

Los negros brujos: *A Reexamination of the Text* : 127

Ortiz's response to the tensions of his time—such as the struggle of Cuba to shed its colonial past, to obtain a sense of selfness—was to produce a document that explored some of the fundamental issues of his day—and those issues were largely connected to questions of race. In order to explore the contradictory reality of early twentieth-century Cuba (the struggle to assimilate its African roots versus its dependence on European models), Ortiz used strategies more often associated with popular culture and the world of imaginative literature, which stamped this book with a distinctiveness, a quality that caused it to endure long after its basis in fact had been diminished.

NOTES

1. See Martin S. Stabb, *In Quest of Identity: Patterns in the Spanish American Essay of Ideas, 1890–1960* (Chapel Hill: University of North Carolina Press, 1967), p. 186.
2. To date there is no book-length critical study of the work of Fernando Ortiz. A good biographical sketch is provided by Julio Le Riverend, "Fernando Ortiz y su obra cubana," in *Órbita de Fernando Ortiz: Selección y prólogo de Julio Le Riverend* (Havana: Unión de Escritores y Artistas de Cuba, 1973), pp. 7–51. The most complete bibliography is that of Araceli García-Carranza, *Bio-bibliografía de Don Fernando Ortiz* (Havana: Biblioteca José Martí, 1970). Two other bibliographies are also useful: Berta Becerra and Juan Comas, "La obra escrita de don Fernando Ortiz," *Revista Interamericana de Bibliografía* 7 (1957): 347–71, and the more specialized work of René León, "Fernando Ortiz: Bibliografía sobre el tema negro," *Explicación de Textos Literarios* 12–13 (1983–1984): 19–25. Somewhat dated but still interesting are the lively comments of Manuel Pedro González, "Cuba's Fernando Ortiz," *Books Abroad* 17 (Winter 1946): 9–13. Of slighter interest are the personal testimonies offered by writers such as Juan Marinello, Nicolás Guillén, José Luciano Franco, José Antonio Portuondo, and Miguel Barnet, in "Fernando Ortiz (1881–1969)," *Casa de las Americas* 10 (July–August 1969): 3–11. Of considerable interest is Gustavo Pérez Firmat, "The Philological Fictions of Fernando Ortiz," *Notebooks in Cultural Analysis* 2 (1968): 190–207.
3. G. R. Coulthard, *Race and Colour in Caribbean Literature* (London: Oxford University Press, 1962), p. 28.
4. F. S. Stimon, *The New Schools of Spanish American Poetry* (Chapel Hill: University of North Carolina Press, 1970), p. 165.
5. *Ensayistas contemporáneos*, ed. Félix Lazo (Havana: Editorial Trópico, 1938), pp. 30–33.
6. Odilio Urfé, "Music and Dance in Cuba," in *Africa in Latin America: Essays on History, Culture, and Socialization,* ed. Manuel Moreno Fraginals and trans. Leonor Blum (New York: Holmes and Meier, 1984), p. 170.
7. René Depestre, "Hello and Goodbye to Negritude," in ibid., p. 254.
8. Gastón Baquero, "Sobre la falsa poesía negra: Tres notas polémicas," *Darío, Cernuda y otros temas poéticos* (Madrid: Editora Nacional, 1969), p. 213.
9. Eric Williams, "The Contemporary Pattern of Race Relations in the Caribbean," *Phylon* 16 (1955): 379.
10. Good examples are Alejo Carpentier, *¡Ecué-Yamba-O!: Historia afro-cubana*

(Madrid: Editorial España, 1933); Ramón Guirao, "Bailadora de rumba," *Diario de la Marina*, 8 April 1928, p. 16; and Lino Novás Calvo, "La Luna de los ñáñigos," *Revista de Occidente* 35 (January 1932): 85–105.

11. Roberto González Echeverría, *Alejo Carpentier: The Pilgrim at Home* (Ithaca, N.Y.: Cornell University Press, 1977), pp. 46–48.

12. Ortiz was not the first to write on blacks in Cuba and in a sense his work only continues that of an earlier generation. See, for example, Antonio Bachiller y Morales, *Los negros* (Barcelona: Gorgas y Compañía, 1887); Francisco Calcagno, *Poetas de color* (Havana: Imp. Militar de Soler y Compañía, 1878). Also an interesting collection of *Costumbrista* articles, *Tipos y costumbres de la Isla de Cuba* (Havana: Miguel de Villa, 1881), contains essays by Enrique Fernández Carrillo ("El ñáñigo"), Carlos Noroña ("Los negros curros"), and José E. Triay ("El calesero"). José Antonio Portuondo refers to these works in "El negro, héroe, bufón y persona en la literatura cubana colonial," *Unión* 7 (1968): 30–36. For a brief but excellent summary of the ideological problems of the era see Ivan Schulman, "Una época de crisis: Cuba en 1830," in *Cecilia Valdés, prólogo y cronología de Ivan Schulman* (Caracas: Biblioteca Ayacucho, 1981), pp. ix–xiii.

13. *Los negros brujos* was to be one of a series of studies on blacks. Only two (*Los negros brujos, Los Negros esclavos*) were ever published. In the prologue to his *Glosario de afronegrismos* (Havana: Imprenta "El siglo XX," 1924) Ortiz explained the project in some detail.

14. Fernando Ortiz, "Brujos o santeros," *Estudios Afrocubanos* 3 (1939): 85. Also see Diana Iznaga Beira, "Fernando Ortiz y su hampa afrocubana," *Universidad de La Habana* 220 (May–August 1983): 155–71.

15. For a good discussion of the importance of artistic material in a literary text, see Jean Schwind, "The Benda Illustrations to *My Antonia*: Cather's 'Silent' Supplement to Jim Burden's Narrative," *PMLA* 100 (January 1985): 51–65.

16. See Andrew Gurr, *Writers in Exile: The Creative Use of Home in Modern Literature* (Atlantic Highlands, N.J.: Harvester Press, 1981).

17. Fernando Ortiz, *Hampa afro-cubana: Los negros brujos: Apuntes para un estudio de etnología criminal* (Madrid: Librería de Fernando Fé, 1906), p. 19. Future references will be given in the text.

18. See Alberto Gutiérrez de la Solana, "En torno a Fernando Ortiz: Lo afrocubano y otros ensayos," in *El ensayo y la crítica literaria en Iberoamérica, Memoria del XIV Congreso del Instituto Internacional de Literatura Iberoamericana* (Toronto: University of Toronto Press, 1970), p. 83.

19. Ortiz had published the following essays which were to form part of *Los negros brujos* a year earlier: "Procedencia de los negros de Cuba," *Cuba y América* 20 (1905): 91–92; "Las supervivencias africanas en Cuba," *Cuba y América* 18 (1905): 7–8; and "La criminalità dei negri en Cuba," *Archivio di psichiatria medicina legala* 24 (1905): 594–600.

20. Ortiz, "La mala vida cubana," *Derecho y sociología* 1 (1906): 46–59.

21. See Moreno Fraginals, "Cultural Contributions and Deculturation," *Africa in Latin America*, pp. 5–22.

22. See Leopoldo Zea, *Dos etapas del pensamiento hispanoamericano: Del romanticismo al positivismo* (Mexico City: El Colegio de México, 1949).

23. For an excellent discussion of this subject, see Stabb, *In Quest of Identity*.

24. See Hayden White, *Tropics of Discourse: Essays in Cultural Criticism* (Baltimore: Johns Hopkins University Press, 1978).

25. See Mark Irving Helbing, "Primitivism and the Harlem Renaissance," Ph.D.

diss., University of Minnesota, 1972, esp. ch. 1 (pp. 15-40). Also of interest is Tzvetan Todorov, *The Conquest of America: The Question of the Other,* trans. Richard Howard (New York: Harper and Row, 1982).

26. Hayden White, *The Tropics of Discourse,* and *Metahistory: The Historical Imagination in Nineteenth Century Europe* (Baltimore: Johns Hopkins University Press, 1983); William R. Siebenschuh, *Fictional Techniques and Factual Works* (Athens: University of Georgia Press, 1983); Suzanne Gerhart, *The Open Boundary of History and Fiction: A Critical Approach to the French Enlightenment* (Princeton, N.J.: Princeton University Press, 1984). The Siebenschuh study in particular contains an excellent bibliography on the subject.

27. Pérez Firmat, "The Philological Fictions of Fernando Ortiz," p. 199.

28. Susan Sniader Lanser, *The Narrative Act: Point of View in Prose Fiction* (Princeton, N.J.: Princeton University Press, 1981).

29. Ortiz was clearly uncomfortable with his choice of title and defended and explained it at some length in "Brujos o santeros," *Estudios Afrocubanos* 3 (1939): 85-90.

30. Lanser, *The Narrative Act,* p. 125.

31. See David William Foster, "Reyes: Para una desmistificación del mito," *Cuadernos Americanos* 6 (November-December 1982): 146.

32. "The Eumolpidai were a priestly family, deriving their origin from a Pelasgian Thracian named Eumolpus—the one with a good voice or melody. They were clothed with long, purple robes which they shook against the threshold of those they cursed. This was a significant action among all ancient peoples—*vide* Nehemiah, Chap. V, v. 13—and is so among orientals to this day." Cited in *Sonnets from the Trophies of José María de Heredia,* trans. Edward Robenson Taylor (New York: P. Elder and Co., 1913), p. 166.

33. See Lanser, *The Narrative Act,* pp. 122-32.

34. See, for example, statements on pp. 40, 71, 85, 95, 111, and 179.

35. See E. B. Garside's review of *Cuban Counterpoint, New York Times,* 16 February 1947, p. 10.

36. Henry James, Preface to *The Ambassadors* (1903; rpt. Boston: Houghton Mifflin, 1966), p. 15.

37. See Leslie Fiedler, *What Was Literature? Class Culture and Mass Society* (New York: Simon and Schuster, 1982).

38. Rómulo Lachatañeré, "El sistema religiososo de Los Lucumís," *Estudios Afroamericanos* 3 (1939): 84.

39. Cited in John Hellmann, *Fables of Fact: The New Journalism as New Fiction* (Urbana: University of Illinois Press, 1981).

RESEARCH NOTES

MANUEL R. GÓMEZ

The U.S. House of Representatives and Policy Toward Cuba: A Study of Political Attitudes

ABSTRACT

The Reagan administration's policy toward Cuba is a key component of regional policy and has been widely debated, but the views of Congressional policymakers have not been the focus of similar scrutiny. This study, based on interviews conducted between July 1985 and January 1986, examines the climate of opinion surrounding this issue among the foreign policy aides of legislators who serve on the Committee on Foreign Affairs in the House of Representatives. The results indicate that Cuba policy has not received a comprehensive review in the House since at least 1980, and that such a review—political factors aside—could potentially challenge key elements of current administration policy toward Cuba.

RESUMEN

La política de la Administración Reagan hacia Cuba constituye un componente fundamental de la política regional que ha sido ampliamente debatido. Sin embargo los puntos de vista de los decisores del congreso no han sido objeto de escrutinio similar. Este estudio, basado en entrevistas hechas entre julio de 1985 y enero de 1986, examina el clima de opinión que existe sobre este problema entre los asistentes de política exterior de legisladores que trabajan en el Comité de Asuntos Exteriores en la Cámara de Representantes. Los resultados indican que la política hacia Cuba no ha recibido una revisión comprehensiva en la Cámara de Representantes desde 1980 por lo menos, y que tal revisión—dejando de lado los factores políticos—podría desafiar potencialmente los elementos claves de la política actual de la administración hacia Cuba.

Cuba has been a key element of the rhetoric and rationale that guide current U.S. policy in Central America and the Caribbean. As a result, the administration's policy toward Cuba has been the focus of much scrutiny and public debate in the Congress, the media, and in academic circles. The views of congressional policymakers regarding Cuba, however, have not been the focus of study or public debate in any way comparable to the scrutiny received by the highly publicized views of the executive branch.

Yet a glance at the *Congressional Record* since 1980 will show that Cuba certainly gets mentioned a great deal—especially in the debates about Radio Martí, Central America, Grenada, and Africa—but the discussions of the issue have been far from comprehensive. This fact is best illustrated by a comment made during our survey from an experienced aide to a congressman who is very active in foreign affairs: "The [broad] issue of Cuba has not been discussed much with [my boss], except in specific issues, like Radio Martí, Africa, troops, etc. No general discussion, only 'projected' Cuba issues."

And, indeed, many of our respondents also agreed with the aide to another member of Congress, on the Western Hemisphere Subcommittee, who told us, "The problem is, since Cuba has not really been an issue for the subcommittee, we've never really done anything on it, I've never really talked to [my boss] very much about it." Cuba, then, is a paradox. It is definitely in the air as a key part of administration rhetoric, and many congressional words are spent on it, but it has not been the subject of substantive policy discussions or analysis in the legislative bodies.

Yet congressional views *are* important, at the very least as an element of potential moderation or encouragement of executive policies. This study seeks to fill the gap of information about congressional views of Cuba policy, by way of interviews with foreign policy aides of legislators who serve on the Foreign Affairs Committee of the House of Representatives.

Methods

Between July 1985 and January 1986, interviews were conducted with the foreign policy aides of legislators who serve on the Committee on Foreign Affairs of the House of Representatives.[1] Nearly all the congressional offices cooperated with the study, with twenty-one of twenty-five Democratic, and fifteen of nineteen Republican offices participating. Each was asked to respond to a questionnaire with ten open-ended questions, and to do so reflecting, as faithfully as possible, the views of the member of Congress for whom they worked. The interviews were not for attribution.[2]

It was clear from the inception of the study that the interviews would not reflect the exact views of the members of the committee. They do, however, approximate them; and, more important, they reflect a climate of opinion about Cuba policy among their principal foreign policy advisors. This climate of opinion, to my knowledge, has not been systematically studied before.

The interview responses were analyzed and tallied into broad categories that encompassed the principal themes found in the answers to each of the questions. The categories are indicated on the tables and in the discussion below.

Results

The results of the survey are summarized in this section, following the order of the questions used in the study. Percentages of responses follow each question.

Questions 1 and 2: Describe your understanding of the present U.S. policy toward Cuba. What are the objectives of that policy?

	Republicans	Democrats	Total
To bring about fundamental changes in the Cuban political system	13%	10%	11%
To isolate Cuba	27	58	32
To limit Cuban expansionism	93	62	75
To deny legitimacy to Cuba	53	14	31

Not surprisingly, the vast majority (75 percent) of members of both parties thought that the existing policy seeks to "limit Cuban expansionism and/or reduce Cuban influence," and especially to thwart Cuban foreign policy goals. Many Democrats, but relatively few Republicans, also emphasized the phrase "isolation of Cuba" as a goal of administration policy, a choice of term that seemed to reflect less hostility than Republican attitudes. An important theme for Republicans (53 percent) in these two questions, as in the latter question on normalization, was to "deny legitimacy" to the Cuban government, while few Democrats (14 percent) emphasized that theme. Only four responses thought that administration policy was geared to bring about fundamental changes in the Cuban domestic political system, and very few spontaneously mentioned the internal human rights issue.

Question 3: Does the policy serve U.S. interests well?

	Republicans	Democrats	Total
Tends to serve U.S. interests	67%	26%	42%
Tends not to serve U.S. interests	13	73	47
Uncertain	13	0	6

As can be seen, the committee was close to evenly divided on this issue, but with clear differences along party lines. Most Republicans (67 percent) felt that current Cuba policy serves U.S. interests well, or, if they wished to change it, they would do so in the direction of a tougher stance. The reverse was true for Democrats. Only four Democratic respondents thought the policy serves at least some U.S. interests well, and a fifth wished a tougher stance, while the majority of their party colleagues (73 percent), did not consider the policy to be in the U.S. interest and tended to favor more flexibility.

On questions 4 and 5, more than half the Democrats (63 percent), but no Republicans, tended to favor normalization of relations with Cuba. Three Republican offices, however, were open to the idea of a normalization process, but their responses put a heavy emphasis on the theme that normalization should come only after "certain conditions are met" by Cuba.

Question 4: Would it be in the U.S. interest to normalize relations with Cuba?

	Republicans	Democrats	Total
Yes (or tending to yes)	0%	63%	35%
Yes, but only after Cuba meets strict conditions	20	11	15
No	73	16	42
Uncertain	7	11	9

When asked how they might modify Cuba policy, most Democrats (77 percent) favored "increased contacts" with Cuba, and even 21 percent of Republicans held such a view (see question 5). Very few respondents favored a policy that would actively seek fundamental changes in the Cuban political system, and none advocated explicit efforts to overthrow the Cuban government.

Question 5: How would you modify existing policy toward Cuba?

	Republicans	Democrats	Total
Encourage increased contacts	21%	77%	56%
Keep policy as is	43	9	22
Make policy tougher	21	9	14
Uncertain	14	5	8

Much ambivalence was apparent in the answers to the questions about possible modifications in the United States' Cuba policy. Perhaps the best example of that ambivalence is the aide who told us, "American interests would be served if Cuba just went away, and all these problems disappeared, [but] it is difficult to envision a policy to achieve that end."

Republican responses often contained a tendency toward paternalism, as in the case of an aide who told us that "to normalize relations would be to reward things that we don't like, it would encourage them." Another aide characterized U.S. policy in similar terms "as a way of demonstrating that we don't view Castro as a legitimate member of the Western Hemisphere." The pattern of these comments was echoed in interviews with several other aides to Republican congressmen, who viewed policy primarily in terms of reward and punishment, rather than as a pragmatic means to manage the conflicts with Cuba in a manner consistent with U.S. interests.

Question 6: Is Cuba a security threat to the United States?

	Republicans	Democrats	Total
Yes, directly	27%	9%	17%
Yes, indirectly	100	43	67
By subversion (67%)			
As Soviet base (73%)			
No, not a serious threat	0	33	19

Few congressional offices (17 percent) considered Cuba a direct security threat to the United States. All the Republicans considered it an indirect threat, either as a "Soviet extension" or as a means of "subversion." Democrats, on the other hand, rated the nature of the Cuban threat on a lower scale. A bit less than half (43 percent) of the Democrats saw Cuba as an indirect threat to U.S. security, and fully 33 percent considered the Cuban security threat exaggerated.

Question 7: Is Radio Martí an effective instrument of policy?

	Republicans	Democrats	Total
Yes (or tending to yes)	73%	48%	58%
No (or tending to no)	7	43	28
Uncertain	20	9	14

Radio Martí was generally supported by both Democrats (48 percent) and Republicans (73 percent), although many respondents qualified their responses by saying that it was "too early to tell" how effective the station is as an instrument of policy. This cautious skepticism underlay a clear thirst for demonstrated evidence of the station's success, and much doubt about the ability to obtain it. On the other hand, several offices that had been critical of the proposal now think that "it doesn't seem to have turned out as bad as some people thought."

Question 8: Does the accumulated experience of our Cuba policy have any relation to Central American policy issues?

The responses to question 8 were the most difficult of the entire study to analyze because no clear or common themes emerged from them. In general terms, we found that Democratic offices did far more soul-searching and touched on many more "lessons" from past Cuba policy than did those from the Republican side. The two groups seemed to agree on only one point: Cuba policy had not been successful over recent decades. Republicans, however, tended to blame the fact that the United States "did not isolate Cuba effectively earlier." Democrats, on the other hand, tended to put the finger on the failure of U.S. policy to more effectively take into account the region's "social and economic deprivation" and "legitimate nationalistic aspirations." Many Democratic offices also spoke of current U.S. policy in Central America as "repeating the same mistakes with Nicaragua as we did with Cuba."

Question 9: How important a factor is Cuba in the Central American conflict?

	Republicans	Democrats	Total
Very important	50%	26%	36%
Important	31	17	23
Importance is exaggerated	19	35	18
Uncertain	0	22	13

On the whole, most members of the committee—on both sides of the aisle—considered the Cuban role in Central America "important" or "very important." A sizable minority—19 percent of Republicans and 35 percent of Democrats—deemed the administration's view of the Cuban role as "exaggerated."

Question 10: Can high-level talks with Cuba in any way contribute to the resolution of the Central American conflicts?

	Republicans	Democrats	Total
Yes	33%	66%	45%
No	53	47	45
Uncertain	13	7	9

Opinion in the committee was nearly evenly divided on the possible benefits of talking to Cuba as a means to contribute to the resolution of the Central American conflict. Not surprisingly, more Democrats (66 percent) than Republicans (33 percent) thought such talks could make a contribution.

Discussion

This study investigated the climate of opinion about Cuba policy among foreign policy aides of the House Foreign Affairs Committee. The results suggest a few areas where there is consensus among Republicans and Democrats, and many others where there are differences of opinion, generally along party lines. The results also indicate substantial and generally unexpressed contradictions within existing Cuba policy.

The most salient point of agreement—and in many ways historically the most surprising—is that few in the committee believe that Cuba policy seeks, or should seek, a fundamental change in the Cuban political system. Marxist Cuba, it seems, is considered a rather permanent fixture of hemispheric reality. It was also striking that many Republicans chafe under this realization, and that Republican policy objectives are strongly influenced by what can only be characterized as an almost paternalistic emphasis on "denying legitimacy" to the reality which they nonetheless acknowledge.

A second point of agreement is a concern about "Cuban expansionism," which is also generally shared regardless of party affiliation. Democrats, however, are surprisingly willing to support "increased dialogue" with Cuba as a policy option, while Republicans tend to support a continuing policy of punishment and isolation. Democrats are also fairly solidly in favor of normalization of relations, while Republicans strongly oppose it.

It is practically impossible, on the basis of this study, to comment on the reasons for these partisan policy differences regarding the central issue of better relations with Cuba. From one end of the ideological spectrum, it is facile to conclude that Republicans are more willing to take measures to contain "Cuban expansionism," while Democrats are more willing to overlook it. An alternate interpretation—one I favor—is that Democrats consider current policy instruments to have utterly failed in their goal of limiting Cuban influence, or, to put it more dramatically, the rigidity of the Republican view has actually paved the way for more effective "Cuban expansionism." Either way, the results of this study cannot answer this question.

There is substantial consensus that Cuba plays an important role in the Central American conflict, but opinion is divided, as a whole and for both parties, about the possible benefits of discussions with Cuba as part of the resolution of the Central American conflict. The surprising finding is that the study did not find the wholesale rejection of the idea, not even among Republicans, which is apparent in administration policy.

Finally, it was very clear from the interviews that Cuba policy has not been, since at least 1980, the subject of any in-depth review by the committee that would logically do so in the House of Representatives. The diversity of opinion found among both Republicans and Democrats suggests that, if political factors could be put aside, such a review might seriously challenge many key elements of current administration policy toward the island.

NOTES

1. Initially, the study was to include the equivalent committee in the Senate, but aides in that chamber of Congress proved far more difficult to capture for interviews. The Senate effort is continuing, however, and will be the subject of a future report.

2. The interviews that form the basis for this study were conducted by two student interns with the Cuban-American Committee Fund, Alison Edwards and Tony Hernandez. The author wishes to acknowledge their invaluable contributions to this article.

WILLARD W. RADELL, JR.

Comparative Performance of Large Cuban Sugar Factories in the 1984 "Zafra"

ABSTRACT

This analysis of the 1984 zafra in Cuba has revealed a tendency for larger mills to perform less well when compared to smaller mills. Moreover, in 1984 larger mills tended to perform worse than expected, judging from their own past performance. A difference of means test was applied, and it was found that large mills were more likely to appear on one of Cuba's below-normal performance lists and small mills were more likely to appear on above-normal performance lists. While size is only one of many variables affecting mill efficiency, a case can be made that Cuba is having special difficulties in managing the larger mills.

RESUMEN

El análisis de la zafra de 1984 en Cuba ha revelado la tendencia a que los ingenios azucareros más grandes presenten un rendimiento inferior a los obtenidos por los ingenios más pequeños. Además, en 1984 los ingenios más grandes tendieron a mostrar rendimientos inferiores a los esperados en base a sus propios rendimientos anteriores. Un examen de diferencia de medias fue aplicado y resultó que los ingenios más grandes tenían una mayor probabilidad de aparecer en una de las listas de Cuba sobre rendimiento por debajo de lo normal y que los ingenios más pequeños tenían una mayor probabilidad de aparecer en las listas de rendimiento por encima de lo normal. Aún cuando el tamaño es solo una de las muchas variables que afectan la eficiencia de los ingenios, se puede argumentar que Cuba tiene dificultades en el manejo de sus ingenios más grandes.

Despite attempts at diversification of the Cuban economy, sugar remains Cuba's number one agricultural and industrial commodity. Although Cuba's production levels have been surpassed by Brazil, Cuba remains the world's top-ranking sugar exporter. (Brazil consumes the majority of its sugar domestically.) Throughout the late 1970s and middle 1980s, the USSR has paid as much as ten times "world" residual market prices and has purchased more Cuban sugar than any other single importer.

While Cuba is somewhat insulated from low world sugar prices by Soviet preferential prices, the unusually low market prices for sugar in the 1980s have inflicted damage on the Cuban economy. About 80 percent of Cuba's export earnings come from sugar and that portion of sugar exports which goes to market economies has disproportionate impact because it is traded for hard currency. Low world prices in recent years and increasing competition from high-fructose corn sugar and sugar substitutes have damaged all sugar-exporting countries, including Cuba.

Since the late 1960s the Cuban sugar industry has been implementing several major initiatives: (1) There has been an attempt to replace the most antiquated equipment with machinery of newer vintage. (2) Despite many problems with mechanizing harvesting, Cuba has successfully mechanized a large portion of the harvest (62 percent) and, as a result, the number of cane cutters has decreased from 350,000 in 1970 to 72,000 in 1985.[1] (3) Production in the 1980s has been stabilized at higher levels. With the exception of the harvest of 1986 (the year of Hurricane Kate), production between 1981 and 1986 has averaged about 8 million metric tons per year. (4) New plants are being built that embody the latest technologies of production control and the most efficient burning of bagasse (cane fiber) in factory steam plants. (5) With normalization of relations with Brazil, Cuba and Brazil are speaking of a "common export strategy." (6) Cuba is expanding fuel alcohol production from sugar. Contracts have been signed with Brazilian firms to buy alcohol distilleries to be retrofitted on Cuban sugar mills. Thus, the sugar industry is being brought into an import-substitution strategy designed to reduce Cuba's dependence on imported oil.

Sugar is often thought to be an exclusively agricultural commodity. Aside from the obvious agricultural aspects of sugar production, there is a less obvious but nevertheless crucial industrial component. Since roughly 90 percent of the weight of the cane is lost in processing, factories associated with sugar production must be placed near the center of the agricultural source of cane. As a result of the unique characteristics of raw cane sugar production, large cane sugar producers like Cuba are in the odd position of having their industry dispersed over large areas. Although such factories represent the major portion of Cuba's industrial capacity, their dispersed locations make difficult the implementation of national industrial policy.

Once cut, cane is a wasting asset, suffering depletion of recoverable sugar with every hour of transit and queuing at the factory. Depletion of the primary raw input creates a strong incentive to integrate growing, harvesting, transportation, industrial processing, and factory maintenance. Suboptimal performance at any stage of the system will reduce output of the final product. Cuba learned this the hard way in 1970 when more than enough cane was cut to yield a 10 million metric ton output of sugar, but actual output fell short at 8.5 million tons. At no time since 1970 has Cuba attempted to increase the flow of a single variable input (cane), while maintaining capital (factories) at existing capacities. Cuba's 1970 rediscovery of the law of diminishing marginal returns has given Cuba a more balanced approach to sugar production in recent years.[2]

One of the greatest weak spots discovered in the 1970 "zafra" (sugar campaign) was the performance of the sugar factories. Through the 1960s not a single new mill was built and there was no major addition to capacity.[3] In fact, some mills were shut down and cannibalized for parts while other mills were unable to operate at their rated capacities because many industrial components were excessively worn.

The poor performance of the sugar factories in 1970 came from a number of sources: (1) Cuba was emerging from a period when it had appeared that the sugar industry would be deliberately shrunk. During the early Che Guevara period the sugar sector was closely associated with "neocolonial" dependence on monoculture for export. The sugar industry was viewed as an unpleasant vestige of an exploitative past that would be replaced by industrial and agricultural diversification. By the late 1960s the pace of investment in the sugar sector was increasing in anticipation of the 1970 harvest, but by less than the amount required to restore factory capacities to prerevolutionary levels. (2) Many of the most competent technicians left Cuba during a period of relatively open emigration. (3) Much of the sugar equipment that had been ordered from the Eastern bloc either performed poorly or did not arrive in time. (4) United States factory equipment was kept out of Cuba by the embargo and Cuba was deprived of the hard currency with which to purchase elsewhere as the United States was boycotting Cuban sugar. (5) The Cuban government realized too late that increasing the input of raw cane without proportionate, complementary increases in other inputs greatly increases unit costs as industrial efficiency deteriorates. (6) Technical education was not equal to the task of maintaining sufficient numbers of sufficiently trained skilled workers, managers, and technicians. In Fidel Castro's words: "There is something that has deteriorated more than the mills themselves, and that is management, the operation, the direction of the mills, as a result of the fact that many of the older workers have been retiring. . . . But we have not carried out an adequate program of renovation and training of new personnel."[4] While inadequacies in technical education first surfaced in 1970, the training of sugar factory personnel remains as a major problem in Cuba in the 1980s.

Among the major disappointments of the Cuban sugar industry in 1970 was the performance of the largest mills. Until 1970, it had been assumed that the greater the capacity of a mill, the greater would be its output. But in the 1970 harvest some of the largest mills proved to be unpredictable in their sustainable capacities and their factory efficiency ratings.[5] Large mills like Urbano Noris were found to run out of cane when operating well (an indication of inadequate production scheduling and transportation of cut cane) and with breakdowns of uncertain duration the factory yields (sugar output as a percent of cane ground) deteriorated following one of the frequent periods of poor performance.

As all the factories extant in the mid-1970s were of prerevolutionary vintage, and because Cuba had come to realize that it would have to depend upon sugar exports into the twenty-first century, MINAZ (Cuba's sugar ministry) began planning for a new generation of sugar mills. In the early 1980s, new sugar factories were under construction with capacities of 6,800 metric tons of cane per day.[6] The prerevolutionary factories had been as large as 14,000 metric tons of capacity. Why were the new mills built smaller than many existing mills? How have large mills performed relative to the smaller mills? Were the mills of 1980 vintage built smaller because of perceived diseconomies of larger size in the Cuban industry? Answers to these questions may be found by analyzing the comparative performance of large and small sugar factories during the 1984 harvest.

How MINAZ Rates Mill Performance

In order to gauge the economic performance of Cuban sugar mills, one must work around problems of partial information. Since 1963, when Cuba discontinued publication of *Anuario Azucarero de Cuba*, there has been no single source of complete annual production data for individual sugar factories.[7] The most crucial pieces of mill information—cane input, capacity, days of operation, and raw sugar output—are not systematically reported on an annual basis outside MINAZ. Fortunately, and probably unintentionally, the Cuban government has released just enough information to make it possible to determine the comparative performance of the larger sugar factories.

Until 1985, *Granma* published four lists of ten entries each pertaining to sugar factory performance for every ten days of the sugar production season. One list ranks the ten factories that had the greatest capacity utilization and another list ranks those with the worst capacity utilization for the previous ten-day period. The third list ranks the ten factories with the highest technical efficiency (measured by the percent of potential sugar actually extracted from the cane) and the final list presents a ranking of the worst factories in the same category. At times the entries on the lists are not ranked, and at other times not only are the mills ranked, but also specific capacity factors and sugar recovery rates are given. It is important to note that the lists are "normalized" in the sense that recovery rates and capacity utilization rates are expressed as percentages of normal for each mill for each ten-day period. Thus, regional differences in soil quality, elevation, and irrigation percentages should not adversely affect the listing of a mill.

As a result of a lack of annual capacity data, the capacities used in this study are the historical capacities, or the maximum figures reported in 1962. For those few mills on which MINAZ has more recently reported capacities in excess of 1962 maxima, no small mills have grown so much that they can now be considered large. Moreover, the nonparametric tests used to analyze the lists are not sensitive to small differences in reported capacities. It is logical to suppose that the Cuban government would like to restore the capacities of sugar factories to at least prerevolutionary levels. For new mills, the recently reported capacities were used. In most cases the occasionally reported capacities in *Granma* are at or below pre-1962 maxima. The lists, coupled with reported capacity data that reveal relative factory sizes, provide sufficient information to enable us to apply nonparametric tests to the hypothesis that larger mills performed less well than smaller factories in the 1984 sugar harvest.

Large Mill Performance

Before analyzing the data, we should note that, by itself, bigness is not usually the primary problem of an inefficient factory. When size is a problem, it is working in tandem with a shortage of adequately trained managers and workers, an improper mix of early- and late-maturing cane varieties, the recent installation of machines that are not yet performing properly, transportation delays, inadequate harvest scheduling, which impairs the freshness of the cane, and inadequate maintenance, which increases unscheduled downtime and leads to suboptimal average daily production rates. All of the above cause problems for any size mill, but the problems are magnified for larger mills, given

TABLE 1
The Relationship Between Size and Recovery Rate in the Ten Best and Ten Worst Cuban Sugar Mills in Each Category, 1984

Size (daily capacity, in metric tons)	Best	Worst
0– 2,000	14	1
2,001– 4,000	61	21
4,001– 6,000	5	25
6,001– 8,000	1	13
8,001–10,000	0	12
10,001–12,000	0	0
12,001–14,000	0	0
14,000–15,000	0	4

Sources: Anuario Azucarero de Cuba, 1962. Ministerio del Comercio Exterior, Havana. *Sugar y Azúcar Yearbook, 1975* (New York: Palmer Publications, 1976); *Granma*, 1984: January 13, 23, 24; February 14, 16; March 6, 8, 12, 15, 17, 19, 24, 27; April 4, 14, 23, 27; May 5.
Note: Recovery rates were measured by the frequency of the mills' appearances on lists of the ten best and ten worsts mills in each category.

their longer supply lines, and greater time and information lags. It should also be noted that most differences in recovery rates are not due to differences in factory size. Mechanically harvested cane, burned cane, nonirrigated cane, early maturing cane, rattooned cane, cane grown on poorer soil, and regional differences in weather and elevation can all lead to lower technical factory efficiency. However, since MINAZ "normalizes" the ratings for each mill, many (but not all) of the above influences are eliminated.

If the largest mills are performing as well as the smaller mills, then the mean capacities of mills on the "good" lists should not differ significantly from those of mills on the "bad" lists. If a disproportionate number of large mills appear on the list of the worst-performing factories, it can be inferred that there are problems unique to the largest mills, given current conditions in Cuba.

In the 1984 harvest, large mills were significantly overrepresented on the lists of worst performers.[8] Table 1 groups Cuban sugar factories by daily cane input capacity. The modal size of the factories appearing with the best sugar recovery rates is 2,001 to 4,000 metric tons. No mills over 8,000 tons appear on the list of best performers. The most frequent size of the worst-performing entries on the lists is 4,001 to 6,000, with thirteen appearances of mills over 8,000 tons.

Table 2 makes similar comparisons by size for capacity utilization rates, with similar results. The model size classes of mills appearing on the lists is 2,001–4,000 for both the best and the worst, but among the

Large Cuban Sugar Factories in the 1984 "Zafra" : 147

TABLE 2
The Relationship between Size and Capacity Utilization in the Ten Best and the Ten Worst Sugar Mills in Each Category, 1984

Size (daily capacity, in metric tons)	Best	Worst
0– 2,000	28	5
2,001– 4,000	54	34
4,001– 6,000	12	24
6,001– 8,000	1	19
8,001–10,000	0	16
10,001–12,000	1	0
12,001–14,000	0	0
14,001–16,000	0	0

Sources: See table 1.
Note: Capacity utilization was measured by the frequency of the mills' appearances on lists of the ten best and ten worst mills in each category.

best performers there are only two appearances over 6,000 tons. In contrast, the list of worst-performing factories contains thirty-five entries of mills with capacities over 6,000 tons.

A similar pattern can be seen in the capacities of those mills that appeared most frequently on the capacity utilization and recovery rate lists. Tables 3 and 4 display the capacities of those mills that appear on the lists of best and worst three times or more. For capacity utilization, those mills that appeared most frequently on the "best" lists had a mean capacity of 2,380 metric tons per day. Those that logged the worst capacity utilization rates had an unweighted mean capacity of 5,917. The mean capacity of the factories with the best recovery rates was 2,409, while the mean of the worst mills was 6,465.

The pattern of poorer comparative performance of large factories can also be observed for each ten-day period. Table 5 shows the mean capacity of those mills rated best and worst in the categories of capacity utilization in each ten-day period. A "t-test" is applied to the difference of means to gauge the statistical significance of the differences. In most cases the differences were significant at a minimum of the 0.05 level. In all periods the mean capacities of the poorest performers were above those of the best performers.

For the sugar recovery rates of the best and worst factories, the results are even more striking. The differences in capacity between the best and the worst recovery rates is shown in table 6. In every ten-day period reported by MINAZ, mill capacities of the best factories were significantly less than the capacities of the worst mills.

It may be argued that the poorer performance of large factories

TABLE 3
The Ten Best and the Ten Worst Cuban Sugar Mills in Capacity Utilization, 1984

	Size (daily capacity, in metric tons)	Times on List[a]
Best		
Arquímedes Colina	2,588	8
Rafael Reyes	1,955	6
Rafael Freyre	4,255	6
Australia	2,645	6
Roberto Ramírez	3,450	5
Remberto Abad Alemán	1,725	5
Paquito Rosales	2,760	4
El Salvador	2,530	4
Manuel Isla	1,840	3
26 de Julio	920	3
Orlando González	3,680	3
Manuel Tames	1,610	3
Pablo Noriega	978	3
Worst		
Bolivia	9,660	8
Sierra de Cubitas	6,325	7
Los Reynaldos	5,175	5
Humberto Alvarez	1,955	4
Guatemala	9,315	3
Nicaragua	8,050	3
Urbano Noris	7,820	3
Orlando Nodarse	2,530	3
Julio A. Mella	5,750	3
Victoria de Yaguajay	2,588	3

Sources: See table 1.
a. Number of times mills appeared on lists for best and worst capacity utilization for a ten-day period.

might reflect a pattern that is generic to sugar mills all over the world, and that the Cuban results are not unusual. To deal with that possibility, a method of reporting similar to that used by MINAZ was applied to the Louisiana cane sugar sector for 1963 and 1964. Sugar recovery rates were ranked for all mills in Louisiana. The top five and the bottom five were then selected.[9] The use of five low and five high mills instead of the ten lowest and ten highest used for Cuba was made necessary by the smaller relative size of the Louisiana sugar industry (more than 150 mills for Cuba; less than 40 mills for Louisiana). For both 1963 and 1964, the mean capacities of the best performing factories exceeded the capacities of the poorest mills in Louisiana. Thus, the situation was the reverse of that which existed in Cuba in 1984.

Large Cuban Sugar Factories in the 1984 "Zafra" : 149

TABLE 4
The Ten Best and the Ten Worst Cuban Sugar Mills in Recovery Efficiency, 1984

	Size (daily capacity, in metric tons)	Times on List[a]
Best		
10 de Octubre	2,415	8
Salvador Rosales	2,070	7
Reynold García	2,645	6
Paquito Rosales	2,760	5
Carlos Caraballo	2,760	5
Luis Arcos Bergnes	2,013	4
Rafael Reyes	1,955	4
Pepito Tey	2,588	4
Manuel Sanguily	1,533	4
Hermanos Ameijeiras	2,933	3
Heriberto Duquesne	2,760	3
Efraín Alfonso	2,473	3
Worst		
Orlando Nodarse	2,530	7
Perú	5,175	7
Jesús Rabí	2,990	7
Frank País	4,025	7
Melanio Hernández	4,600	6
30 de Noviembre	6,800	6
Guatemala	9,315	6
Bolivia	9,660	6
Grito de Yara	6,800	5
Manuel M. Prieto	5,175	4
Brasil	14,041	4

Sources: See table 1.
a. Number of times mills appeared on lists for best and worst recovery efficiency for a ten-day period.

Why Bigger Is Not Better

The most striking reason for the inferior performance of the largest Cuban sugar mills involves a perverse application of the law of diminishing marginal returns. Usually, diminishing marginal returns is expressed as the tendency of additions to output to decrease as more variable input is added to otherwise fixed inputs. In most Cuban sugar mills over the last twenty-five years cane inputs have been maintained at prerevolutionary levels while in many mills the "fixed" inputs, including management expertise, have been allowed to slowly experience net depreciation. This twist on the law of diminishing marginal returns has had a profound impact on the Cuban sugar industry. The Cuban case reveals an asymmetry in the application of the concept of the

TABLE 5
Differences in Mean Capacities of the Best and the Worst Cuban Sugar Mills, in Capacity Utilization, 1984

Ten-Day Period	Best	Worst	SD 1	SD 2	t	Significance (%)
1-1 to 1-10	2,772	4,784	1,363	2,400	−2.18	95.0
1-11 to 1-20	2,800	5,693	709	3,028	−2.79	95.0
1-21 to 1-31	—	—	—	—	—	—
2-1 to 2-10	2,340	4,722	540	2,219	−2.80	95.0
2-11 to 2-20	—	—	—	—	—	—
2-21 to 2-29	2,386	4,738	850	2,323	−2.85	95.0
3-1 to 3-10	2,202	6,545	1,129	1,896	−5.90	99.9
3-11 to 3-20	2,703	5,586	1,103	2,719	−2.94	99.0
3-21 to 3-31	2,645	4,100	761	2,377	−1.74	90.0
4-1 to 4-10	4,002	5,808	2,678	2,528	−1.47	n.s.
4-11 to 4-20	3,400	6,056	1,451	4,010	−1.86	90.0
4-21 to 4-30	2,703	4,855	1,132	2,499	−2.35	95.0

Sources: See table 1.
Note: Dashes indicate data not available.

"long run." Since it takes two to five years to construct a new sugar mill or add significant capacity to an old mill, the long run is two to five years for an expansion of capacity. But many factory components are so old that unpredictable major failures are likely, and effective factory capacity could drop in five minutes. With such a drop in capacity, the principle of diminishing marginal returns can be restated as follows: "As less of a 'fixed' input is combined with the same amounts of a variable input, the marginal product of the last unit of a variable input will decrease." Thus, the concept of the long run is not reversi-

TABLE 6
Differences in Mean Capacities of the Best and the Worst Cuban Sugar Mills, in Recovery Rates, 1984

Ten-Day Period	Best	Worst	SD 1	SD 2	t	Significance (%)
1-11 to 1-21	2,559	3,969	589	1,772	−2.26	95
1-21 to 1-31	—	—	—	—	—	—
2-1 to 2-10	2,340	5,306	371	2,073	−4.20	99
2-11 to 2-20	—	—	—	—	—	—
2-21 to 2-29	2,702	6,431	932	3,592	−3.01	99
3-1 to 3-10	2,734	6,122	709	4,094	−2.55	95
3-11 to 3-20	2,743	5,267	1,098	2,114	−3.13	99
3-21 to 3-30	3,043	5,707	2,044	2,429	−2.51	95
4-1 to 4-10	2,433	6,570	469	3,781	−3.24	99
4-11 to 4-20	2,153	6,398	404	3,736	−3.20	99

Sources: See table 1.
Note: Dashes indicate data not available.

ble. There are no truly fixed inputs on the downside of production, even in the short run.

Creeping depreciation in the Cuban sugar industry has also caused a reversal of the "Horndal effect."[10] The "Horndal effect" recognizes that once a factory is set up, managers can expect increases in efficiency even in the absence of any new investment. In the Fagersta system of factories, the Horndal factory alone had no new investment, but nevertheless experienced increases in labor and capital productivity. Apparently, the Horndal factory, with fixed nominal capacity, had inert areas that were increasingly exploited with time and "learning." For the Horndal plant there was a strong learning curve that was responsible for increases in productivity of 2 percent per annum. In the Cuban sugar sector from 1960 to 1984, there has been a "forgetting" curve that has shown itself as declining productivity relative to nominal capacity for some mills.

The "forgetting" in Cuban sugar production has stemmed from several related causes. Most of Cuba's postrevolutionary sugar factories are of pre-1950 vintage. Thus, most of the Horndal-type increases in productivity would have been captured before the Cuban Revolution. Given the poor diplomatic relations between the United States and Cuba, Cuban managers have not had access to replacement equipment from all of the original suppliers (in the United States). Postrevolutionary emigration included a substantial number of skilled sugar technicians and managers, who had served as part of the industrial memory of the sugar sector. With their emigration, Cuban sugar production lost technical knowledge that had been accumulated over many decades. Periodic foreign exchange crises have sometimes led Cuba to defer imports of needed spare parts.[11] Finally, there is some evidence of poor record keeping in the sugar mills. Thus, factory managers have no idea how many operating hours individual components have logged. Without that knowledge, factory managers have no way of anticipating breakdowns except by hoarding scarce replacement parts. In the absence of good records on component vintages, such hoarding would not be expected to be done at optimal levels.[12]

The "forgetting" curve sets into motion forces that lead to inferior performance on the part of the largest sugar mills by increasing the incidence of unscheduled downtime. Because there are a limited number of days when it makes the most sense to process the cane, sugar plant managers carefully select the day grinding begins and the day it ends. Some Cuban economists have suggested that it would be reasonable for production to begin on the first day that average revenue exceeds average cost and to end on the last day that average revenue equals average cost.[13] Whatever the decision rule for beginning and ending a harvest, factory yields peak in the middle of the "zafra." Thus, unscheduled downtime within that optimal number of operating days will increase unit costs both by reducing the efficiency of the mill during its most productive days, as well as by extending the harvest into days when production would not ideally take place at all. In other words, the daily rated capacity of the factory stays the same, but the factories' ability to efficiently exploit the optimum number of days of production decreases with an increase in the frequency and duration of unscheduled downtime.[14]

Large mills are the most susceptible to breakdowns and hastily scheduled downtime. When a large mill is operating at its rated capacity, the harvesting and transportation systems must be operating at capacity to feed the mill. The larger the mill, the more cane there must be in transit at any point in time. A breakdown traps large quantities of cut cane in the "pipeline" of a large mill. During the 1970 harvest there were complaints that cane could not be cut fast enough when the large Urbano Noris mill was functioning well, yet when it broke down all harvesting had to be terminated. Once the cane pipeline is empty, it takes longer to refill for a large mill. Since cut cane rapidly loses usable sugar content, stockpiling is only feasible to a limited extent. As a result of the wasting nature of sugar cane, factory efficiency will suffer increasingly, the longer breakdowns last and the more unpredictable they are.

There is also a spatial dimension to the disadvantages of larger mills in an environment of unreliable factory performance. Mills tend to be placed at the center of the cane fields they serve. As a result, the larger mills tend to be farther apart. A small mill that suffers a breakdown can easily divert the cane in the pipeline to adjacent mills as long as adjacent mills can adjust their own production scheduling to accommodate the additional cane expeditiously. To divert the cane from a large mill to its neighbor will involve more kilometers traveled and, more importantly, involve significantly more transit time.[15] Thus, even when the diverted cane finally arrives at a mill, it already will have lost much of its sugar content and factory efficiency will suffer as a result.[16] In short, small mills are more easily substituted for each other than are the larger mills. After a breakdown the smaller mills should be able to more quickly resume capacity operations as the average distance for cane to travel will be less for the smaller mills.

Inferior performance by larger mills has apparently been recognized by MINAZ and the Cuban government.[17] The new mills that have been built since 1980 have had capacities of 6,800 metric tons, which is about 7,000 tons below the size of the largest existing Cuban sugar mills.[18] The new mill built by Cuba in Nicaragua has 6,800 metric tons of capacity, which indicates that the Cubans feel that they have found an optimal size. At present Cuba is well along on a major program to replicate mills in the 6,800-ton class.

Whether or not the new mills will be optimal given Cuba's current conditions remains to be seen. The new mills are not huge, but are nevertheless well above average. Since it can take up to five years *after* completion for a sugar factory to reach optimal production levels, it is not surprising that new mills have appeared more than once on the 1984 poor performance lists. In 1985 the Cubans ceased regular publication of the performance lists for individual mills in *Granma,* and it is possible that this was a result of misplaced embarrassment over the high frequency of new mills on the poor performance lists. If that is the reason for not publishing the lists in 1985, then the Cuban government is expecting too much from the new mills. On the other hand, if the 1980–1985 vintage mills are still among the worst performers in 1989, then the $1 billion-plus investment in new sugar mills will have been a failure.

Conversely, if by 1989 the new mills are appearing regularly on the best-performance lists, then it is likely that publication of the lists will resume. From that success, MINAZ would be expected to initiate another program in the 1990s to build more mills in the 6,800-ton class. Given the poor relative performance of the largest mills, as documented in this study, it is unlikely that MINAZ will soon initiate any mills as large as the largest existing Cuban mills.

NOTES

The author is grateful for the comments of three anonymous *Cuban Studies* referees.

1. Chamber of Commerce of the Republic of Cuba, *Cuba Economic News* 22 (1986), 2.

2. Marta Zaldívar Puig and Humberto Blanco Rosales, "El Cálculo de Capacidades en la Empresa Industrial," *Economía y Desarrollo* 84 (January–February 1985), 195. Puig and Rosales note that sugar equipment has a useful life of about twenty years, while 85 percent of Cuba's averages thirty-two years. For the 1970 harvest Fidel Castro stated: "Naturally, our sugar mills are now eighteen years older than they were in 1952." He went on to state that age of the mill was not a concern since most of the production problems came with the mills that had new equipment. The new equipment was intended to increase capacity at some of the mills, but as often happens with new machinery, effective capacity dropped at those mills in 1970 (Fidel Castro, "Speech on the Progress of the 1970 Sugar Harvest," *Granma* [English edition], May 31, 1970, p. 9).

3. For an excellent analysis of the problems of the 1970 "zafra," see Sergio Roca, *Cuban Economic Policy and Ideology: The Ten Million Ton Sugar Harvest* (Beverly Hills, Calif.: Sage Publications, 1976). Fidel Castro commented at length on the problems with the larger mills: "What very often happened was this: In Oriente Province . . . all those giant sugar mills had all the necessary manpower, trucks, cane loaders, everything, waiting for the mills to reach their scheduled level of grinding capacity. The result? Constant breakdowns and stops. Therefore, in order not to have an accumulation of cut cane lying on the ground, it was necessary time and again to paralyze 40,000 or 50,000 workers. . . . And this had a tremendous demoralizing effect. Since the cane couldn't be accumulated in advance, the day that a giant sugar mill was operating well it didn't have enough cane to grind" ("Speech on the Progress of the 1970 Sugar Harvest," *Granma* [English edition], May 31, 1970, p. 9.
4. Fidel Castro, ibid.
5. The problems extended beyond the largest mills. After the large harvest in 1970 many mills apparently had trouble operating at their rated capacities. "En 1971 la actividad del mantenimiento en la industria azucarera era muy deficiente, lo que producía una gran inestabilidad en la operación, fundamentalmente a causa de altos porcientos de tiempo perdido por roturas industriales . . . y por interrupciones operativas . . . y afectaba en gran medida el aprovechamiento de las capacidades instaladas" (Fernando Charadán López, *La Industria Azucarera en Cuba* [Editorial de Ciencias Sociales, Havana, 1982], p. 169). López identified two classes of problem mills: those on which maintenance had been neglected and those that had been altered or expanded between 1965 and 1970 (pp. 172-79).
6. Chamber of Commerce of the Republic of Cuba, *Cuba Economic News* 17, no. 123 (1981), 13. See *Cuba Economic News* 21, no. 145 (January-February 1985), 9, for a description of the Victoria de Julio sugar mill in Nicaragua. See ibid., no. 114 for news of the Batalla de las Guasimas mill, and no. 121 for Jesús Suárez Gayol. For another new mill, Batalla de Santa Clara, see *Granma*, February 20, 1985, p. 1. See also *Economic Report* (Banco Nacional de Cuba, printed in the United States by the Cuban American National Foundation, February 1985), Appendix 1, p. 2, and Appendix 2, p. 4.
7. Ministerio del Commercio Exterior, *Anuario Azucarero de Cuba* (Havana, 1962). *La Industria Azucarera en Cuba*, no. 5 (1982) offers a wealth of technical information about the Cuban sugar industry, but it does not replace the systematic annual plant data formerly published in *Anuario*. Detailed plant data for 1966 and 1967 were published in 1971 (*Manual Azucarero de Cuba* [Havana: Instituto Cubano del Libro, 1971], but regular publication of such data apparently did not continue in a widely available form.
8. In many cases capacities reported currently in *Granma*, in *Sugar y Azúcar Yearbook* (1975), and in *Anuario Azucarero de Cuba* (1962) are identical. While factories tend to track their historical capacities, actual capacity is not currently reported very accurately for many mills. As Puig and Rosales state it "Muchos equipos no se poseen los datos originales del fabricante; asimismo, existen otros que se han modernizado y a los cuales no se les ha recalculado exactamente la producción horaria" ("El Cálculo de Capacidades," p. 187).
9. *The Gilmore Hawaii-Louisiana-Florida Sugar Manual, 1965*, ed. Aldrich Bloomquist (Fargo, N.D., 1966).
10. William Lazonick and Thomas Brush, "The Horndal Effect in Early U.S. Manufacturing," *Explorations in Economic History* 22 (January 1985), 53-96. Erik Lundberg is credited with bringing the "Horndal effect" to economics.
11. Carmelo Mesa-Lago, *The Economy of Socialist Cuba* (Albuquerque: University of New Mexico Press, 1981), pp. 80-81.

12. José Ramón Fernández Hernández and Caridad de la Torre Estrada, "La Acumulación de Inventarios y su Efecto en la Gestión Financiera de las Empresas Azucareras," *Economía v Desarrollo* 76 (September–October 1983), 191–205. More attention is being paid to the general problem of inventory control especially in warehousing and shipping, but it remains to be seen whether or not MINAZ will be able to control the materials and spare parts inventories accumulated in some of the factories (*Granma,* August 16, 1986, p. 1).

13. Ramón Rodríguez Betancourt, "Determinación del Período Optimo de Zafra en el Central Rafael Reyes," *Economía y Desarrollo* 57 (May–June 1980), p. 190.

14. Manuel Pérez Viera and Antonio Morales Pita, "Análisis Económico del Tiempo Perdido Industrial en un Complejo Agro-Industrial Azucarero," *Cuba-Azúcar,* January–March 1984, pp. 11–16. For a listing of aggregate downtime by cause for the Cuban sugar industry from 1976 to 1982 see: *Anuario Estadístico de Cuba, 1982* (Havana: República de Cuba, Comité Estatal de Estadísticas), p. 158.

15. Fidel Castro, "Speech on the Progress of the Sugar Harvest," *Granma* [English edition], February 15, 1970, p. 2: "When the Guiteras (10,000-ton capacity) is grinding at the rate of 200,000 cwt. there are 400,000 cwt. of cane on the ground. When for any reason, the mill stops for 15 hours, 24 hours, the 400,000 cwt. of cane on the ground are delayed from 24 to 48 hours, and it is almost impossible to haul them elsewhere."

16. Usable sugar content is crucial to mill performance. See Puig and Rosales ("El Cálculo de Capacidades," p. 195): "La mala calidad de la materia prima hacía disminuir el porcentaje de aprovechamiento de la capacidad."

17. The larger mills are not alone in their problems. Over half of Cuba's sugar factories are not covering their unit costs of production. Negative net revenue in a socialist enterprise does not have the immediate dire consequences suffered by firms in a market economy. But the concern of Cuban officials that seventy-eight enterprises are not covering their costs indicates that much of the industry is performing with more than desired levels of inefficiency. Although only six raw sugar mills are mentioned by name (not enough for statistical significance), the three high-cost mills have average historical capacity of 5,180 tons, while the three low-cost raw sugar factories mentioned have average capacities of 4,274 tons ("Evidentes Desniveles en Costos por Tonelada Métrica de Azúcar," *Trabajadores,* Havana, December 9, 1985.

18. This may also reflect the general policy of "downsize scaling of enterprises" mentioned by Robert L. Bach in "Socialist Construction and Cuban Emigration: Explorations Into Mariel," *Cuban Studies* 15 (Summer 1985), 28.

DEBATE

ANDREW ZIMBALIST

Analyzing Cuban Planning: A Response to Roca

In his article "State Enterprises in Cuba Under the New System of Planning and Management (SDPE)" (*Cuban Studies* 16 [1986]), Sergio Roca describes my assessment of Cuba's SDPE as "untenable."[1] Roca writes: "After declaring that the Cubans themselves have been very satisfied with the progress of the SDPE, [Zimbalist concluded that after 1970] the Cubans have been successfully confronting the allocation, coordination, and motivation issues that affect all planned economies" (p. 178). In a footnote Roca then impugns my source of information, sarcastically referring to Humberto Pérez, former chief of Cuba's central planning board, as my "star" witness. I shall proceed by, first, making some semantic and interpretational observations regarding Roca's critique of my earlier article and, then, by evaluating aspects of the methodology and substance of Roca's article itself.

It is puzzling that Roca objects to my citing several speeches by the head of Cuban planning as evidence of the official judgment on the progress of the SDPE. He is the best source for such an appraisal. The fact that the Cubans have also made serious criticisms of the inadequacies of their system of planning and management hardly means that the system has not had a positive impact on the Cuban economy. It is also true that since I wrote my article the official Cuban line on the SDPE by December 1984 did become more critical. This new attitude and the consequent efforts at reform illustrate Cubans' characteristic impatience and public self-criticism. The nature of the reform discussion, at this stage at least (July 1986), is consistent with the periodic reevaluations, moratoria, and retrenchments of the post-1968 reform experience in Hungary. Had Roca a better understanding of the mechanisms of central planning and the experience with the same in the CMEA countries and China, he would not be so glib in assessing Cuba's System of Planning and Management (SPDE).

Further, by implication Roca suggests that my information base is rather limited and does not include experience or interviews at the micro level. In fact, I have been interviewing planning officials, enterprise directors, and union representatives in Cuba over the past four years. My investigation, however, is at mid-point. The one article I

159

wrote on the subject begins with a metaphor likening the analysis of Cuban planning to completing a puzzle with lost and altered pieces. Obviously, I meant to underscore the tentative nature of my discussion.

Lastly, I believe Roca has misinterpreted my phrase "successfully confronting" to mean "successfully overcoming." By "confronting" I mean that the Cubans have recognized the important problem areas and begun to deal with or confront them. A large share of Cuba's planning problems are systemic to centrally planned systems and hence can be diminished but not extinguished.[2] The extent to which Cuba has diminished these problems relative to other planned economies is an interesting but very complicated question, one too broad for the limited scope of this rebuttal.

Although he misinterpreted it, Roca was able to identify a consistent theme in my essay. The theme of his article is not easily discerned. At the outset Roca writes that his article is about "the process of economic institutionalization: its extent, depth and nature" (p. 156). Yet he never informs the reader what he means by the term "economic institutionalization." In his conclusion Roca asserts: "While it is clear that major beneficial changes have occurred since 1975 in the Cuban model of economic planning and management, it is also incontrovertible that the remaining shortcomings . . . make it very difficult to conclude that a fully effective economic system now operates on the island." This actually is a reasonable conclusion, one with which I completely agree. It is unfortunately rather vague as well—what country has a "fully effective economic system"?—and does not follow from the thrust of his argument.

Let us consider first Roca's methodology. Roca's primary data base is interviews with twenty-five Cuban exiles resident in the United States. The interviewees held a variety of administrative and managerial jobs in Cuba. They were not selected at random and do not, hence, constitute a representative sampling of the Cuban exile population. More important, they do not constitute a representative or even reasonable sampling of the population of Cuban administrative, managerial, and planning personnel. There is, rather, every reason to believe that these exiles represent a sample of negatively biased opinion about Cuba and its economy. The anecdotes and interpretations of these individuals are no more reliable a priori than would be a series of interviews about life in the United States with draft-dodgers resident in Canada prior to the Carter amnesty. Moreover, they have been promised anonymity by Roca and cannot be held accountable for their claims.

Roca does not explicitly defend his method; rather he seeks refuge behind the work of Joe Berliner on Soviet managers. The refuge is false. First, the Berliner study of 1957 was undertaken at a time when very little was known in the West about the actual operation of enterprises in centrally planned economies. Second, the relationship between Soviet publications and Berliner's interviews with exiles was much closer, more faithful and systematic than Roca's. Third, Berliner himself continues to harbor serious doubts about his methods in that study.

Perhaps Roca believes he does defend his method with the remark, "The fact that these informants have emigrated from Cuba does not entitle us to dismiss this group a priori as incapable of providing credible testimony about the conditions of their work experience" (p. 158). Roca's informants are certainly not "incapable" of credible testimony, although maybe they are "unlikely" to provide it in a balanced and reliable fashion. This, however, begs the issue which is that his sample is not suitable to form the backbone of a study on Cuba's planning and management system.

In his concluding remarks Roca also invokes the puzzle metaphor: "If this research project is likened to a puzzle, then the Cuban materials outline the edges and the interviews fill in the interior space" (p. 177). In my view, Roca is considerably off the mark in making this claim. Roca does indeed use Cuban materials; yet the contours of his argument are shaped not by a balanced use of these materials but the selective use of only self-critical and negative evaluations. Further, Roca adds at least one point from his interview data that appears nowhere in the Cuban materials; to wit, the alleged pervasive "personalismo" of Castro in distorting the rational allocation of resources. Other than this point, which is misconceived as I shall explain below, Roca adds no new critical analyses of Cuba's planning system. All Roca writes and much more analysis of the deficiencies in the functioning of Cuba's economic mechanisms is available in a plethora of Cuban materials.[3] These materials have the added advantage of providing a historical context and balance in their presentation. In short, Roca's method is not scientific; nor does he execute his dubious methodology in a rigorous and careful fashion.

Space constraints permit me to comment on just a few substantive aspects of Roca's argument. Roca repeats the hackneyed claim that the SDPE is "essentially identical to the current Soviet economic model." It is not clear whether Roca refers to the 1965 Soviet reform, to the 1979 reform, or to the Gorbachev reforms, or to parts of all three. In fact, the similarities in form between Soviet and Cuban planning are great, but the content of planning relationships and many details of form are significantly different. Unless one appreciates these differences, it is next to impossible to interpret the dynamics of the Cuban experience. It would, for instance, have been impossible to anticipate the current renewal of the debate on moral versus material incentives, or the new restrictions on private market activities, on the basis of the Soviet economic model.

Shortly after invoking the "essentially identical" argument, Roca writes that "profitability was to be established as the key criterion of performance in production centers" (p. 160). This is not true either in Cuba or in the Soviet Union. The key criterion of performance in theory and in practice in both economies is the meeting of the planned output target. This criterion is complemented by indicators of profit, profitability, cost reduction, growth rates, quality standards, and so on. It is not uncommon for Soviet enterprises to be given several dozen performance indicators, each of which will have an impact on the size of the unit's stimulation and bonus funds. But the key criterion is always the output target (variously expressed), as it has to be if the central plan is to hold together. Any analyst familiar with the logic of central planning or the shortage characteristic endemic to central planned economies knows that financial indicators such as profitability play a secondary role to physical indicators.

As one would expect, there is a problem throughout in interpreting the citations from Roca's interviews. Frequently Roca does not mention what year or what period the quoted passage is meant to describe and commonly the context or circumstances of the anecdote is not given. Occasionally it appears that the interviewee has his own story mixed up (perhaps this is due to a lack of context). For instance, Roca quotes informant 14 as saying: "I remember that in 1978 and 1979 JUCEPLAN strongly urged central organs and ministries to allow enterprises to generate preliminary figures. This was never done" (p. 161). For both one- and five-year plans preliminary output figures always originate with JUCEPLAN (the central planning board) and, then, are disaggregated by the ministries before being sent to the enterprises. At this point the enterprise evaluates the preliminary figures and can make counterproposals along with requests for more input. To have the process originate at the bottom may have a democratic ring but in practice would make coordination and balance in the plan an impossibility (except by monumental coincidence). It is difficult to believe JUCEPLAN ever intended to do this as reported. There are other means to give greater weight to enterprise proposals that are consistent with the logic of central planning.

The ambiguity regarding the time of the interviews and Roca's own faulty understanding of the SDPE at times lead to incorrect statements. Conceding some differences between Soviet and Cuban planning, Roca writes: "Among the differences, the absence in Cuba of material rewards . . . to motivate superior managerial performance stands out" (p. 167). Up to the implementation of the SDPE such rewards did not in fact exist in Cuba. With the SDPE, however, managers do share in the distribution of bonus funds roughly in proportion to their salary's share in the total wage bill of the enterprise. That is, contrary to Roca's statement, managers do receive material bonuses based on performance.

Roca cites statistics from 1980 to the effect that less than 10 percent of enterprises were able to form stimulation and bonus funds in that year. Since the funds were first introduced on an experimental basis in 1979 and the price reform was not carried out until 1981, it is hardly surprising that so few enterprises benefited from them in 1980. By 1985, 52.1 percent of enterprises had formed stimulation funds.

Roca's discussion of material incentives points to a serious problem with his entire presentation. He is analyzing the "institutionalization" of a post-1976 system on the basis of interviews with individuals who left Cuba in 1980 and whose direct experience with the SDPE often predates considerably the time of their departure from Cuba. It is important to note that before 1976 Cuba did not have a Five-Year Plan and the basic institutions of planning were not in place. Cubans in most instances had to build the organizations of the SDPE from scratch. Roca, then, without acknowledging it, is analyzing teething, not long-term behavioral problems in many instances.

Further, in discussing the application of material incentives Roca does not mention "normas" (individual work norms) and even seems to confuse them with "primas" (bonuses) which are applied primarily to groups. Whereas work norms have had a troubled existence in Cuba, they do apply to over half the work force and have been a major component of material incentives. In mentioning the Cuban insistence on balancing material with moral incentives, Roca naively asserts: "These ideological positions contradict standard Marxist theory" (p. 169).

Roca devotes seven pages of anecdotes to establish an excessive planning role for the party and Castro. The evidence here is again interpreted out of context and largely consists of dubious informant claims. For example, informant 269 is quoted as saying: "In the case of sugar output targets, Fidel and the Political Bureau made the basic decisions" (p. 172). At one, very general level, since the Political Bureau establishes the basic priorities of the plan, this is true. But we don't need eyewitness accounts to tell us what is in the Constitution and what is well known, nor is that what Roca intends. At a specific level, it is as difficult to accept this simple portrayal of reality as it is hard to believe that an economist at a light industry enterprise (the job of informant 269) would have access to this information, even if it were true.

Other anecdotes tell of Castro stepping in to solve particular bottlenecks and allocational problems. These stories are quite believable, but they hardly establish regular or pervasive interference or systematic control over the plan by Castro. Nor do they establish that the pattern of Castro-inspired miniplans, common to the 1960s when there was no effective formal planning apparatus, has been recreated. If Castro's travels about Cuba confront him with the inefficiencies of the government bureaucracy, it is natural for him to investigate the source of problems and at times to attempt their resolution. It would probably be difficult to find a chief executive in any country who does not do the same from time to time.

Moreover, given the systematic shortages and torpidity of centrally planned economies, it is often necessary for the center to intervene to provide for priority sectors or to cut through the thick bureaucratic morass. Such sporadic intervention, however, is common in centrally planned economies. To be sure, energetic and charismatic leaders such as Castro and Gorbachev are likely to be more involved and more visible than others. It is even plausible to contend that Castro's interventions are still too frequent and occasionally damaging. To assert, however, as Roca does (p. 170) that "Fidel exercised a pervasive and detrimental influence at all levels of economic organization and over all functions of economic administration" on the basis of testimony from his informants is utterly irresponsible.

The establishment of the Grupo Central in December 1984 is interpreted by Roca as a machiavellian plot to assert control over the plan by Castro. But why plot if you already have control as Roca's interviewees claim of Castro before 1980? I believe that the Grupo Central has a much more complicated explanation and role than Roca suggests, but here again space constraints preclude elaboration.

NOTES

1. Cf. Andrew Zimbalist, "Cuban Economic Planning: Organization and Performance," in *Cuba: Twenty-Five Years of Revolution, 1959–1984*, ed. Sandor Halebsky and John Kirk (New York: Praeger, 1985).

2. For a discussion of these planning problems, see Andrew Zimbalist and Deborah

Milenkovitch, "The Economics of Socialism," in *The New Palgrave: A Dictionary of Economic Thought and Doctrine,* ed. John Eatwell et al. (London: Macmillan, 1987); Andrew Zimbalist and H. Sherman, *Comparing Economic Systems: A Political-Economic Approach* (New York: Academic Press, 1984), chs. 7–11, 14, 17.

3. In addition to the materials cited by Roca, these documents are useful: "Humberto Pérez, *Intervención: Clausura de la IV Plenaria Nacional de Chequeo de la Implantación del SDPE* (Havana: JUCEPLAN, May 1985); *Dictámenes Aprobados en la IV Plenaria del Chequeo de la Implantación del SDPE* (Havana: JUCEPLAN, May 1985); Fidel Castro, "Main Report to the Third Party Congress," *Granma Weekly Review,* February 16, 1986; Arturo Guzmán, "Intervención: Clausura del II Evento Científico de la ANEC del Area de Ciencias Económicas de la U.H.," *Economía y Desarrollo* 80 (May–June 1984); José Machado, *Intervención: Clausura del Activo Nacional del Partido acerca de la Rentabilidad de Empresas,* Havana, January 1984. Also see the extensive discussions in *Granma,* July 1–15, 1986, on economic deficiencies, reporting on the provincial Revisiones de Empresas.

SERGIO G. ROCA

Planners in Wonderland: A Reply to Zimbalist

In his "Response," Zimbalist is again off to flights of fancy regarding the interpretation of Cuban economic reality, but only almost off, once more, to unprofessional modes of discourse. Let us be thankful for small, albeit fleeting, miracles. I plead no contest to sarcasm, twice. But to be the recipient of a little bit of sarcasm is much less objectionable than to be the purveyor of a lot of abusive language. My comments are organized under three headings, each one rebutting a specific aspect of the critical observations made by Zimbalist.

Semantic Games: Misreadings and Non-Readings

Among Zimbalist's well-honed and often used tactics in his abrasive style of academic debate are text manipulation, word games, selective omissions, and surprise references. Followers of Cuban scholarship need not to be reminded of the tergiversations attempted by Brundenius and Zimbalist in their controversy with Mesa-Lago and Pérez-López. I will give some examples.

As evidence of text manipulation, take the matter of Zimbalist's complaint about my "impugning" his use of Humberto Pérez as reference on the workings of the SDPE. It would be foolish to deny that Pérez is an important source of information and, in fact, in my writings I have cited his assessments extensively. However, it is clear in my passage that it was not the witness himself who was under question but the accuracy of his quoted testimony on the "progress" of the SDPE implementation. Who was closer to the mark, Zimbalist or I, may be settled in short order. In his article, Zimbalist cites a 1983 interview in which Pérez stated, "The system has already produced advantageous results. . . . The growth in 1981 and 1982 is largely a result of our success in achieving . . . economic consciousness and the workings of our economic management mechanisms."[1] But in February 1986, Castro concluded: "Following the initial thrust in implementing the SDPE there has been no consistent follow-through to improve it. The initiative was lost and the creativity needed to adapt this system to our own conditions—a system largely taken from the experience of other countries—never materialized."[2]

In playing word games to defend his own obfuscation, Zimbalist tries to differentiate between "successfully confronting" and "successfully overcoming." Where is the evidence that the Cubans have been successful even at the level of confrontation? How many times must an issue (centralization, incentives) be dealt with before it is overcome? If a problem is *successfully* confronted, should not that be the end of it? Indeed, in my piece Castro is quoted as follows: "Is it possible or not for us to accept the challenge of finding definitive, strategic solutions to the problems of our economy and our development?"[3]

Zimbalist's use of the ploy of selective omission is easily demonstrated. He alleges that the reader is never informed what is meant by "economic institutionalization." In fact, my discussion (pp. 157–58) not only provides a definition of the specific aspects pertaining to the economic sector, but also relates the SDPE to the overall institutionalization process, a term well understood by most scholars, including Zimbalist.[4] He also asserts that "without acknowledging it" my article "is analyzing teething . . . problems in many instances." However, I wrote that "the full introduction of the SDPE was to proceed over a ten-year period from 1976" and warned that "the years covered in this study . . . correspond to the formative period of the SDPE" (pp. 158–59).

Finally, in order to undermine my arguments, Zimbalist pulls out, as if from a magician's hat, several surprise references and sources which (1) were not critical factors in his original piece (his interviews with Cuban economic officials were cited briefly only twice), (2) are not available to most U.S. researchers (I have requested from both the Cubans and Zimbalist, without success, the two documents related to the IV Plenaria Nacional of the SDPE cited in his third note), and (3) postdate the final revision of my article completed in summer 1985. (The first session of the Third Party Congress was held in February 1986.)

Methodological Issues

Under this rubric, Zimbalist's main charge is that the interviewees "were not selected at random and do not, hence, constitute a representative sampling of the Cuban exile population." As I explained in my article, the respondents were not randomly selected because they could not be identified as a cluster group (managerial, professional, and technical personnel) within the universe of the general exile population. As stated, what I obtained was a judgment sample, that is, one in which the quality of the results can be evaluated only as a judgment of someone who has expert knowledge of the situation. (Most likely, this sampling technique was also used by Zimbalist in his Cuban interviews.)

On the issue of the suitability of my sample to the topic being addressed, it is clear that a similar predicament must have been faced by Zimbalist in his Cuban conversations. His interlocutors, including JUCEPLAN officials and enterprise directors, most likely offered positively biased opinions about the Cuban economy. Under such conditions, the testimony of Zimbalist's respondents may be questioned on the same criteria upon which his challenge is based: reliability, credibility, and balance. Let us not apply a double standard: if Zimbalist's interview data are admissible, so are mine.

Furthermore, contrary to Zimbalist's continued insistence, there is a close, faithful, and systematic relationship between the content of my interview materials and the information conveyed by Cuban officials and reports. The interested reader may corroborate the existence of such tight correlations by examining the statements of Humberto Pérez and the SDPE Commission (pp. 161–62) dealing with the lack of enterprise autonomy, and the official pronouncements (p. 164) on the shortcomings in the use of "cálculo económico." (As an aside, my book on the management of Cuban state enterprises, currently in preparation, will contain many more references of official self-criticisms linked to interviews and commentaries.)

Finally, in order to obtain current information and official opinion for inclusion in the book, I have been trying without success—as noted in my article—to arrange a research visit to the island since the fall of 1984. In contrast, Zimbalist is a regular visitor to Havana. It is to be hoped that the recent LASA resolution calling upon the Cuban government to ease the restrictions against travel by Cuban-American scholars will be heeded.

Substantive Points

In this section I will deal briefly with several minor issues raised by Zimbalist before answering his two major criticisms. Zimbalist's argument concerning the testimony of informant 14 (p. 159) about the process of generating preliminary output figures misses the point since the key section of the interview is at the bottom where it is maintained that enterprises handled output figures only when received from above as directive targets. This problem is part of what the SDPE reports cited in my article describe as "excessive tutelage or paternalism" (p. 161). In discussing "normas" and "primas," it is Zimbalist who shows himself to be thoroughly confused. "Normas" are the individual work quotas upon which the (potential) payment of "primas" to the meritorious worker is based. See note 21 to my article for a full explanation of the component parts of a worker's total money income.

Finally, it is totally incorrect for Zimbalist to link *his* point about "the Cuban insistence on balancing material with moral incentives" with my statement on the contradiction of standard Marxist theory. On the contrary, my extensive discussion on this issue (p. 167) starts by calling attention to "the fragility of the leadership's political commitment to material incentives" and goes on to indicate the extent to which the Cubans in the early 1980s advocated the primacy of moral incentives and warned of the pernicious consequences that would stem from the excessive use of markets and material rewards. It was the Cuban *tilt* toward moral incentives that elicited my conclusions concerning the contravention of Marxist theory and Soviet policy. (By 1986 the tilting approached listing proportions: free farmers' markets and productivity bonuses were eliminated, voluntary work and "conciencia" were reinstated. How is that for the allegedly poor predictive power of my model?)

One major criticism hurled by Zimbalist revolves around the origin and nature of the Cuban economic model and its comparability to other socialist models, especially in relation to the timing of and capacity for economic reform. Zimbalist charges that my assertion that the SDPE is "essentially identical to the current Soviet economic model" is a "hackneyed claim" and denies that profitability was to be held as "the" key criterion of performance. (I concede that "the" should have been "a".) However, it is interesting to note that in his article, Zimbalist used language quite similar to mine in referring to the SDPE model.[5]

More important, in portraying my understanding and analysis of the Cuban economic model as being fatally constrained by my supposed perception of its fidelity to the Soviet blueprint, Zimbalist is just setting up a straw man. While we may differ with regard to the closeness of the fit at the theoretical level, there is no disagreement on the point that Cuban and Soviet economic practices are not identical.[6] In fact, one of my basic arguments in the study is that Cuban planning and management practices are exceptional due in large part to the presence of Fidel. (More below on Zimbalist's nontreatment of Fidel.) It is in accounting for the practical differences—in terms of type, extent and source—that Zimbalist and I will again surely clash.

Zimbalist commits a serious error of judgment when he discusses the Cuban process of economic reform within the context of similar developments in CMEA countries, especially Hungary. Moreover, the reference to China should be to Mao's China, since the key variable linking the two cases is the powerful presence of the revolutionary leader. The main point in my article—buttressed by subsequent events and policies—was that Cuba failed to implement the SDPE from 1976 to 1985, except in superficial fashion. At present, the argument can be extended to state that since 1985 Cubans have started to retrench without having advanced much in the previous ten years. In fact, if Cuban economic policy were to develop along the path outlined by Fidel's "revolutionary counteroffensive" of mid-1986, I would predict that Cuba will be successfully *contributing* to the allocation, coordination, and motivation problems associated with mobilization or radical economic models, in sharp contrast to the pragmatic reform paths chosen by most other centrally planned economies.

The second major issue argued by Zimbalist concerns the role of Fidel in economic affairs. Among several points, Zimbalist charges that the evidence is "interpreted out of context," that it "largely consists of dubious informant claims," that it amounts to "seven pages of anecdotes," and that the issue itself "appears nowhere in the Cuban materials." In rebuttal, I would underscore the following texts from my article:

(1) of the seven full pages devoted to this topic (pp. 168–75), one-half contain Castro's own references and my analysis of his official duties/unofficial functions; (2) the interpretation of interview responses was fully contextual, including insightful historical references ranging back to the early 1960s and forward to the spring of 1985; and (3) it was pointed out that "it is a telling point that Cuban press commentaries on the impact of the economic role of the party and Fidel are virtually nonexistent" (p. 173). (How naive to think that Fidel's intromissions would be criticized in the Cuban press, itself recently chastised by him for being uncritical.)

Moreover, Zimbalist's position on the role of Castro in economic affairs is essentially incongruent since he strongly posits a quasi–sui generis Cuban economic model or practice, yet minimizes its key idiosyncratic component. Fidel's interventions are not casual, limited, and antibureaucratic, but systematic, pervasive, and suprabureaucratic. In other words, such behavior constitutes his modus operandi. Tad Szulc's recent biography of Fidel provides ample evidence of that reality. Fidel's intromissions are attributable to personal style, well-established work habits, revolutionary stature, and organizational structure. The GEC of 1984 may be the current version of Fidel's "shadow government" of 1959–1961, created for the similar purpose of capturing and controlling the totality of economic power.

In sum, my conclusions regarding the failure to implement the SDPE, the shallowness of the process of economic institutionalization, and the economic role of Castro remain basically untouched by Zimbalist's charges. If Zimbalist still wants to argue that the Cuban model is almost unique, that material and moral incentives are balanced, that the Cubans will continue to confront problems, that Castro's economic power is circumscribed and that his interventions are helpful rather than destabilizing—then it would appear that Zimbalist insists on believing in fairy tales.

NOTES

1. Andrew Zimbalist, "Cuban Economic Planning: Organization and Performance," in *Cuba: Twenty-Five Years of Revolution, 1959–1984,* ed. Sandor Halebsky and John M. Kirk (New York: Praeger, 1985), p. 224.
2. Fidel Castro, "Main Report to the Third Congress of the Communist Party of Cuba," Havana, February 1986, p. 35.
3. Sergio G. Roca, "State Enterprises in Cuba Under the New System of Planning and Management (SDPE)," *Cuban Studies* 16 (1986), 164.
4. Zimbalist, "Cuban Economic Planning," pp. 222–23: "[The SDPE and the first FYP of 1976–1980] each represents the evolving maturity and institutionalization of Cuba's economic organizations."
5. Ibid., p. 223: "The SDPE in many respects is modeled after the 1965 Soviet reforms; . . . it attempts . . . [among other goals] to introduce a profitability criterion with its attendant incentives."
6. See my article, "Management of State Enterprises: A Comparison of the Soviet Union and Cuba," *Journal of Comparative Economics,* forthcoming.

REVIEWS

RECENT WORK IN CUBAN STUDIES

CONTRIBUTORS

HAROLD D. SIMS, Editor

Reviews

DOCUMENTS

Michael Taber, ed. *Fidel Castro Speeches 1984–85: War and Crisis in the Americas*. New York: Pathfinder Press, 1985. 249 pp. $30.00, cloth; $7.95, paper.

This edited volume of Fidel Castro's speeches, which has recently been added to Pathfinder Press's growing list of such collections in English, is significant because of the gravity and the international scope of the topics addressed. The Cuban leader's views are here presented on issues that pertain to the broad realm of U.S. strategic and economic interests in Latin America as well as its moral responsibilities to that crisis-ridden region.

Among the subjects discussed in this work are the invasion of Grenada, described by Castro as a "Pyrrhic" victory for Reagan (p. 11); the maintenance of a strong Cuban defense in the light of U.S. actions in Grenada; and the short-lived U.S.-Cuba accord on migratory relations. Appended to the volume is Castro's angry response to the U.S. decision to begin "subversive broadcasts" (p. 237) on Radio José Martí which terminated the accord indefinitely. Also included is Castro's speech at the dedication of a sugar mill in Nicaragua, in which he assumes the position of a generous statesman by canceling the debt owed by Nicaragua to Cuba for its aid in that enterprise and at the same time calls on nations far richer than Cuba to be as magnanimous with regard to Latin America's debt. In another interesting speech, given at the close of the National Assembly of People's Power in December 1984, Castro challenges the Cuban people to undertake an "economic battle" (p. 61) that will involve some sacrifices on their part. It is emphasized here that Cuba "must strictly comply with the sacred principle of meeting [its] commitments to the socialist countries" (p. 63), because "the Soviet Union [has] never failed in its cooperation" (p. 75). One wonders what behind-the-scenes pressures these statements reflect.

Many of the speeches are actually lengthy interviews with foreign journalists, including one with Robert MacNeil for the "MacNeil/

Lehrer News Hour" and the interview for the Mexican newspaper *Excelsior,* in which Castro calls for the cancelation of Latin America's entire foreign debt, a plea that has excited many Latin Americans and disturbed their northern neighbors. In this interview, armed with facts and figures, Castro proceeds step by step to demonstrate why Latin America's debt is unpayable. He points out the irony that twenty-four years ago the Alliance for Progress called for $20 billion to be pumped *into* the region as a remedy for its problems; but "now, the economically underdeveloped countries of this hemisphere, with twice the population and triple the social problems will be giving the industrialized countries $40 billion a year as interest on their debts" (p. 209). This is an impossible burden, argues Castro, and thus the industrialized creditor nations should make themselves responsible for the debts to their own banks, using funds siphoned from their military expenditures, "and military spending would still be fabulously high and cause for concern" (p. 228). Furthermore, to press their demands, Latin American countries must unite in a debtors' club. South America cannot tolerate any more hardship. There will not be a swing to the right to enforce further belt-tightening measures; instead, the region "is going to explode. I am deeply convinced of this. The old formulas for avoiding those outbreaks have already been exhausted. The present crisis is more serious, deeper, and more generalized than ever before. The military are withdrawing from their positions in state administration; they cannot manage the countries; and they have left the civilian governments a fearsome legacy" (p. 222).

Lest Washington think he is advocating revolution, Castro assures the interviewer he is not. Elsewhere, the Cuban leader identifies "the surefire agent of the revolution in this hemisphere, . . . the International Monetary Fund" (p. 93). If Fidel is a bit simplistic here, he also points out the absurdity of Washington's view that revolution can be exported: "Who can export the present international economic crisis that is creating so many social problems and so much instability? . . . Who can export the growing underdevelopment and misery in Latin America and the hunger, the real fact that tens of millions of people are hungry?" (p. 93).

In this volume, one can find some of Castro's predictable evasions on the topics of political prisoners, elections, human rights, and Cuba's dependency on the Soviet Union, as well as abundant praise for the Cuban Revolution: it has helped more poor, quips Castro, than "all the saints put together" for which "we might be canonized one day"

(p. 141). And the reader may be provoked by Castro's observations as a self-appointed prophet of doom. On the other hand, one cannot dismiss lightly the Cuban leader's haunting vision of future social upheaval in the hemisphere we all share.

Donna W. Brett
University of Pittsburgh

ECONOMICS

República de Cuba, Comité Estatal de Estadísticas. *Cuba en Cifras 1985.* **Havana: CEE, n.d. 126 pp.** *Boletín Estadístico Mensual de Cuba,* **1985, nos. 7–12 (July–December); 1986, no. 1 (January).**

The 1985 edition of *Cuba en Cifras* includes data for the year 1985 on most topics: population; global indicators (GSP in current prices); industry (output by branches and of selected products, fishing, electric consumption); construction (by economic sector and province, housing); investment (total, by economic sector, type of investment, and province); agriculture (output by branches, output of selected products, cultives, irrigation); transportation and communications (output by branches, passengers, freight, merchant marine); state procurement ("acopio") of agricultural products; education (general indicators of three educational levels, day-care centers); culture and art (artistic activities, libraries, zoos, publications, newspapers, films); public health (hospitals, beds, outpatient consultation, immunization, ratios of contagious diseases); lodging and tourism; and sports. However, data for 1985 are missing for: labor and wages, sugar industry (latest information provided is for the 1983–1984 harvest), domestic trade, foreign trade, and communal and personal services.

The gaps noted above for 1985 (except for communal and personal services) are not filled by the *Boletín Estadístico Mensual* issues (for the second half of 1985 and first month of 1986) since this publication does not regularly publish data on those topics. The *Boletín,* however, occasionally provides more detailed information (especially broken down by quarters or months) than *Cuba en Cifras* for the following topics: population, industry, construction and investment, agriculture, transportation and communications, work security, education, culture and art, communal and personal services, tourism and entertainment, public health, and sports. Data for 1986 are given for most of these items in the January issue of the *Boletín*.

I waited until the end of 1986 hoping to receive the *Anuario Estadístico de Cuba 1985*, but regrettably it did not arrive in time to be included in this volume. It will be reviewed in the next volume of *Cuban Studies*.

Carmelo Mesa-Lago
University of Pittsburgh

Charles Edquist. *Capitalism, Socialism, and Technology: A Comparative Study of Cuba and Jamaica.* **London: Zed Books, 1985. 182 pp.**

Many miles and different climates separate Sweden and the Caribbean, but Charles Edquist has seen fit to overcome those and other more formidable obstacles in producing a solid piece of research and writing in this study of socioeconomic aspects of technical change in sugarcane harvesting in Cuba and Jamaica. By socioeconomic aspects I mean both the determinants and the consequences of the choice of technique, which are then compared in the context of two different economic systems between the late 1950s and the early 1980s. Among the questions posed by the author are: "Which are the most important determinants and obstacles to technical change under capitalism and socialism? What effect did the transition to socialism in Cuba have on technical change? Which social and economic factors influenced the performance of various technologies? What is the relation between technical change and unemployment?" (p. 3).

The book is divided into three parts. First, the theoretical framework combines structural and actor-oriented approaches. One key concept is that of "social carriers of techniques," defined as "a social entity which chooses and implements a technique; it 'carries' it into the society" (pp. 5–6). The successful carrier, whether private company, agricultural cooperative, or government agency, must exercise its choice within the terms of six necessary and sufficient conditions: interest, power, organization, information, access, and knowledge. Regrettably, no reference is made in this section to the vast literature on the economics of technological change (such as works by Schumpeter, Landes, Berliner, and Rosenberg).

The second part discusses the empirical evidence for Cuba and Jamaica, both the structural conditions of their sugar sectors and the behavior of government agencies, mill owners, cane farmers, and labor unions. An excellent historical section describes Cuba's prerevolutionary situation and the development and introduction of cane-harvesting mechanization in the 1960s and 1970s. I lack the expertise to judge the quality of Edquist's handling of the Jamaican experience.

The heart of the study is the third part (about 100 pages), which analyzes the empirical record and compares causes and consequences in the two countries. Edquist is to be commended for the great care and diligence with which he amassed, organized, and evaluated the data, as well as for his fidelity in working within the confines of his methodology. For instance, his discussion of the relative performance of different Cuban harvester models (pp. 109–20) is both ingenious and rigorous. Among others, it is an important finding that the increasing proportion of KTP-1 harvesters in Cuba's total stock accounts for most of the change in average performance per machine in the 1970s. However, I have serious reservations concerning several critical interpretations and conclusions.

First, there are some probable inconsistencies in the text, such as Edquist's assessments of the Cuban level of development and of the extent of technical expertise. While he asserts that "Jamaica is—in contrast to Cuba—a typical case of a developing country which has not developed" (p. 55), later he maintains that "Cuba was still a developing country in the late 1970s" (p. 82). With regard to mechanization attempts after 1970, he argues that "earlier efforts had created a very important pool of knowledge and experience. For example, thousands of workers had been educated to operate, maintain and repair *harvesting* machines" (p. 45, emphasis added). But later Edquist admits that the low operational rate of *loading* machines "as late as in the 1970 zafra . . . indicates that problems regarding knowledge about how to operate, maintain and repair the machines persisted through the whole of the 1960s" (p. 85). If Cuban workers were indeed capable of handling harvesters, why such ineptitude with the simpler loading machines?

Second, in terms of Edquist's "actor-oriented approach," I find it incongruent that the leading man on the Cuban stage is mentioned, in passing, only twice in the text. Castro was an overwhelming force in every aspect of the revolutionary process, especially in economic decision making through the early 1970s. He determined the ten-million-ton sugar target as well as many specific details of the 1965–1970 sugar plan. His role in the determination and implementation of economic policies (such as moral incentives, agricultural organization) was not inconsequential. In this regard I can offer a relevant piece of information derived from my current research project.

180 : *Reviews*

Edquist concludes, properly so, that "the massive implementation of the [Soviet-built] combine harvesters KCT-1 and KT-1 in 1965–1968 was a complete failure" (p. 125), adding later that the magnitude of the mistake could have been reduced if "the models implemented had been tested more thoroughly before the decision was made to introduce them on a large scale" (p. 143). But he never raises the question of who or what agency made the premature decision to import hundreds of harvesters. According to the testimony of one of my informants, a Cuban agricultural engineer who collaborated with Henderson and Suárez Gayol in the 1960s and who was present at the test trials, it was Castro's own decision, against the counsel of both Cuban and Soviet technicians, to order the manufacture and delivery of 500 units of the prototype models. In sum, Castro should have been treated as an independent and decisive actor in the Cuban process of the choice of technique.

Third, Edquist's contentions linking cane-harvest mechanization and structural economic change in Cuba are not really supported by any evidence in his study (or elsewhere). The argument that "mechanization was closely related to a structural transformation of the economy, e.g., through making possible comprehensive reallocations of labor and through supporting the development of an indigenous capital goods industry" (p.144) is, I think, a highly debatable proposition. There has been a structural shift away from agricultural employment, but this has not been accompanied by a proportional change in output composition or in export-commodity concentration. Sugar is still king. There is no argument that cane mechanization has improved sectoral efficiency, but very few linkage effects can be detected across the Cuban economy. If "cane mechanization played the role of a 'big push' in Cuba" (p. 144), why has the record of socialist economic growth been so puny and uneven? If Cuba's sugar sector functioned in fact as a "leading sector," it must have just taken the island's economy around in circles.

Finally, Edquist's main conclusion that the different outcomes in Cuba and Jamaica regarding cane harvesting stem from systemic factors strikes me as overly simplistic. He writes: "In summary, *all* actors in Cuba and *none* in Jamaica had an interest in the mechanization of cutting in the 1970s. . . . This striking difference must be attributed to the differences in the socioeconomic system and the employment situation in the two countries, i.e., to structural conditions" (p. 100, emphasis in original). This assertion, and the surrounding discussion on pages 96–103, I find too general and vague.

It is not only the socialist model but primarily the Soviet Union that, in specific ways and precise terms such as protected sugar markets and massive economic assistance, defines Cuba's structural conditions. It is the Soviet subsidy of about 25 percent of Cuba's civilian economy that in large measure made possible the choice of cane-harvesting mechanization and eased the burden of work force adjustments (though Cuba still faces substantial underemployment). To make the connection with Jamaica, I would argue that the advantageous economic and financial conditions obtained by socialist Cuba are unique and nonreplicable. Is the USSR prepared to finance emerging Third-World allies along the Cuban pattern? Cuba is not the model but rather the exception. As Castro recently stated: "The USSR constitutes the fundamental pillar of our present and our future, of our development. . . . It is a really privileged situation. Our relations with the socialist camp, our terms of trade with the socialist camp . . . is what really has made possible this miracle of ours" (*Granma*, Jan. 4, 1985, p.4).

Aside from the above reservations and disagreements, which reflect methodological and interpretive cleavages, I would commend this book as provocative, exhaustively researched, clearly organized, and well written.

Sergio G. Roca
Adelphi University

Carmelo Mesa-Lago and Jorge Pérez-López. *A Study of Cuba's Material Product System, Its Conversion to the System of National Accounts, and Estimation of Gross Domestic Product Per Capita and Growth Rates.* **World Bank Staff Working Papers, no. 770. Washington, D.C.: World Bank, 1985. 104 pp.**

Two factors made the task of reviewing this work difficult. I will explain my handling of them.

First, as most readers of this publication probably know, this study has been involved in an extensive and bitter controversy in a specialized economic journal. (See the debate in *Comparative Economic Studies* 27, nos. 1, 3, 4 [1985], which also entails two other works written separately by the authors.) Within the boundaries of scholarly dispute, Claes Brundenius and Andrew Zimbalist, the other protagonists in the debate, undertook a highly critical evaluation of the World Bank study along methodological and theoretical lines. However, from the overall tone of their challenge and from specific commentaries in the text, one could easily infer that the professional demeanor and personal integrity of the authors were being questioned. I have no reservations whatsoever in this regard. I have the highest opinion of Carmelo Mesa-Lago and Jorge Pérez-López as both scholars and individuals, a view sustained through fifteen years of professional dealings and personal contacts. They have shown themselves to be honest scholars, meticulous with facts, and balanced in interpretation. In sum, my review addresses the substantive merits of their study, with their integrity as a given.

Second, the study is not bedside reading material, except for sufferers of acute insomnia. It is a dense, technical volume (about one-fourth of which is methodological notes grouped in four technical appendices, with over thirty statistical tables) analyzing and evaluating several methods for estimating economic data about socialist Cuba. If professional economists writing for a specialized outlet experienced difficulties in making themselves understood, what could be gained from covering the same ground for a multidisciplinary audience? Thus I refrain from concentrating on narrow technical issues and instead focus on broader questions related to the study's implications for our understanding of the economy of socialist Cuba.

In this volume, part of a World Bank research project dealing with national income data of centrally planned economies, the authors set out "to gather and review all available official Cuban national product statistics and independent estimates both on the Material Product System (MPS) and the System of National Accounts (SNA) with respect to reliability, consistency and reasonableness" (p. ix). In this they succeed admirably. Indeed, Mesa-Lago and Pérez-López have given us an exhaustive review of all accessible data on Cuban output, a painstaking explanation of terms and techniques, and a careful assessment of strengths and shortcomings.

If for no other reason than its comprehensive presentation of the many disparate data and estimates of Cuban national output, this study would be a valuable addition to the literature. For instance, we are given complete data regarding Cuba's gross social product, gross material product, and net material product (generated by several official Cuban agencies: JUCEPLAN, Comité Estatal de Estadísticas, Banco Nacional de Cuba). In addition, the authors present and evaluate gross domestic product estimates (based on SNA methodology) made by a motley group of organizations, including the CIA, the Arms Control and Disarmament Agency, the World Bank, and CMEA. Also important are the results of Cuba's MPS/SNA conversion exercise done for the year 1974.

In a more technical vein and more controversially, the authors develop their own estimates of Cuban gross domestic product by two alternative methods: "scaling up" from gross or net material product and "physical indicators." However, because of insurmountable methodological and data problems, they find it either impossible (p. 35) or unwise (p. 48) to apply such approaches to the Cuban case.

The discussion of the Cuban price system and inflation in section 3 is particularly illuminating. I learned a great deal from it. Similarly, the treatment of exchange rates and peso convertibility addresses a key issue usually slighted in most works. Tables 27–30 (pp. 68–73), which summarize all Cuban national accounts data and estimates for 1959–1980 and in four benchmark years from 1965 to 1980, constitute the heart of the study and represent a remarkable achievement.

After carefully presenting the data and assessing their reliability, the authors conclude (pp. 66–67) that (1) Cuban data on the MPS "are scanty, highly aggregated, frequently revised and affected by numerous methodological changes"; (2) Cuban data on GSP are available for 1962–1981 "but are of limited use because of methodological changes"; and (3) the several MPS/SNA conversions, as well as the "scaling-up" and physical indicators approaches, suffer from differences in concept, method, prices, and exchange rates that are "very significant," so that "none of the available growth rate estimates are reliable" (p. 70). The implications of these results for our future study of the Cuban economy and its performance are quite clear: we need more rigor in our estimates, more skepticism in our assessments, and more uncertainty in our conclusions.

Mesa-Lago and Pérez-López were faced with a wide range of difficult theoretical, data and methodological issues, some of them irresolvable. What is the meaning of inflation in a planned economy? How to estimate it? How to measure structural/sectoral economic shifts? How distorted is the official peso exchange rate? Thus it is possible to fairly question results based on unavoidable procedural quagmires. What the authors do, as expected, is just precisely that. I find it unremarkable that Mesa-Lago and Pérez-López have the strength to expose their doubts and ambiguities about their work.

Two minor matters should be mentioned. The dating of the start of state-controlled prices and the creation of the Comité Estatal de Precios (p. 49) is somewhat confusing; while the former did begin in 1961, the latter was not at work until 1976. The abolition of the "mercado libre campesino" in the spring of 1986 renders moot any discussion of its probable impact upon inflation (p. 74).

In sum, I think that Mesa-Lago and Pérez-López have successfully addressed a complex and difficult task of compilation and evaluation. Their hard work is evident, their presentation is clear, and their conclusions are compelling. From now on, serious scholarship on the Cuban economy will have to contend with this study.

Sergio G. Roca
Adelphi University

FOREIGN RELATIONS

H. Michael Erisman. *Cuba's International Relations: The Anatomy of a Nationalistic Foreign Policy.* **Boulder, Colo.: Westview Press, 1985. Xv + 203 pp.**

Erisman's survey of Cuban foreign policy comprises about two-thirds of this book and is supplemented by a selection of Fidel Castro's speeches and interviews. The study is organized chronologically, dividing postrevolutionary foreign policy into six eras: 1959–1962, 1962–1968, 1968–1972, 1972–1975, 1975–1979, and 1979 onward. The first three, however, receive only brief review in a single chapter; the book's main focus is on the 1970s and 1980s. This imbalance in coverage, though not objectionable in itself, sometimes results in insufficient attention to key events during the early period. For instance, the Cuban missile crisis, which was pivotal for all three sides of the triangular relationship between Cuba, the United States, and the Soviet Union, is mentioned only in passing.

Within each era, the book is organized conceptually around Cuba's relations with the United States, the Soviet Union, Latin America, and the Third World (particularly Africa and the Nonaligned Movement). This effectively covers the full gamut of Cuban foreign policy, although in reality these sets of relations are so often intertwined that separate consideration of them occasionally fragments the flow of the analysis. In addition to reviewing the basic events of Cuban foreign affairs, Erisman presents a comprehensive survey of the main arguments and interpretations that have been advanced by others in the field, making the book an excellent review of the literature.

This ambitious project is undertaken in the space of only about 120 pages, which necessitates very summary treatment of many issues. The result is a veritable whirlwind tour, and inevitably one feels that the treatment of some important issues has been a bit cursory.

Erisman's main thesis is reflected in the book's title. He argues that nationalism has consistently been a central motivation behind Cuban foreign policy (although certainly not the sole motivation), and he takes issue with those who advance the "surrogate thesis"—the idea that Cuba is nothing more than a Soviet pawn on the international chessboard. Erisman's narrative effectively shows that most of Cuba's international initiatives respond to the Cuban national interest.

At the same time, he acknowledges the importance of Soviet military and economic assistance to Cuba, recognizing that without it, Cuba's capacity to conduct a global foreign policy would be negligible. He even speaks of Cuban economic "dependency" on the Soviet Union. Those who argue *in favor* of the "surrogate thesis" insist that these ties between Cuba and the Soviet Union effectively reduce or at least constrain Cuba's freedom of action. Erisman clearly disagrees, but he never fully engages the issue of just how much influence Soviet assistance buys in Havana—something that a truly decisive refutation of the "surrogate thesis" requires.

Selections from Castro's speeches and interviews are appended to each chapter starting with the 1972–1975 era, and they are generally well chosen. Once again, however, the decade of the 1960s receives short shrift, since the earliest selection is from 1971. This is unfortunate, since there are several historically important speeches from the 1960s that could have been included—the First and Second Declarations of Havana, and Castro's speech to the Tricontinental Conference in 1966, just to mention three.

In addition, although writing on the book was completed in 1984, inexplicably, the most recent selection is from late 1981. Consequently, no major Cuban statements on Central America during the Reagan administration or on Grenada are included. This is especially unfortunate, since these two issues were so critical for Cuban foreign policy in the 1980s.

Finally, one wishes that documents other than Castro's speeches could have been included. Without doubt, his speeches still constitute the most authoritative statements of Cuban policy. But they would have been complemented by the inclusion of other materials such as the thesis on foreign policy adopted at the First Party Congress, or Carlos Rafael Rodríguez's 1981 article in *Cuba Socialista,* "Fundamentos estratégicos de la política exterior de la Revolución Cubana."

William M. LeoGrande
American University

Carlos Alberto Montaner. *Cuba, Castro and the Caribbean*. New Brunswick, N.J.: Transaction Books, 1985. 116 pp.

Forget about finding much in this book specifically dealing with Castro and the Caribbean. Even the subtitle (*The Cuban Revolution and the Crisis in Western Conscience*) obfuscates its true contents—which can be depicted as an analytical dissection and scrutiny of Cuba's people and culture by one of the island's more perceptive (and long exiled) sons, Carlos Alberto Montaner. In fact, at times even a purely Cuban focus seems to give way to generalizations that might be fittingly applied to all Latin America.

Montaner may be controversial for what he says in his many publications, but not for how he expresses himself. His writing is incisive, erudite, and frequently disputatious, even when transformed into another language. (A credit here to translator Nelson Duran.) In this instance, Montaner reflects upon the Cuban condition via several short essays that appear to have been written at different times and for different purposes with no preconceived notion of unity. Yet, they evince enough thematic commonality to justify being assembled into a single work (notwithstanding the book's misleading title and the gratuitous inclusion of a basic chronology of Cuban-American relations up to 1959 as an appendix).

Montaner's detractors, who object to what they consider his "conservative" perspectives, will find the message contained in these essays equally hard to swallow. For what Latin American "radical" could accept the proposition that today efforts to transform society through violent removal of the ruling class and redistribution of property are essentially irrelevant and that old-style nationalism is no longer possible? Montaner says Cuba and other Latin American countries are "marginal" nations with "static" societies, long accustomed to blaming others for their ills instead of seeking the causes for their relatively backward social and economic development in themselves. With a value system that neither encourages nor rewards innovation, creativity, excellence, or pride in workmanship, Latin America will forever be "doomed to ape the creative centers of the world." The solution will not be found in efforts to become culturally autonomous, politically independent, or economically self-sufficient; the only reasonable hope is to develop its human resources for the task of assuming an active role in the emergence of a global civilization.

For Montaner, Cuba's future (like its past) must intertwine with that of the United States, not through annexation nor domination, but through shared values. And, paradoxically, it will be the notoriously anti-Yankee Fidel Castro whom history will record as contributing the most to Cuba's cultural Americanization—by virtue of forcing a tenth of its population to assimilate modernizing values which, through them, will eventually permeate Cuban society in the post-Castro period. In short, Montaner assumes "Cuban-Americans" will play a decisive role in the economic, scientific, and technological progress that will come to enmesh Cuba in a "natural dependency" with the United States. To associate Cuba with the Soviet Union means, for Montaner, that Castro inexorably impoverishes his people by linking social development to that of a third-rate scientific and cultural power, hopelessly destined to be more imitative than intellectually constructive.

Whatever Cuba's future political fate, are Cubans really capable of moving their country into the mainstream of technological and scientific advancement? Montaner's assessment of Cuban cultural traits (whether true or not so true) is also bound to displease his critics. He sees Cubans in general as victims of an exaggerated sense of their own historical importance who, moreover, traditionally display little evidence of discipline, foresight, tolerance, originality, or excellence in productive work. "If our provincialism prevents us from seeing these signs, all too plainly evident," he states, "then we shall never be able to shake our present state of prostration, dependence, and subsidiariness." More significant than a political revolution, Cubans must come to see that only a major transformation in their individual and collective behavior can mold the attitudes capable of catapulting their country toward true emancipation and prosperity.

Agree with him or not, Carlos Alberto once again succeeds in making one think.

Lynne-D. Bender
Inter American University of Puerto Rico

GENERAL

Sandor Halebsky and John M. Kirk, ed. *Cuba: Twenty-Five Years of Revolution, 1959–1984*. New York: Praeger, 1985. Xiii + 466 pp.

This "critical anthology addresses the general misunderstandings concerning the Cuban Revolution and attempts to provide a more balanced overview of the revolutionary process." Therefore, while some chapters "highlight the dramatic advances and improvements gained by the Cuban people, others detail negative aspects of the process. Both viewpoints must be presented if we are to comprehend the nature of the Cuban phenomenon" (pp. 3-4). The editors thus state their large book's admirable purpose.

In many respects, the book succeeds. For scholars, the premier essay is Louis A. Pérez, Jr.'s, bibliographic report on works about Cuba since 1959. Not only is it helpful but also it shows that much has been done, even if much remains to be done. The prize for lucidity and brevity in reviewing a vast subject goes to Rhoda Pearl Rabkin, whose chapter is the book's only general discussion of politics. Roberto González Echevarría's characteristically well-written essay on criticism and literature in revolutionary Cuba is especially informative for those (like myself) who do not follow that field professionally.

The book is also valuable for teaching because it presents alternative scholarly images of the same process and, in doing so, it invites reflection. Consider the section on cultural change. Why do able scholars see such different things when they look at cultural phenomena in Cuba? While all of these scholars discuss accomplishments in the cultural field since 1959, only some discuss as well some of the negative trends, including censorship, that are part of Cuba's recent history and of the book's mandate.

Or consider references to worker participation in enterprise decision making. Andrew Zimbalist concludes "that the shift in enterprise social relations described above helped to promote the development of internal incentives (worker motivation) as well as the elicitation of good ideas for increasing productivity and thereby contributed, along with other factors, to the spurt in productivity growth during the first half of the seventies" (p. 222). His able chapter on planning says a lot about the planning system, and about the role of the workers, but not much about management's role. While agreeing that significant changes in labor-management relations occurred in the early 1970s, Marifeli Pérez-Stable's analysis of the role of the working class is more troubling because she also focuses on management's role. She shows that much apparent worker participation was merely formal, that much else might better be called "involvement" rather than "meaningful participation," and that the increase in managerial power in the early 1980s was "politically disturbing" for those who look to the working class to play a vanguard role in the construction of socialism (pp. 300-03).

Thoughtful points are worth highlighting even in sections where a debate is not joined directly. In the conclusion to their chapter, James Petras and Morris Morley demonstrate both their sympathy with the processes occurring in Cuba after 1959 and their honesty. They praise what they judge to be the government's accomplishments but they also note that Cuba has "overdeveloped institutions of national defense and underdeveloped institutions of democratic representation. The relevance of the Cuban Revolution for other countries is found in the superb organization of its defense system; its weakness lies in the leadership's inability to broaden the scope of citizen participation and debate" (p. 436). They also do not shy away from noting that "Cuba supported the efforts of a dictatorial military regime in Ethiopia to defeat a national liberation movement" in Eritrea, though that action differed from Cuba's more normal support for such movements (p. 434).

This is, however, one of the rare references in this book to the armed forces. Otherwise, there is no sustained discussion of the premier institution created since 1959. Also, the section on the "social revolution" makes no mention of the dramatic increases since 1959 in divorces, suicides, and abortions, or of Cuba's dramatically shifting population growth rates. These are surely major transformations that should be part of an assessment of the Revolution.

Nor is there any discussion of the role of the Interior Ministry, of repression, of political imprisonment, or of torture in prison. Some of these subjects might have been discussed in Max Azicri's chapter on "socialist legality and practice." They were not. Azicri's only reference to this sordid underside of revolutionary rule suggests doubt that political prisoners and other dissidents were mistreated (p. 316). But the main responsibility lies with the editors. Despite their admirable intentions, they did not include even one chapter on political imprisonment even though scholars can now draw on increasing evidence about this subject. The absence of commentary on the worst of the "negative trends" in Cuba gives the book too celebratory a tone for what should properly have been throughout a "critical anthology." (For a noncelebratory book, assessing the same period, with a different mixture of strengths and weaknesses, see H. Thomas, G. Fauriol, and J. Weiss, *The Cuban Revolution: Twenty-Five Years Later* [Boulder, Colo.: Westview Press, 1984]).

It is important to recall and, yes, to celebrate the good things the revolutionary government has done in the name of the people. It is just as important to recall and, yes, to condemn the evil things that this same government has also done in the name of the people.

Jorge I. Domínguez
Harvard University

HISTORY

Allan J. Kuethe. *Cuba, 1753–1815: Crown, Military, and Society.* Knoxville: University of Tennessee Press, 1986. 232 pp. $23.95.

One of the livelier aspects of Cuban studies in recent years has been the increased scholarly attention given to the island's colonial past. On the scales of historical significance, Cuba's four centuries as a Spanish possession clearly outweigh in importance developments on the island during its twentieth-century existence as an independent nation. As deceptively easy as it is for some to think that Cuba's moment in the sun came in 1959, renewed interest in the island's past shows that Cuba has frequently stood near or in the center of world affairs. Allan J. Kuethe is one of those scholars whose work takes us into new and suggestive areas of Cuba's rich history.

Cuba, 1753–1815 covers a very important era. In the period dealt with in this book, Havana was attacked and occupied temporarily by an enemy army (1762–1763), the Cuban economy converted from being a modest exporter of tobacco to the world's largest producer of sugar, and the Spanish empire disintegrated—a disintegration that affected but did not sweep the island up in its wake. Following in the footsteps of Lyle McAlister, one of the first scholars to note the importance of the military in colonial Latin American history, Kuethe uses the abundant records left by Spanish army officers to reveal numerous secrets about the island's society and government. If ever there was a colony whose military establishment reflected its social structure, Cuba was it.

Although it would be misleading to speak of any Spanish territory as typical, some possessions obviously had more characteristics in common than others. Kuethe, however, makes a strong case that Cuba was unique within the imperial system. Since the island had such a major responsibility for the defense of the northern Spanish colonies, the loss of Havana at the end of the Seven Years' War provoked the government into initiating fundamental reforms to prevent the island from recapture. Many of the key Spanish reforms centered on reorganizing the island's militia to make it an effective military force. This reorganization, done under the watchful eyes of two influential Spanish bureaucrats, the Conde de Ricla and Field Marshal Alejandro O'Reilly, was so successful that it gave the island the manpower needed to dissuade future assaults and enough troops left over to send units to fight in Florida, Louisiana, and other Caribbean Islands during the turbulent period 1779–1815. In fact, by the early nineteenth century, the only Spanish force in Cuba was the island's militia. In many ways, the Cuban militia represented for the crown a model that it wished to extend to the rest of Spanish America; however, no other Spanish possession duplicated it with quite the same success.

As with most military improvements, the militia reforms in Cuba were extremely expensive, both financially and in terms of lost time taken from civilian activities. The crown wanted Cuba to shoulder much of the increased expense. In theory, the crown had the authority simply to decree new taxes and responsibilities and then let its loyal subjects obey. However, such a cavalier approach would have led to the subversion of the Cuban militia by hostile participants. As a result, the crown and royal officials in Cuba negotiated with the Cuban patriciate regarding increased taxes and obligations. In perhaps the most interesting part of his book, Keuthe describes how the Cuban elite drove a very hard bargain before surrendering part of their income and time to the crown. The final agreement, which involved substantial trade concessions to the island and the granting of numerous titles of nobility, was so mutually beneficial to the government and the island's local leadership that Cuba's loyalty during the troubled period from 1808 to 1825, when the rest of the Spanish empire broke away, can be explained to a large degree by the popularity of the militia reforms.

With so much attention given to newer specialties in history, it is refreshing to see what an insightful book can still be produced by an experienced and intelligent scholar using traditional narrative history. No other recent book on Cuban or Latin American history gives the reader such an understanding of how imperial policy was hammered out in practice. Compromise and consultation were the principal factors in promoting colonial harmony in Cuba, and one can only suppose that the crown attempted the same political process in other Spanish colonies as well. *Cuba, 1753–1815* is also the latest book to tackle the question of colonial loyalty during a time of imperial collapse. That the king's policies worked so well in Cuba raises the question of why these same programs did so poorly elsewhere in Spanish America. Kuethe's constant theme that Cuba was different might provide the answer. The Cuban elite had access to the Spanish court and possessed the political sophistication to manipulate imperial policy to a degree unrealized by other colonies. In many respects, the history of the island resembles more that of the European regions of Spain than the past of the other Spanish New World colonies. The sea that separated most of the empire from the mother country actually bound Cuba closer to its European center.

James A. Lewis
Western Carolina University

Leví Marrero. *Cuba, Economía y Sociedad. Azúcar, Ilustración y Conciencia* (1763–1868). Vol. 12 (4). Madrid: Editorial Playor, 1985.

Volume 12 of Leví Marrero's monumental history of Cuba is the fourth of an anticipated six-volume set treating the period 1763–1868 (see *Cuban Studies* 15(1985), 78–80). The first three volumes covered (1) demography; (2) general economic development, land tenure and use, and the growth and transformation of the sugar industry; and (3) the evolution of the tobacco industry, the rise and fall of coffee, and the transportation revolution. The present volume addresses commerce and navigation, money and banking, and the operation of the colonial treasury.

By far the largest section of volume 12, accounting for well over half the text, is that on Cuban commerce. Marrero begins by describing the futile efforts of the Royal Havana Company to reassert its monopolistic position in the aftermath of the Seven Years' War. The company, as shown in Marrero's trilogy on the period 1701–1763, had played a dynamic role in Cuban economic development during the 1740s and 1750s, but following the British capture of Havana in 1762, the Spanish government was determined to seek new directions in its attempt to strengthen the island economically and militarily. The trade ordinance of 1765 pointed commercial policy toward deregulation and shattered what hopes remained for the company. Among its provisions, the 1765 law opened the Cuban trade to eight Spanish ports besides Cádiz and authorized free participation by Cubans and Spaniards alike; further deregulation arrived with the well-known Reglamento de Comercio Libre of 1778.

Marrero then traces the persistent struggle by Cubans to obtain further commercial liberties on up to the royal order of 1818, which finally opened the Cuban marketplace to the world. Provided are lengthy accounts of "habanero" maneuverings to expand their commercial outlets through neutral trade and thereby gain access to coveted opportunities in the United States. In this regard, Cubans were remarkably successful, especially during the American Revolution, the French Revolution and Napoleonic Wars. Marrero argues that this access to wider markets was a primary factor behind the remarkable economic expansion during the century following the Seven Years' War. Crucial as well was a more ready access to slave labor, especially following the opening of the Cuban slave trade to foreign suppliers in 1789. Interestingly, Marrero argues that the capital that financed the sugar revolution was largely generated internally, and although he details the great size of the Mexican subsidy up to 1811, he does not see it as an important source of investment revenue as Franklin Knight, Manuel Moreno Fraginals, and I myself all have done.

This section also contains detailed export statistics—those for sugar, tobacco, and coffee being the most important—and an analysis of Cuba's wide variety of imports—primarily foodstuffs and textiles. Much of the sugar trade was directed to the United States, which, at least after 1818, ranked only slightly behind Spain in providing legal Cuban imports. Marrero concludes that nineteenth-century Cuba in reality had two colonial masters, one political, the other economic. Also included is an informative exposition on shipbuilding in Havana, which ranked as a major industry until 1796.

The section on money and banking explores the basic structural flaw in the sugar economy of the first half of the nineteenth century: the shortage of investment capital. Banking was slow to develop in Spain and even slower in Cuba, which did not really have what could be described as a modern system until near the end of the period under analysis. Moreover, Marrero shows that the system that emerged was not responsive to the needs of agriculture in that loans, although available at relatively reasonable prices, were short-term whereas needs were long-term. As a consequence, planters found themselves compelled to borrow from merchants at usurious rates, which led to the fading of the old aristocracy and the emergence of a new class of merchant (moneylending) planters.

In his final section, Marrero examines the operation of the royal treasury in Cuba. Subjects treated include the establishment and functioning of the intendancy, the impressive rise of royal income between 1763 and 1868, the various forms of taxation, the pattern of expenditure, and belated efforts to reform the system. Initially, Cuba was a net beneficiary of royal spending, but during the early nineteenth century the island saw itself transformed into a major contributor to the Madrid treasury under a system of taxation that Marrero views as archaic and oppressive. With Cuba cut off from representation in the Cortes since 1837, this unfavorable relationship led to an alienation that would soon become manifest.

Like its predecessors, this volume is based on an impressive variety of archival and secondary sources. It is richly illustrated with maps and plates, and includes numerous statistical tables and documents reproduced wholly or in part. Volume 12 stands as yet another heroic step forward in Leví Marrero's history of his native land.

Allan J. Kuethe
Texas Tech University

Rebecca J. Scott. *Slave Emancipation in Cuba: The Transition to Free Labor, 1860-1899.* **Princeton, N.J.: Princeton University Press, 1985. 319 pp.**

Slavery and the slave trade to the Americas have attracted much scholarly research and writing since the late 1940s. The emergence of Afro-American populations from slavery has been less studied, despite the fact that contemporary patterns of race relations and the social, economic, and political conditions of blacks and mulattos are closely linked to postemancipation experiences.

This book examines the gradual *process* of abolition in Cuba from a variety of perspectives. Colonial politics, economic transformations, the social dislocation caused by insurrection (1868-1878), and most refreshing of all, the attitudes and activities of slaves, "libertos," and masters provide the multifaceted prism through which slave emancipation is viewed.

Heretofore, the abolition of Cuban slavery has been analyzed as a political response by Spain to domestic and international pressures, or as the result of internal contradictions prompted by technological innovations linked to advancing capitalist relations of production, and slave labor. Scott's major argument is that despite modernization of sugar refining, slavery as a labor system was neither unprofitable nor incompatible with sugar production, even after the abolition process began. Masters in the major sugar-producing regions successfully strove to preserve core slave labor forces through the 1870s, after promulgation of the 1870 Moret Law which initiated legal abolition by freeing slaves born after 1868 and those reaching sixty years of age.

The process of slave emancipation began before it was legally institutionalized. The independence insurrection of 1868 heralded the transformation of Cuban social relations, especially in regions of rebel control. Scott documents the contradictions within the rebellion regarding slavery and abolition, but emphasizes the fact that slaves abandoning their masters to join the insurrection could never accept the old mechanisms of class and racial domination. For those who remained enslaved, the possibility of actively shaping the future was embodied by insurrectionary slaves who legally secured their freedom through the peace agreement of 1878.

The Moret Law was Spain's answer to the issue of slavery raised by the revolt, but it was the slaves themselves who pushed the process forward. They increasingly took advantage of legal provisions which could lead to freedom, appealing to local officials for access to slave registries, protesting violations of laws prohibiting use of the whip or other illegal punishments, or abandoning "ingenios" for maroonage or the insurrection to the east. Slaves are portrayed not as passive characters who were mere objects of policy and laws, but as active participants in a historical drama that shaped their collective destiny. It is to Scott's credit that this is done realistically, without romanticizing slave activities, and within the ambience of the brutality and degradation of the slave system.

The efforts of masters to preserve the old social relationships of slavery when the world around them was in the process of transformation is a fascinating part of this book. This was especially true after the establishment of the "patronato" in 1880, theoretically a period of tutelage when ex-slaves, "patrocinados," owed labor obligations to former masters. "Patrocinados" sought to use legal institutions to their advantage and former masters struggled to preserve the continuity of production, labor control, and their old social prerogatives. This final episode of the emancipation process, which culminated in complete abolition in 1886, is analyzed from the perspective of masters, slaves, freedmen, and women, and how they interacted in the colony's various regions.

The fate of ex-slaves becomes blurred after 1886. Slaves were a vital economic resource to elite groups who generated enormous quantities of historical documentation on every aspect of slavery. With freedom, ex-slaves as a group ceased their place as a separate legal category and their role as a valued economic resource. Blacks and mulattos were counted in censuses, discriminated against legally and socially, and carefully watched during periods of political crisis. But a separate historical record was not maintained.

What became of Cuban ex-slaves after emancipation? Scott suggests answers that have been well recognized by Cuban specialists for some time. Some became sugar "colonos," while others migrated to cities or to Camagüey and Oriente. Yet the fate of those freed remains largely unknown. To the end of the "patronato" in 1886 this book is based on the creative use of a rich variety of documentation stored in Cuban, Spanish, United States, and British archives. For the period 1886 to

1899, the documentation declines in both quantity and quality. While Scott has provided us with an incisive account of the abolition process that will undoubtedly stand the test of time, the fate of ex-slaves in the late nineteenth and early twentieth century remains a fascinating topic for future historical research.

Laird W. Bergad
Lehman College,
City University of New York

LITERATURE

Miguel Barnet. *Gallego.* **Madrid: Ediciones Alfaguara, S.A., 1981. 224 pp.**

From an ethnic point of view, Cuba's population consists of three elements: whites, mainly of Spanish descent; blacks of African ancestry; and Orientals whose ancestors came from China in the mid-to-late nineteenth century. Indian aborigines disappeared in the early years of Spanish colonization. Miguel Barnet, in his novel *El Cimarrón* (*The Story of a Runaway Slave*), paid homage to the black contribution to Cuban heritage. Now with *Gallego* he is doing the same for the Spaniards. Both books are in the vein of Oscar Lewis's social ethnographies and are based on texts attributed to a former slave and a Galician immigrant respectively, although Esteban Montejo, the maroon, is a real person—"un personaje de carne y hueso," as Unamuno would have called him—while Manuel Ruíz, "el gallego," is a purely fictional character. Both novels belong to the Cuban literary tradition of personal memoirs of social life and, to a certain degree, to the U.S. tradition embodied in the works of Mark Twain (*Huckleberry Finn*) and Salinger (*The Catcher in the Rye*).

Using the first-person narrator technique, Barnet relates the life and work of a Galician villager ("un aldeano") who came to Cuba after World War I (more precisely during the administration of President Mario G. Menocal) to escape the difficult economic situation of his native Galicia, and to "make good" in his adopted country. His deeds and misdeeds, his fortunes and misfortunes are clearly portrayed throughout the 224 pages of the book. The novel is, on the other hand, like a parade of characters typical of prerevolutionary Cuba. They are drawn by Barnet with a few deft strokes that make them quite different from the old "personajes típicos" of conventional novels. The history of Cuba after independence is the background of the literary work. Here, the author discreetly emphasizes the deplorable human conditions in which poor people lived, and stresses how the 1959 Cuban Revolution has attempted to improve such conditions. In an oblique way, the book is also an indictment of the conditions of social life in Spain during the same period.

The characterization of Manuel Ruíz, "el gallego," as a man with two "patrias" is, in my opinion, the best part of the novel. The man's lifestyle, half Galician and half Cuban, his peculiar sociolect full of "galleguismos" and "cubanismos" are assets to the book. Much less convincing is Manuel's return to Spain to fight against Franco's forces since "el gallego," up to that moment, had shown very little interest in local politics and none whatsoever in the politics of the Continent. This chapter seems to be an afterthought. Breaking the internal unity of the novel, it gives excessive attention to the sociopolitical interests Barnet wants to promote. *Gallego,* in fact, brings to mind another of Barnet's novels, *La canción de Rachel,* in which, after the Revolution, a retired courtesan relates her life, and through it outlines Cuban sociocultural history. Both novels are good examples of the testimonial novel that has recently flourished in Latin American circles, and whose origins can be traced to the middle of the nineteenth century with Domingo Faustino Sarmiento's *Facundo. Gallego* is a perfect example of the kind of literature in which the author, with great ability, combines literary craft with political propaganda.

Despite its shortcomings, *Gallego* fulfills its avowed goal of paying tribute to Spanish immigration in Cuba and constitutes another success in Miguel Barnet's literary career.

Leonel A. de la Cuesta
Florida International University

Roberto González Echevarría. *The Voice of the Masters: Writing and Authority in Modern Latin American Literature.* **Austin: University of Texas Press, 1985.**

González Echevarría believes that the "criticism of Latin American literature is in the midst of a crisis. . . . Signs of this crisis are everywhere. The most apparent is the absence of any school, ideology, or critical tendency enjoying even a modicum of shared acceptance."

198 : *Reviews*

Having opted for what proves to be a highly provocative deconstructionist approach, he notes, tongue-in-check, that "deconstructive criticism's indiscretion, like charity, begins at home, since in practice it self-deconstructs as it deconstructs." What he means to underscore is the radically deconstructive nature of all writing. In his opinion, one of several reasons for the critics' failure to develop any coherent system of Latin American literary criticism is the fact that the best of the region's literature has itself *constituted* its critical thought: "All great works of Latin American literature . . . question the central myths on which they rest."

In his statement of purpose, he expresses his opinion that a particular concept of culture has constituted the ideology that lends meaning to Latin American literature, while at the same time that literature has been working to eliminate such a relationship.

He begins by pointing out how the authoritative voice is central in Rodó's highly influential *Ariel,* how the master places the reader in the position of pupil, so that "truth, spirit, hope and everything that is good dwell in the modulations of the teacher's voice." He then notes that "the rhetorical power to sustain the magisterial voice consists in doing violence to an implied other onto whom one's words are to be cut. This reading at the center of Rodó's influential essay continues to be at the core of the Latin American tradition that follows it." Several other works are brought in to reinforce the point. González Echevarría espouses the view that *Doña Bárbara* is far more profound than it is usually held to be, in that it continually returns to the theme of writing as it engages in the process of implicitly examining those cultural myths of founding mentioned above. He feels that in Gallegos's novel a critical subtext subverts the primary plane of the usual allegorical reading. "Los funerales de la Mamá Grande" is taken to be something of a sequel to *Doña Bárbara,* significant in part because the dictatorial figure is dead at the time of writing. González Echevarría feels it is instructive that, when the lists of items owned by Mamá Grande are read, it appears that she "does not really own the things alluded to by these formulae, but the formulae themselves."

The author spends a good deal of time coming to grips with the phenomenon of the novel of dictatorship, with its roots in Sarmiento's *Facundo,* and its flowering in the 1970s. His contention is that this represents an inquiry not only into the nature of political power, but into "the power, the energy that constitutes a literary text, particularly a novel, and a function within it of the figure of the author." A dictator is supposed to rule through his "voice," much as an author does, but González Echevarría points out that the dictator of these novels typically is threatened by a writer: "It is not the dictator-author, but the secretary-writer, who reigns, even if he is nothing but a Carnival king."

In his consideration of Roa Bastos's *Yo el supremo,* González Echevarría notes that the dictator becomes uneasy as he senses that the center of power in his domains has been gradually displaced from his voice to the texts generated by his secretary, "a subordinate who usurps power by being able to supplant truth and knowledge with simulacra." He notes as well that *"Yo el supremo* is the final victory of the text."

He feels that Latin American literature and criticism are founded on the myth of the organic coherence of nature and a corresponding myth involving language in correspondence with nature. The latter involves a close relationship between signs and things, between writing and the world. Modern literature, paradoxically, is founded on doubts concerning the latter. One results of this, it would seem, is an emphasis on the literature of exile, which reflects the signifier's flight away from the signifier. Still, a work such as Carpentier's "El derecho de asilo" questions the connection between writing and exile. "The story leads inevitably to the conclusion that all political activity consists of the generation of sign systems whose aim is to deceive rather than to enlighten, and much less to guide; to deflect attention rather than to focus it."

The book ends, curiously, with a translation of Cabrera Infante's "Meta-final," a supplement to *Tres tristes tigres* that appeared in the first of two issues of *Alacrán Azul,* and which González Echevarría considers to be among the most important texts ever to appear in Latin America, for its contribution to the critical processes he views as taking place in the recent literature of the region: the progressive destruction of the founding cultural myths. In "Meta-final," he says, "language is written on the brink of its own extinction."

The book is a tour de force, a virtuoso performance with all that implies. It raises exciting possibilities, forces the reader to view well-known texts in exciting new ways, and provides an overview of Latin American literature that must be responded to in one form or another. Such an ambitious work often raises serious questions. This reader wonders, for example, whether there is any validity to a discussion of Fuentes's choice of the title *Terra nostra* over *Tierra nuestra* in which it is stated that "our common code—Spanish—has dissolved the cryptic atemporality of Latin by splitting its pristine vowels, by diphthongizing the accented long *e* and *o* into *ie* and *ue*," so that *"Terra Nostra*'s title pretends to be a shared language in which there is no time, no difference, no exchange."

One wonders too whether the word "theodicy" (the defense of the acts of God), which is used several times, is supposed to mean "theophany" (a breakthrough of the divine into the human realm). These are minor objections, and do not detract from a text which is a serious contribution to the development of the coherent literary criticism that González Echevarría desires to see.

William L. Siemens
West Virginia University

Compiled by VILMA E. PETRASH

Recent Work in Cuban Studies

Agriculture

Books and Monographs

Burnhill, Lauren A. *The Private Sector in Cuban Agriculture, 1959–1985: A Socio-economic Study.* Washington, D.C.: School of Advanced International Studies, Johns Hopkins University, 1986. 83 pp.
Díaz Vázquez, Julio A. See *Economics, Industry and Planning.*
Hildebrand, Harald. "Zur Entwicklung der Landwirtschaft der Republik Kubain der Etappe des Sozialistischen Aufbaus." Inagural-diss., Humboldt Universität Berlin [East Germany], 1984. 219 + 11 pp.
Ledo Babarro, Félix. "Untersuchungen zu Grudlagen überbetrieblich anwendbarer Zeitnormative im Holzeinschlag in Kuba (Pinus Tropicalis Morelet, Pinus caribaea Morelet var. caribaea). Diss. A., Technische Universität Dresden [East Germany], 1984. 156 pp.
Sánchez, Pedro A., and Grant M. Scobie. *Cuba and the CGIAR Centers. A Study of Their Collaboration in Agricultural Research.* Washington, D.C.: World Bank, 1985. 132 pp. [Study from the Consultative Group on International Agricultural Research—CGIAR.]
Silverio, S. Mayea, L. Herrera, et al. *Enfermedades de las plantas cultivadas en Cuba.* Havana: Editorial Pueblo y Educación, 1985. 424 pp.

Articles and Papers

Arias, Salvador. "¿Disparos en la mirilla?" *Santiago* 57 (March 1985), 225–40.
Feuer, Carl Henry. "Does Socialism Make a Difference? Sugarcane Agriculture in Cuba and Jamaica." *Social and Economic Studies* (University of the West Indies, Kingston, Jamaica), 1987.
Forster, Nancy, and Howard Handelman. "Food Production and Distribution in Cuba: The Impact of the Revolution." In *Food, Politics, and Society in Latin America,* ed. John Super and Thomas Wright, 174–98. Lincoln: University of Nebraska Press, 1985.
Huss, Werner, and Lothar Mairich. "Entwicklungstendenzen der kubanischen Landwirtschaft." *Jahrbuch Asien, Afrika, Lateinamerika* [Berlin] 13, no. 3 (1985), 490–501.
Kaláshnikov, Nikolái. "La cooperativización, vía para la transformación del sector campesino." *América Latina* [Moscow] 4 (April 1986), 47–55.
Lehman, D. "Smallholding Agriculture in Revolutionary Cuba: A Case of Under-exploitation?" *Development and Change* 16 (April 1985), 214–19.
Le Riverend, Julio. See *History.*

Morales, Eliodoro, and Enrique Rodríguez. See *Economics, Industry, and Planning*
Pollitt, Brian H. See *Economics, Industry, and Planning*.
Rodríguez, José Luis. See *Economics, Industry, and Planning*.
Rojas, Iliana, and Jorge Hernández. "La reforma agraria, base imprescindible." *América Latina* [Moscow] 4 (April 1986), 38–46.
Stubbs, Jean. See *Economics, Industry, and Planning*.
Suárez Torres, Juan O., and Pablo Zamora Rodríguez. See *Science and Technology*.

Anthropology and Archaeology

Books and Monographs

Cabrera, Lydia. *El monte*. Miami: Universal, 1986. 620 pp.
———. *Otan iyebiye. Las piedras preciosas*. Miami: Universal, 1986. 113 pp.
———. *Reglas de Congo: Palo monte-mayombe*. Miami: Universal, 1986. 225 pp.
———. *Regla Kimbisa del Santo Cristo del Buen Viaje*. Miami: Universal, 1986. 85 pp.
Pino, Milton, and Nilecta Castellanos. *Acerca de la asociación de perezosos cubanos extinguidos con evidencias culturales de aborígenes cubanos*. Reporte de Investigación no. 4. Havana: Academia de Ciencias, 1985. 29 pp.

Articles and Papers

Hernández, Grizel. "Cultos sincréticos cubanos: los Ibellis." *Temas* 7 (1985), 57–70.
Menéndez, Lázara, and Raquel Mendieta. "Cayo Hueso, una experiencia cultural." *Temas* 7 (1985), 41–56.

Architecture and Urban Development

Books and Monographs

Downing, Douglas Charles. "Residential Concentration of Refugees in California and the United States." Ph.D. diss., University of Massachusetts, 1984. 599 pp. *DAI* 46, no. 1 (July 1985): 270-71-A, UM8500072. [Deals in part with Cuban refugees.]

Articles and Papers

Aguilera Rojas, Javier. "La Habana vieja. Mapas y planes de los archivos de España." *Ciudad y Territorio* [Madrid] 63/64 (January–June 1985), 99–110.
Aguirre, Yolanda. "Un puerto y una ciudad: San Cristóbal de la Habana." Ibid., 27–39.
Aruca, Lohania. "25 años de planificación física". *Arquitectura y Urbanismo* 6, no. 1 (November 1985), 4–7. [Interview with Cecilia Menéndez.]
———. "Los portales de La Habana." *Arquitectura y Urbanismo* 3 (1985), 24–29.

———. "Por una teoría cubana de planificación regional y urbana." *Arquitectura y Urbanismo* 3 (1985), 98–99. [I Jornada Científica Internacional sobre Planificación Regional y Urbana.]
Capablanca, Enrique. "La Habana vieja: Anteproyecto de restauración." *Ciudad y Territorio* [Madrid] 63/64 (January–June 1985), 57–64.
Centro Nacional de Conservación, Ministerio de la Cultura. "Propuesta de restauración de la plaza vieja de La Habana." Ibid., 73–80.
Coyula, Mario. "Vivienda, renovación urbana y poder popular: La Habana (1ra. parte)." *Arquitectura y Urbanismo* 6, no. 2 (1985), 12–17.
———. "La reanimación urbanística en ciudad de La Habana." *Arquitectura y Urbanismo* 6, no. 3 (1985), 10–16.
———. "Vivienda, renovación urbana y poder popular: algunas consideraciones sobre La Habana (2da parte)." Ibid., 3–9.
Cuervo Masoné, Héctor. "Concentración y desconcentración urbana en la experiencia cubana." *Pensamiento Iberoamericano* 1 (January–June 1985), 141–46.
———. "La planificación de las ciudades en Cuba." *Arquitectura y Urbanismo* 6, 1 (November 1985), 8–15.
Escobar, Emilio. "La función cultural de los centros urbanos." *Arquitectura y Urbanismo* 6, no. 1 (November 1985), 74–81.
Fernández, Enrique. "La reestructuración de nuestras ciudades." Ibid., 30–35.
Fernández Núñez, José Manuel. "Dos décadas de planificación regional y urbana en Cuba." *Ciudad y Territorio* [Madrid] 63/64 (January–June 1985), 95–98.
García, Alicia. "Arquitectura doméstica tradicional e identidad nacional." *Arquitectura y Urbanismo* 6, no. 2 (1986), 26–31.
Hamberg, Jill. "The Dynamics of Cuban Housing Policy." In *Critical Perspectives on Housing,* ed. Rachel G. Bratt, Chester Hartman, and Ann Meyerson, 586–624. Philadelphia: Temple University Press, 1986.
"La Habana vieja vuelve a la vida." *América 92* 7 (August–September–October 1986).
Lápidus, Luis. "Las señales gráficas y los contextos históricos." *Ciudad y Territorio* [Madrid] 63/64 (January–June 1985), 47–54.
Lápidus, Luis, and Estrella Fuentes. "Una arquitectura para las plantas y el hombre: Jardín Botánico Nacional." *Arquitectura y Urbanismo* 6, no. 2 (1985), 48–55.
López, Omar, and Felipe Arafet. "El sistema principal de plazas en Santiago de Cuba." *Arquitectura y Urbanismo* 6, no. 1 (1985), 82–87.
Mahtar M'Bow, Amadou. "Campaña internacional para la salvaguarda de la plaza vieja de La Habana." *Ciudad y Territorio* [Madrid] 63/64 (January–June 1985), 65–72.
Murcia, Emilio. "Cartografía histórica de Cuba." Ibid., 111–12.
Nacer, Salvador, and Ricardo Fernández. "Ensayo de rehabilitación urbana en y una zona de casco histórico de Santiago de Cuba." *Arquitectura y Urbanismo* 6, no. 1 (November 1985), 88–95.

Núñez Jiménez, Antonio. "La Habana vieja: monumento nacional." *Ciudad y Territorio* [Madrid] 63/64 (January–June 1985), 55–56.
Padrón Lotti, Miguel. "Metodología de la Planificación en Cuba." Ibid., 89–94.
Pérez, Elio. "Proyecto de color para una fábrica de cerveza de Camagüey." *Arquitectura y Urbanismo* 6, no. 2 (1985), 56–59.
Pérez Rojas, Estrella. "Ownership of Land to House the Poor in Cuba." *Planning and Administration* [The Hague] 11, no. 1 (1984), 30–34.
Pi, Manuel. "Paredes ligeras: experiencias de Cuba." *Arquitectura y Urbanismo* 6, no. 2 (1985), 66–72.
Rallo, Joaquín. "Cuba: 161 centrales y una capital." *Ciudad y Territorio* [Madrid] 63/64 (January–June 1985), 5–16.
Rodríguez, Oscar Jaime. "Restauración de la casa de Don Gaspar Ribero Vasconcelos." *Arquitectura y Urbanismo* 6, no. 2 (1985), 32–35.
Royo, Elena. "Criterios para el tratamiento de los solares yermos en La Habana Vieja." *Arquitectura y Urbanismo* 6, no. 3 (1985), 16–23.
Sánchez, Antonio. "La estructura simbólica del Centro Histórico de Camagüey." Ibid., 30–41.
Segre, Roberto. "La Habana Vieja: La historia recuperada en el contexto urbano." *Homines* 10, no. 1 (January–July 1986), 319–39.
―――. "El sistema monumental de la Ciudad de La Habana: 1900–1930." *Ciudad y Territorio* [Madrid] 63/64 (January–June 1985), 17–26.
Venegas, Carlos. "La Habana Vieja: plazas y centralidad." *Temas* 8 (1986), 89–130.

Art, Cinema, Music, and Theater
Books and Monographs

Arenas, Reinaldo. *Persecución (Cinco Piezas de Teatro Experimental)*. Miami: Universal, 1986. 70 pp. [Play]
Artiles, Freddy. *Teatro*. Havana: Letras Cubanas, 1984. 370 pp.
Canet, Antonio. *Cecilia Valdés, Grabados*. Havana: Letras Cubanas, 1983. 44 pp. [Novel and engravings]
Chanan, Michael. *The Cuban Image: Cinema and Cultural Politics in Cuba*. Bloomington: Indiana University Press, 1986.
De Quesada y Miranda, Gonzalo. *Iconografía Martiana*. Havana: Editorial Letras Cubanas, 1985. 120 pp.
Dufrasne-González, J. Emanuel. "La homogeneidad de la música caribeña: sobre la música comercial y popular de Puerto Rico." Ph.D. diss., University of California, Los Angeles, 1985. 478 pp. *DAI* 46, no. 5 (November 1985): 1121-A, UM8513108. [Includes comparisons with the musical culture of Cuba.]
Fuentes, Orlirio. "El teatro de Virgilio Piñera." Ph.D. diss., City University of New York, 1985. 470 pp. *DAI* 46, no. 11 (May 1986): 3366-A, UM8601643.
González, Alfredo W. *Dos y Dos Son Cinco y Otras Cuatro Comedias*. Miami: Universal, 1984. 256 pp. [Plays]

González-Cruz, Luis F., ed. *Una caja de zapatos vacía*. Miami: Ediciones Universal, 1986. 83 pp. [Play by Virgilio Piñera]
Naser, Amín B. See *Biography*.
Piñera, Virgilio. *Una Caja de Zapatos Vacía*. Miami: Universal, 1986. [Play]
———. *"Pequeñas Maniobras" y "Presiones Diamantes."* Madrid: Ediciones Alfaguarasa, 1986. 334 pp.
Ulla, Jorge, Lawrence Ott, and Miñuca Villaverde. *Dos filmes de Mariel. El éxodo cubano de 1980*. Miami: Universal, 1986. 160 pp.

Articles and Papers

Alén, Olavo. "Music and Popular Culture: Toward a Dynamic Vision." Presented at the annual meeting of the Latin American Studies Association, Boston, October 1986.
Contreras, Félix. "La Habana en el Art Nouveau." *Bohemia* 78, no. 37 (September 12, 1986), 53–55.
Escanparter, José A. "Doscincuentenarios de Luis A. Baralt." *Linden Lane Magazine* 5, no. 2 (July–September 1986).
———. "Función del teatro en la Cuba socialista." Presented at the seminar "La cultura como factor de influencia en la sociedad socialista cubana," University of Miami, January 1986.
———. "La burguesía provinciana cubana en el teatro cubano de Manuel Reguera Saumell." *Círculo: Revista de Cultura* 15 (1986), 91–97.
———. "La memoria como salvación: *Trinidad de Cuba* de Lydia Cabrera." In *Homenaje a Lydia Cabrera,* ed. Isabel Castellanos and Josefina Inclán. Miami: Universal, 1987.
———. "Temas y estilos en el teatro de Leopoldo Hernández." Presented at the Thirty-Sixth Mountain Interstate Foreign Language Conference, Wake Forest University, Winston-Salem, N.C., October 1986.
———. "Veinticinco años de teatro cubano en el exilio." *Latin American Theater Review* 19, no. 2 (Spring 1986), 57–66.
Loyola Fernández, José. "Influencia de la música folklórica y popular cubana en la música culta contemporánea." *Unión,* 1985, no. 1, pp. 72–82.
Martínez, Juan A. "The Mythical Landscapes of a Cuban Painter: Wilfredo Lam's La Jungla." *Caribbean Review* 15, no. 2 (Spring 1986), 32–36.
Peirano, Luis. "Cine cubano, cine latinoamericano: un sueño de luchar por él: una entrevista con Jesús Díaz." *Quehacer* [Peru] 36 (August–September 1985). n.p.
Sánchez-Grey Alba, Esther. "Función de títeres y espíritus en el teatro de ideas de José Cid Pérez." *Círculo: Revista de Cultura* 15 (1986), 85–90.

Bibliography and Information Science

Books and Monographs

Academia de Ciencias de Cuba. *Indice analítico de Suplemento Literario del Diario de la Marina*. Havana: Academia de Ciencias de Cuba, 1984. 226 pp.

Camarillo, Albert, ed. See *Cubans Abroad.*
Chilcote, Ronald H., and Sheryl Lutjens, eds. *Cuba, 1953–1978: A Bibliographic Guide to the Literature.* White Plains, N.Y.: Kraus International, 1986. 2 vols. 1,378 pp.
Gomis, Redi. *Notas críticas sobre la bibliografía acerca de la comunidad cubana.* Havana: Centro de Estudios sobre América Latina, Avances de Investigación, 1985. 87 pp.
Maratos, Daniel, and D. Hill Marnesba. *Escritores de la diáspora cubana. Manual bibliográfico.* Metuchen, N.J., and London: Scarecrow Press, 1986. 391 pp.
Mota, Francisco. *Para la historia del periodismo en Cuba: un aporte bibliográfico.* Havana: Oriente, 1985. 192 pp.

Articles and Papers

"Cuba: patrimonio arquitectónico, historia y desarrollo urbano. Bibliografía." *Ciudad y Territorio* [Madrid] 63/64 (January–June 1985), p. 131.
Naranjo, Consuelo, and Elda Evangelina González. "Notas bibliográficas sobre la inmigración española a América Latina en el siglo XV: el caso de Cuba y Brasil." *Revista Española de Investigaciones Sociológicas* (April–June 1984), 215–25.
Pérez, Louis, Jr. "Twenty-Five Years of Cuban Historiography: A Retrospective." Paper presented at the annual meeting of the Latin American Studies Association, Boston, October 1986.
Pérez Guzmán, Francisco. "La historiografía de las guerras de independencia en veinticinco años de Revolución." *Revista de la Biblioteca Nacional José Martí* 27, no. 1 (January–April 1985), 41–61.
Pérez Menéndez, Alicia, and Lilian Vizcaíno González. "Breve estudio historiográfico sobre el movimiento juvenil cubano (1959–1983)." Ibid., 79–89.
Poskonina, L. S. "Stroitel'stvo sotsializma na Kube v osveshchenii burszhuaznoi istoriografii." *Voprosy istorii* 10 (October 1985), 54–68.
Zanetti Lecuona. "La historiografía de temática social (1959–1984)." *Revista de la Biblioteca Nacional José Martí* 27, no. 1 (January–April 1985), 5–17.

Biography

Books and Monographs

Abel, Christopher, and Nissa Torrents, eds. *José Martí: Revolutionary Democrat.* London: Athlone Press; Durham, N.C.: Duke University Press, 1986. 238 pp.
Alvarez Ruiz, Eladio, and José Albuerne Rivera. See *History.*
Baeza Flores, Alberto. *Vida de José Martí.* Santo Domingo: Editorial Industrias de Artes Gráficas Ril, 1986. 798 pp.
Cabalé Ruiz, Manolo. *Teófilo Stevenson.* Havana: Editorial Científico Técnica, 1985. 144 pp. [On the life of one of the greatest amateur athletes in Cuba.]

Calixto Bernal. Su tiempo y su obra. Madrid: Playor, 1986. 23 pp.
Chao, Ramón. *Palabras en el Tiempo de Alejo Carpentier.* Miami: Universal, 1984. 250 pp.
Guillén, Nicolás. *Martín Morua Delgado.* Havana: Unión, 1985. 36 pp. [Stories]
Hernández-Bauza, Miguel. *Biografía de una emoción popular: El Dr. Grau.* Miami: Universal, 1986.
Infiesta, Ramón. *Máximo Gómez.* Santo Domingo: Editorial Industria de Artes Gráficas Ril, 1986. 228 pp.
Márquez Sterling, Carlos. *A la ingerencia extraña la virtud doméstica. (Biografía de Manuel Márquez Sterling).* Miami: Universal, 1986. 267 pp.
Miranda Fernández, Lucinda. *Lázaro Peña, capitán de la clase obrera cubana.* Havana: Ciencias Sociales, 1984. 386 pp.
Naser, Amín B. *Benny More.* Havana: Unión, 1985. 234 pp.
Sánchez, Juan. *Fidelio Ponce.* Havana: Editorial Letras Cubanas, 1985. 144 pp. [Life of the Cuban artist Fidelio Ponce.]
Souza, Benigno. *Máximo Gómez: El Generalísimo.* Santo Domingo: Editorial Universidad Autónoma de Santo Domingo, 1986. 253 pp.
Szulc, Tad. *Fidel: A Critical Portrait.* New York: William Morrow, 1986. 703 pp.
Triana, Fausto. *Braudilio Vinent. La fama de la consistencia.* Havana: Editorial Científico Técnica, 1985. 112 pp. [On the life of baseball pitcher Braudilio Vinent.]

Articles and Monographs

Mirónov, Vladímir. "Ernesto Che Guevara: hombre-revolución. (Segunda Parte)." *América Latina* [Moscow] 4 (April 1986), 56–74.
Poyo, Gerald E. "José Martí: Architect of Social Unity in the Cuban Emigre Communities in the United States." In *José Martí: Revolutionary Democrat,* ed. Christopher Abel and Nissa Torrents. London: Athlone Press; Durham: Duke University Press, 1986.
Torrents, Nissa. "Order and Passion in *Amistad Funesta.*" In ibid., 176–91.

Cubans Abroad

Books and Monographs

Anderson, Annelise. *Illegal Aliens and Employers' Sanctions: Solving the Wrong Problem.* Stanford, Calif.: Stanford University, Hoover Institution, 1986. 27 pp. [Reference to Mariel's Cubans.]
Gann, L. H., and Peter J. Duignan. *The Hispanics in the United States: A History.* Boulder, Colo.: Westview, 1986. 500 pp. [Includes a chapter on Cubans.]
Camarillo, Albert, ed. *Latinos in the United States: A Historical Bibliography.* Santa Barbara, Calif.: ABC-CLIO, 1986. 350 pp.
Downing, Douglas Charles. See *Architecture and Urban Development.*

Duany, Jorge Luis. "The Cubans in Puerto Rico: Socioeconomic Adaptation in a Caribbean City." Ph.D. diss., University of California, Berkeley, 1985. *DAI* 46, no. 9 (March 1986): 2732-A, UM8524938.

Gomis, Redi. See *Bibliography and Information Science*.

Loredo, Rómulo. *Las mil y unas noches guajiras*. Havana: Editorial Unión, 1985. 572 pp. [Play]

Martínez, Milton M. *Los otros marielitos*. New Orleans: Dixie Printing and Supply, 1985. 130 pp.

Masud-Piloto, Félix Roberto. "The Political Dynamics of the Cuban Migration to the United States, 1959–1980." Ph.D. diss., Florida State University, 1985. 253 pp. *DAI* 47, no. 1 (July 1986): 285-A, UM8605780.

Prieto, Yolanda. See *Women*.

Sanders, Joseph Paul. "The Impact of Migration and Other Variables on the Physical and Mental Health of Hispanic Migrants to Boston." Ph.D. diss., Boston College, 1986. 633 pp. *DAI* 46, no. 12 (June 1986): 3873-A, UM8604117. [Deals in part with Cuban-Americans.]

Santos, Belkis M. "An In-Depth Assessment of the Educational Involvement of Selected Hispanic Parents and Community Leaders in the Development and Implementation of a Desegregation Plan for the Chicago Public Schools." Ph.D. diss., Loyola University of Chicago, 1986. 290 pp. *DAI* 47. no. 1 (July 1986): 45-A, UM8605558. [Includes some information about Cuban-Americans.]

Silva, Helga. *The Children of Mariel from Shock to Integration: Cuban Refugee Children in South Florida Schools*. Washington, D.C.: Cuban American National Foundation, 1985. 65 pp.

Soruco, Carlos Rafael. "Marketing Television Programs in the United States: The Case of the Hispanic Audience." Ph.D. diss., Indiana University, 1985. 216 pp. *DAI* 46, no. 10 (April 1986): 2848-A, UM8527035. [Concerned in part with Cubans in the United States.]

Starret, Richard Alton. "The Utilization of Social Services by the Hispanic Elderly Population." Ph.D. diss., University of Texas, Arlington, 1983. 348 pp. *DAI* 45, no. 9 (March 1985), 2724-A, UM8426843. [Includes Cuban-Americans.]

Subervi-Velez, Federico Antonio. "Hispanics, the Mass Media, and Politics: Assimilation vs. Pluralism." Ph.D. diss., University of Wisconsin, Madison, 1984. 357 pp. *DAI* 45, no. 8 (February 1985), 2293-A, UM8410803.

Thompson, Sylvia Ann. "Community Leadership in Greater Miami, Florida: What Role for Blacks and Cuban-Americans?" Ph.D. diss., Southern Illinois University, Carbondale, 1985. 457 pp. *DAI* 46, no. 11 (May 1986): 3479-A, UM8526741.

"The Rights of Cuban Refugees . . ." See *Law and Human Rights*.

Articles and Papers

Cobas, José A. "Ethnic Enclaves and Middleman Minorities: Alternative Strategies of Immigrant Adaptation?" *Sociological Perspectives* 30 (April 1987). [Concerns Cuban immigrants.]

———. "Puerto Rican Reactions to Cuban Immigrants: Insights from Trading Minority Interpretations." *Ethnic and Racial Studies* 9 (October 1986), 530–36.
Dixon, Heriberto. "The Cuban-American Counterpoint: Black Cubans in the United States." Presented at the International Symposium on the Cultural Expression of Hispanics in the United States, Association for the Diffusion and Study of Latin Cultures in North America, Paris, March 1986.
Hernández, Rafael, and Redi Gomis. "Retrato de Mariel: el ángulo socioeconómico." *Cuadernos de Nuestra América* 3, no. 5 (January–June 1986), 124–51.
Mendoza, Manuel G. "The Third Wave." *Mariel Magazine* 1, no. 1 (1986), 12–14. [On Cuban refugees.]
Pérez, Lisandro. "Cubans in the United States." *Annals of the American Academy of Political and Social Science* 487 (September 1986), 126–37.
———. "Immigrant Economic Adjustment and Family Organization: The Cuban Success Story Reexamined." *International Migration Review* 20, no. 1 (Spring 1986), 4–20.
Portes, Alejandro, and Robert D. Manning. "The Immigrant Enclave: Theory and Empirical Examples." In *Competitive Ethnic Relations*, 47–68. New York: Academic Press, 1986.
Portes, Alejandro, and Rafael Moro. "The Political Adaptation Process of Cubans and Other Ethnic Minorities in the United States: A Preliminary Analysis." *International Migration Review* 19, no. 1 (1986), 35–63.
Portes, Alejandro, and Alex Stepick. "Unwelcome Immigrants: The Labor Market Experiences of 1980 (Mariel) Cuban and Haitian Refugees in South Florida." *American Sociological Review* 50 (August 1985), 493–514.
Portes, Alejandro, Alex Stepick, and Cynthia Truelove. "Three Years Later: The Adaptation Process of 1980 (Mariel) Cuban Refugees in South Florida." *Population Research and Policy Review* 5 (1986), 83–94.
Poyo, Gerald E. "Cuban-Americans in Historical Perpective. Toward a Structural Understanding." Paper presented at the annual meeting of the Latin American Studies Association, Boston, October, 1986.
———. "The 'Exile' Identity in the Cuban American Community." Ibid.
———. See also *Biography*.

Demography, Medicine, and Public Health

Books and Monographs

Alvarez Vásquez, Luisa. *La Fecundidad en Cuba*. Havana: Ciencias Sociales, 1985. 184 pp.
Atlas demográfico nacional. Havana: Comité Estatal de Estadísticas, Instituto Cubano de Cartografía, 1985. 117 pp.
Colectivo de especialistas de salud pública. See *Women*.
Comité Estatal de Estadísticas. *Principales aspectos demográficos de la población cubana en el año 1984*. Havana: Instituto de Investigaciones Estadísticas, 1985. 57 pp.

———. See also *Statistics*.
Masud-Piloto, Félix Roberto. See *Cubans Abroad*.
Starrett, Richard Alton. See *Cubans Abroad*.
Valdivie Navarro, Manuel I. "Uber Energie- und Proteinkonzentrationen in Broilerrationen in Kuba." Dissertation B., Universität Rostock [East Germany], 1983. 188 + 104 pp.

Articles and Papers

Bisset Lazcano, J. A., M. C. Marquetti, B. González, M. E. Mendizabal, and A. Navarro. "Abundance of Larvae of Urban Mosquitoes During the Campaign of the Eradication of *Aedes asgypt* (Linnaeus, 1792) and of dengue of Cuba (1981–82)." *Revista Cubana de Medicina Tropical* 37, no. 2 (May–August 1985), 161–68. [In Spanish]
Boxer, P. A., and J. T. Garvey. "Psychiatric Diagnoses of Cuban Refugees in the United States: Findings of Medical Review Boards." *American Journal of Psychiatry* 142, no. 1 (January 1985), 86–89.
Colombo B., and G. Martínez. "Hemoglobin Variants in Cuba." *Hemoglobin* 9, no. 4 (1985), 415–22.
Díaz-Briquets, Sergio. "How to Figure Out Cuba: Development, Ideology and Mortality." *Caribbean Review* 15, no. 2 (Spring 1986), 8–11, 39–42.
Eberstadt, Nicholas. "Did Fidel Fudge the Figures? Literacy and Health: The Cuban Model." Ibid., 5–7, 37–38.
Farnós Morejón, Alfonso. See *Women*.
Fernández Padilla, Rigoberto. See *Economics, Industry, and Planning*.
Foreman, J. T. "Susto and the Health Needs of the Cuban Refugee Population." *Topics in Clinical Nursing* 7, no. 3 (October 1985), 40–47.
González Quiñonez, Fernando. See *Women*.
Kourí, Gustavo, María G. Guzmán, and José Bravo. "Dengue hemorrágico en Cuba, ciencia de una epidemia." *Boletín de la Oficina Sanitaria Panamericana* 100, no. 3 (March 1986), 309–19.
Kourí, Gustavo, María G. Guzmán, and José Bravo. "Hemorrhagic Dengue in Cuba: History of an Epidemic." *Bulletin of the Pan American Health Organization* 20, no. 1 (1986), 24–30.
Lowenthal, A. S., C. Dawson, and B. B. Lowenthal. "Psychology and Human Services in Cuba: Personal Perspectives." *Journal of Community Psychology* 13, no. 2 (April 1985), 105–16.
Martínez, G., R. Ferreira, A. Hernández, A. di Rienzo, and L. Felicetti. "Molecular Characterization of HbH Disease in the Cuban Population." *Human Genetics* 72, no. 4 (April 1986), 318–19.
Martínez Rodríguez, R., J. C. Millán Marcelo, A. Ramos García, A. Díaz Hernández, J. Pérez Avila, and A. Pérez Rodríguez. "Presentation of the First Case in Cuba of Imported and Reported *Schistsomiasis mansoni*." *Revista Cubana de Medicina Tropical* 37, no. 2 (May–August 1985), 183–86. [In Spanish]
Montijo, J. A., B. I. Ruiz, H. L. Aponte, and D. Monllor. "The Puerto Rican

and Cuban Public Health Systems: A Comparison." *Journal of Community Psychology* 13, no. 2 (April 1985), 204–11.
Pasquali, E. A. "Santería: A Religion That Is a Health Care System for Long Island Cuban Americans." *Journal of the New York State Nurses Association* 17, no. 1 (April 1986), 12–15.
Pérez Stable, E. J. "Community Medicine in Cuba." *Journal of Community Psychology* 13, no. 2 (April 1985), 124–37.
Roque, Roberto. "El problema de la tipología de actividades del presupuesto de tiempo de la población cubana." *Temas* 8 (1986), 5–40.
Santana, Sarah. "Cuban Health Policy and Performance." Presented at the annual meeting of the Latin American Studies Association, Boston, October 1986.
Serret Miguel, Miriam, Bertha R. Valdés, and José M. Parapar de la Riesta. See *Education*.
Silver, L. B., B. J. Silver, M. M. Silverman, W. Prescott, and L. del Pollard. "The Cuban Immigration of 1980: A Special Mental Health Challenge." *Public Health Reports* 100, no. 1 (January–February 1985), 40–48.
Tesh, Sylvia. "Health Education in Cuba: A Preface." *International Journal of Health Services* 16, no. 1 (1986), 87–104.

Documents

Books and Monographs

Castro, Fidel. *Fidel Castro on Chile*. New York: Pathfinder Press, 1985. 158 pp.
———. *Fidel Castro: Speeches. War and Crisis in the Americas 1984–85*. New York: Pathfinder Press, 1986. 268 pp.
———. See *Women*.
Elliot, Jeffrey, and Mervin Dymally. *Fidel Castro: Nothing Can Stop the Course of History*. New York: Pathinder Press, 1986. 258 pp.
Legislación Económica. Havana: Ciencias Sociales, 1984. 348 pp.
Rodríguez Demorizi, Emilio. *Cartas de Máximo Gómez*. Santo Domingo: Editorial Mograf S.A., Taller Gráfico, 1986. 77 pp.
Taber, Michael, ed. *War and Crisis in the Americas: Fidel Castro Speeches*. New York: Pathfinder Press, 1985. 272 pp.

Articles and Papers

Castro, Fidel. "Discurso en el Encuentro sobre la Deuda Externa de la América Latina y el Caribe." *Casa de las Américas* 26, no. 153 (November–December 1985), 4–29.
"Cuba-United States: Agreement on Immigration Procedures and the Return of Cuban Nationals" [New York, December 14, 1984]. *International Legal Materials* 24, no. 1 (January 1985), 32–37.
"Discurso pronunciado por el Comandante en Jefe Fidel Castro Ruz en la graduación de los alumnos del Instituto de Enseñanza Primaria." *Educación* 16, no. 59 (October–December 1985), 3–20.

Domínguez, Jorge I. See *Foreign Relations*.
"Proyecto del programa del partido comunista de Cuba (Segunda parte. Capítulos 8 y 9)." *Bohemia* 78, no. 38 (September 19, 1986), 76–78.
Skoug, Kenneth N., Jr. "A Spotlight on Cuba." Current Policy no. 881. Washington, D.C.: U.S. Department of State, Bureau of Public Affairs, 1986. 4 pp.
U.S. Department of State. "U.S., Cuba Resume Normal Migration." *Department of State Bulletin* 85, no. 2095 (February 1985), 44–46.
"White House Tapes and Minutes of the Cuban Missile Crisis." *International Security* 10 (Summer 1985), 164–70.

Economics, Industry, and Planning
Books and Monographs
Azicri, Max. *Cuba—Politics, Economics, and Society*. London: Frances Pinter, 1987.
Banco Nacional de Cuba/Comité Estatal de Estadísticas. *Cuba: Quarterly Economic Report, June 1985*. Havana: Comité Estadístico de Cuba, 1985. 31 pp.
———. *Cuba: Quarterly Economic Report, September 1985*. Havana: Comité Estadístico de Cuba, 1985. 31 pp.
Comisión Económica Para América Latina (CEPAL). *Estudio económico de América Latina y el Caribe, 1984: Cuba. Versión preliminar*. Santiago: CEPAL, 1985. 34 pp.
———. *Notas para el estudio económico de América Latina y el Caribe, 1984: Cuba*. Mexico City: CEPAL, 1985. 72 pp.
Comité Estadístico de Cuba. See *Statistics*.
Cruz, Carlos. "Phasenanalyse an eisenhaltigen Ruckstanden der Kubanischen Nickelproduktion." Dissertation B., Akademie der Wissenschaften der DDR, Berlin [East Germany], 1981. 116 pp.
Gutiérrez, Tania. See *Labor and Unions*.
Leahy, Margaret E. See *Women*.
Legislación Económica. See *Documents*.
Leuchter, Wolfang. "Grundfragen der Herausbildung der materiell-technischen Basis des Sozialismus und des Systems der Leitung und Planung der Volkswirtschaft in Kuba." Dissertation B., Universität Rostock [East Germany], 1985. 434 pp.
Marshall, Peter, and Barry Lewis. *Into Cuba*. New York: Alfred Van der Marck Editions, 1986. 192 pp.
Mesa-Lago, Carmelo, and Pérez-López, Jorge F. *A Study of Cuba's Material Product System*. . . . World Bank Staff Working Paper no. 770. Washington, D.C.: World Bank, 1985. 104 pp.
Moral García, Jorge. "Bedingungen für den rationellen Umschlag von Containern in Kubanischen Seehafen, untersucht am Beispiel des Hafens Havanna." Dissertation A., Universität Rostock [East Germany], 1984. 316 pp.

Ojeda Fagundo, Aurelio. "Entwicklung neuer Methoden zur Futterplanung und-bilanzierung in Kuba." Dissertation A., Humboldt-Universität zu Berlin [East Germany], 1985. 86 + 4 pp.
Pérez, Lisandro. See *Cubans Abroad.*
Radio Martí. Department of Research and Policy. *Cuba Annual Report: 1985.* New Brunswick, N.J.: Transaction Books, 1986. 400 pp.
Rodríguez García, José L. *Dos ensayos sobre la economía cubana.* Havana: Ciencias Sociales, n.d.
Sloan, John W. *Public Policy in Latin America. A Comparative Survey.* Pittsburgh, Pa.: University of Pittsburgh Press, 1984. 250 pp. [Chapter 6 compares development strategies in Cuba and Brazil.]
Tan, C. Suan. *Cuba-USSR Sugar Trade.* Division Working Paper no. 1986-2 (June 1986). Washington, D.C.: Economic Analysis and Projection Department, World Bank, 1986. 70 pp.
Zimbalist, Andrew, ed. *Cuba's Socialist Economy Toward the 1990s.* Special Issue of *World Development.* Elmsford, N.Y.: Pergamon Press, 1986.

Articles and Papers

Abouchar, Alan. "The Treatment of Intermediate Goods in Cuban National Income Accounts: Parallels and Differences with the Soviet Methodology." *Comparative Economic Studies* 28 (Summer 1986), 37–48.
Aldana Martínez, Jorge. "Los ferrocarriles como manifestación del desarrollo capitalista en Cuba (1837–1898)." *Santiago* [Cuba] 56 (December 1984), 133–67.
Armenteros, Marta, and Rolando Vergara. "El análisis del costo de la producción en la empressa industrial." *Economía y Desarrollo* 90 (January–February 1986), 11–25.
Armenteros, Marta, and Rolando Vergara. "Normas de consumo en el sector de la construcción en Pinar del Río." *Economía y Desarrollo* 88 (September–October 1985), 10–22.
Averhoff, Alberto. "Principios básicos de la planificación de la producción agrícola." *Economía y Desarrollo* 89 (November–December 1985), 11–19.
Brundenius, Claes. "Development of the Capital Goods." Presented at the annual meeting of the Latin American Studies Association, Boston, October 1986.
———. "The Controversy Over Cuban Economic Growth with Equity: Settled and Unsettled Issues." Ibid.
———. "Equity and Growth in the Economic Development of Cuba." Ibid.
Cabrera, Olga. "Las ideas económicas de Guiteras." *Santiago* 57 (March 1985), 149–64.
Cruz Pérez, Ramón, Martha R. López, and Amalia Bocanegra. "Algunos elementos sobre el análisis de los fondos básicos." *Economía y Desarrollo* 88 (September–October 1985), 23–33.
Debrosse, Martía E., and Rosalía Martínez. "Sobre la regionalización económica y la planificación territorial." Ibid., 34–45.

Díaz, Elena, and Martha Núñez. "América Latina-Cuba: desarrollo y calidad de vida." *Cuadernos de Nuestra América* 3, no. 5 (January–June 1986), 152–70.

Díaz Balaguer, Rafael. "Esencia del presupuesto estatal de Cuba y su significación en el desarrollo económico y social del país." *Economía y Desarrollo* 90 (January–February 1986), 27–37.

Díaz Vázquez, Julio A. "La producción de azúcar, cítricos y níquel en el desarrollo perspectivo de la economía cubana." *Economía y Desarrollo* 91 (March–April 1986), 11–19.

Eckstein, Susan. "Comment on Chapter 12/Carmelo Mesa-Lago." In *Latin American Political Economy: Financial Crisis and Political Change*, ed. Jonathan Hartlyn and Samuel A. Morley, 292–318. Boulder, Colo.: Westview, 1986.

———. "The Impact of the Cuban Revolution: A Comparative Perspective." *Comparative Studies in Society and History* 28, no. 3 (July 1986), 502–34.

———. "On Socialist Fiscal Crisis. Lessons From Cuba." Presented at the American Sociological Association Meeting, New York, September 1986. 39 pp.

Fernández, Austín, and Lilliam Pla. "El comercio exterior y la construcción del socialismo en Cuba." *Economía y Desarrollo* 90 (January–February 1986), 39–49.

Fernández Padilla, Rigoberto. "Variables económicas y demográficas: elementos para la elaboración de un modelo de fecundidad." *Revista Estadística* 8, no. 17 (December 1985), 4–34.

Feuer, Carl Henry. "The Performance of the Cuban Sugar Industry, 1981–1985." *World Development*, December 1986.

———. See also *Agriculture, Labor and Unions*.

Fields, Gary. "Economic Development and Housing Policy in Cuba." *Berkeley Planning Journal* 2, nos. 1–2 (1985), 53–80.

García, María de los A. "Consideraciones sobre el crédito bancario a corto plazo y su aplicación en empresas de Santiago de Cuba." *Economía y Desarrollo* 89 (November–December 1985), 21–33.

Gedda, G. "Canceling the Debt." *Foreign Service Journal*, November 1985, 20–23. [On Cuban external debt.]

Gómez, Félix R. "Fondos de estimulación económica en las empresas de la economía cubana." *Economía y Desarrollo* 90 (January–February 1986), 77–89.

González, Pedro Luis. "Algunas consideraciones sobre la normación del consumo energético." *Economía y Desarrollo* 91 (March–April 1986), 21–31. [On energy consumption in Cuba.]

González, Raúl. "La posición cubana." *Quehacer* [Peru] 36 (August–September 1985), 25–32. [On Latin American external debt.]

González, Roberto, and Héctor Ayala. "El período de transición: la experiencia cubana (I)." *Economía y Desarrollo* 90 (January–February 1986), 101–19.

González, Roberto, and Héctor Ayala. "El período de transición: la experiencia cubana (II)." *Economía y Desarrollo* 91 (March–April 1986), 33–45.
Henríquez, Lysette. "Cuba: sistema de dirección y planificación de la economía". *Pensamiento Iberoamericano* 8 (July–December 1985), 452–59. [Review article]
Hernández, Amalio, and Javier Camargo. "Una metodología para definir el campo económico de acción entre los medios de transportación interprovincial de pasajeros en la República de Cuba." *Economía y Desarrollo* 91 (March–April 1986), 63–73.
Hernández, Raquel, Martha Chávez, and Sandra González. "Los presupuestos de gastos y su papel en la planificación del costo de producción." Ibid., 47–61. [On the role of expenditures budgets in production cost planning.]
Infante, Maira, Jorge L. Bouza, and Nicolás Labintzev. "Algunas consideraciones del perfeccionamiento de la contabilidad y del análisis de las pérdidas por producción defectuosa en las empresas industriales." Ibid., 75–83. [On improvements in accounting and analysis of losses due to defective production in industrial enterprises.]
Ivanovich, Vitaly, and Marlinda Clark. "El aumento de la eficiencia económica como ley económica, y su interrelación con el sistema de leyes económicas del socialismo." Ibid., 85–95. [On increased economic efficiency in the Cuban economy.]
Kroupa, Olga Y. "Aspectos sobre la concentración y especialización de las empresas constructoras del Ministerio de la Construcción." *Economía y Desarrollo* 88 (September–October 1985), 211–17.
Larrea, Raúl. "Notas sobre el perfeccionamiento de la planificación en la industria mecánica en Cuba." Ibid., 92–103.
León, Laureano, et al. See *Foreign Relations.*
Levine, Barry B. "Rethinking Cuba." *Caribbean Review* 15, no. 2 (Spring 1986), 3.
López, Della Luisa. See *Ideology.*
MacDonald, Scott B., and F. Joseph Demetrius. "The Caribbean Sugar Crisis: Consequences and Challenges." *Journal of Inter-American Affairs* 28, no. 1 (Spring 1986)), 1–58. [Deals in part with Cuba.]
Ma Sa. "External Economic Policies of Cuba." *Latin American Studies* [Japan] no. 2 (1986), 46–50.
Mesa-Lago, Carmelo. "Cuba's Centrally Planned Economy: An Equity Trade-off for Growth." In *Latin American Political Economy: Financial Crisis and Political Change,* ed. Jonathan Hartlyn and Samuel A. Morley. Boulder, Colo.: Westview, 1986.
———. "Economic Development in Socialist Cuba." Presented at the annual meeting of the Latin American Studies Association, Boston, October 1986.
Morales, Eliodoro, and Enrique Rodríguez. "La duración de la zafra y su efecto en la eficiencia agroindustrial." *Economía y Desarrollo* 91 (March–April 1986), 97–101. [On the duration of Cuba's sugar harvest and its effects on agroindustrial efficiency.]

Packenham, Robert A. "Capitalist vs. Socialist Dependency: The Case of Cuba." *Journal of Inter-American Affairs* 28, no. 1 (Spring 1986), 59–92.
Palazuelos Manso, Enrique. "La balanza de pagos entre Cuba y España." *Revista CIDOB d'AFERS INTERNACIONALS* (Spring 1986), 19–48.
Paulo Evaristo, Cardenal Ars, Archbishop of São Paulo. See *Foreign Relations*.
Pérez, Reinaldo. "Algunas cuestiones sobre la planificación del nivel de vida." *Economía y Desarrollo* 91 (March–April 1986), 103–07. [On standard-of-living planning in Cuba.]
Pérez-López, Jorge F. "Cuba as an Oil Trader: Petroleum Deal in a Falling Market." *Caribbean Review* 15, no. 2 (Spring 1986), 26–29, 43–44.
———. "Cuban Economic Performance During 1981–85. Prospects for 1986–90." Ocassional Paper no. 12. *Cuba After the Third Party Congress. Selected Essays,* 11–33. Washington, D.C.: Central American and Caribbean Program, School of Advanced International Studies, Johns Hopkins University, 1986.
———. "Studies of the Cuban Economy." Presented at the annual meeting of the Latin American Studies Association, October 1986.
Pollitt, Brian H. "The Cuban Sugar Economy and the Great Depression." *Bulletin of Latin American Research* 3, no. 2 (1984), 3–28.
Posada, Carlos. "¿Economía del turismo o economía en el turismo? *Economía y Desarrollo* 91 (March–April 1986), 211–31. [On tourism and the Cuban economy.]
Rabaza, Francisco. "Las brigadas de producción en el sector de construcciones básicas." Ibid., 119–43. [On production brigades in the basic construction sector.]
Rodríguez, José Luis. "Los efectos de la reforma agraria sobre el campesinado en Cuba." Ibid., 145–73. [On the effects of land reform on Cuban farmers.]
———. "El desarrollo económico de Cuba y sus perspectivas para el futuro." In *Cuba—Estados Unidos: dos enfoques,* ed. Juan G. Tokatlian, 201–47. Bogotá: CEREC and Grupo Editor Latino Americano, 1984.
Rodríguez García, José Luis. "La estrategia de desarrollo de Cuba socialista." Presented at the annual meeting of the Latin American Studies Association, Boston, October 1986.
Ruiz Caro, Ariela. "Plan Baker: una respuesta a Alan García y a Fidel Castro." *Quehacer* [Peru] 38 (December 1985–January 1986), 23–27.
———. "La reunión de Habana: cielo o infierno: el escenario es cualquiera." *Quehacer* [Peru] 36 (August–September 1985), 15–24.
Salazar-Carrillo, Jorge. "Is the Cuban Economy Knowable? A National Accounting Parable." *Caribbean Review* 15, no. 2 (Spring 1986), 24–25.
Salgado, José M., Orestes Gámez and Marcio Suárez. "Las inversiones: conceptos básicos y tratamiento contable." *Economía y Desarrollo* 91 (March–April 1986), 175–93.
Sánchez Robert, Gerardo. "La renegociación de la deuda externa cubana." *Santiago* [Cuba] 56 (December 1984), 9–74.

Silva, Julio. "La interpretación de la inflación contemporánea ante la ley del valor-trabajo y la formulación de una teoría explicativa." *Economía y Desarrollo* 90 (January–February 1986), 161–87.
Stubbs, Jean. See *Women*.
Torres, Miguel, and Raúl Carballosa. "Análisis crítico de algunos planteamientos de la cubanología burguesa sobre la economía cubana." *Economía y Desarrollo* 89 (November–December 1985), 201–15.
Villar Roberto. "Participación de Cuba en la integración económica socialista. Su papel y su lugar." *Economía y Desarrollo* 88 (September–October 1985), 204–10.
Zimbalist, Andrew. "Twisting Statistics to Attack Cuba." *Cuba Times* 5, no. 2 (January–February 1985), 15–16.
―――. "Cuban Industrial Growth, 1965–1985." *World Development*, December 1986.
―――. "Cuban Industrial Growth." Presented at the annual meeting of the Latin American Studies Association, Boston, October 1986.
―――. "Introduction: Cuba's Socialist Economy toward the 1990s." *World Development*, December 1986.
Zimbalist, Andrew, and Claes Brundenius. "Cuban Economic Growth: A Final Word." *Comparative Economic Studies*, Winter 1985.
Zimbalist, Andrew, and Susan Eckstein. "Patterns of Cuban Development: The First Twenty-Five Years." *World Development*, December 1986.

Education

Books and Monographs

Almendros, Herminio. *La escuela moderna ¿Reacción o progreso?* Havana: Editorial Ciencias Sociales, 1985. 164 pp. [On the Cuban Revolution's success in education.]
Eng, Luisa. See *Women*.
Ponce Ortiz, María. See *Women*.
Román Hernández, Jorge. *La elección de la profesión en estudiantes de la enseñanza media*. Havana: Academia, 1982. 78 pp.
Silva, Helga. See *Cubans Abroad*.
Simpson, Renate. *La educación superior en Cuba bajo el colonialismo español*. Havana: Editorial de las Ciencias Sociales, 1984. 314 pp.

Articles and Papers

Chávez Rodríguez, Justo. "La educación escolarizada en Cuba en la etapa de 1510 a 1790." *Educación* 14, no. 55 (October–December 1984), 31–40.
Crespo, Elba. "El plan de investigación del Ministerio de Educación en marcha." *Educación* 14, no. 53 (April–June 1984), 24–31.
Eberstadt, Nicholas. See *Demography, Medicine, and Public Health*.
Febles, Mier. "Vinculación ideológica de la ciencia con la docencia." *Educación* 14, no. 55 (October–December 1984), 10–25.

Fernández, J. R. "Intervención de J. R. Fernández, Ministro de Educación, en la clausura de la III Jornada Pedagógica Nacional." *Educación* 13, no. 51 (October–December 1983), 3–11.

Fernández, José R. "Desarrollo de la educación en Cuba. Tema de Pedagogía 86." *Educación* 16, no. 61 (April–June 1986), 3–37. [Closing speech in "Pedagogía 86."]

Frometa López, Onix, Ariel Velázquez Sánchez, José M. Recalde Rivero, and Jorge López Cuesta. "La organización de la enseñanza práctica en el centro politécnico Villena—Revolución." *Educación* 16, no. 60 (January–March 1986), 57–64.

González Castro, Vicente. "La comunicación oral en las clases: algunas ideas de Martí." *Educación* 14, no. 53 (April–June 1984), 19–23.

Hernández Lima, Elida. "Papel de la escuela en la formación de los gustos e ideales estéticos de los escolares primarios." *Educación* 15, no. 59 (October–December 1985), 79–90.

Hernández Mujica, Jorge L. "Apuntes sobre el desarrollo de una ciencia en Cuba." *Educación* 13, no. 50 (July–September 1983), 85–99.

Isa, Moreno, and Norberto Pompa Espinosa. "Los consejos de escuela: experiencia de su funcionamiento en la Provincia de Matanzas." *Educación* 15, no. 56 (January–March 1985), 77–80.

Loforte Estévez, Beatriz. "Las tradiciones patriótico militares y laborales en Cuba y la educación comunista de los estudiantes del ISP 'José Martí.' " *Educación* 15, no. 57 (April–June 1985), 111–15.

López, Josefina, and Ana María Siverio. "Estudio experimental de la preparación del niño en zonas rurales." *Educación* 14, no. 55 (October–December 1984), 54–61.

Machado Ramírez, Evelio, and Mirtha Dipoté Drake. "El trabajo científico en los departamentos de idiomas extranjeras de los institutos superiores pedagógicos y su vinculación con la escuela media." *Educación* 14, no. 52 (January–March 1984), 108–14.

Mier Febles, Juan. "José Martí, el hombre necesario." *Educación* 13, no. 51 (October–December 1983), 62–75.

Miranda, Jacinto. "La transformación radical del sistema nacional de educación, uno de los más grandes logros de la Revolución." *Educación* 14, no. 53 (April–June 1984), 76–82.

Morales Pita, Antonio E. "Experiencias investigativas multidisciplinarias profesor-alumno en el MINAZ." *Revista Cubana de Educación Superior* 5, no. 1 (1985), 14–22.

Nápoles Padrón, Elsa, Marina Alexandrova, and Carlos Alvarez de Zayas. "Método para determinar la actitud comunista ante el trabajo en las prácticas de producción del estudiante universitario." *Revista Cubana de Educación Superior* 5, no. 1 (1985), 53–60.

Ortíz Díaz, María Dolores. See *Women*.

Pacheco Alvarez, Farah. "Los círculos infantiles: una hermosa obra de la revolución." *Educación* 16, no. 60 (January–March 1986), 6–13.

Pita Céspedes, Balbina. "Licenciatura en educación primaria." *Educación* 16, no. 59 (October–December 1985), 29–32.
Puig López, Zenaida. 'Enrique José Varona y la reforma de la enseñanza secundaria y universitaria en Cuba." *Educación* 14, no. 52 (January–March 1984), 97–107.
Rafael Vásquez, Barbara. "La formación del personal docente en las condiciones de la revolución cubana." *Educación* 16, no. 61 (April–June 1986), 40–55.
Rodríguez Cosío, Magaly, and Dulce Betancourt Boada. "La formación de colectivos en las aulas de enseñanza media." *Educación* 14, no. 53 (April–June 1984), 84–95.
Romero Sotolongo, Benito. "Algunas consideraciones sobre el sistema de ingreso a los cursos regulares de trabajadores." *Revista Cubana de Educación Superior* 5, no. 1 (1985), 73–81.
Rudnikas Katz, Bertha. "El estudio de la obra de José Martí en los programas de lectura y literatura de la educación general politécnica y laboral." *Educación* 13, no. 50 (July–September 1983), 31–51.
Ruiz Aguilera, Ariel. "Fortalecimiento de la política de la educación física y deportiva escolar como necesidad socio-político del país." *Educación* 13, no. 51 (October–December 1983), 99–107.
Santana Henríquez, Mirta. "Ajustes introducidos en los primeros grados de la educación primaria." *Educación* 16, no. 61 (April–June 1986), 56–62.
Serret Miguel, Miriam, Bertha R. Valdés, and José M. Parapar de la Riestra. "Algunas opiniones de los alumnos de 1er. año de medicina sobre la práctica de familiarización, curso 1981–1982." *Revista Cubana de Educación Superior* 5, no. 1 (1985), 23–34.
Súper Rojas, José Ramón, and Oneida Casuso Hernández. "Una experiencia innovadora en los institutos de perfeccionamiento educacional: El forum científico de estudiantes." *Educación* 15, no. 58 (July–September 1985), 96–105.
"Tareas principales del Ministerio de Educación para el curso escolar 1984–85." *Educación* 14, no. 54 (July–September 1984), 40–45.
Velázquez Pérez, Xiomara. " 'Augusto César Sandino', ejemplo de secundaria básica en el campo." *Educación* 14, no. 52 (January–March 1984), 35–46.

Foreign Relations

Books and Monographs

Allai, Joe Terence. "Cuban Foreign Policy in the Caribbean: Analytical Problems and Perspectives." M.A. thesis, University of Manitoba, 1982. *Canadian Theses on Microfiche Service,* no. 54606.
Balari, Eugenio R. *Cuba—USA: Crossed Words.* Havana: Editorial Ciencias Sociales, 1986. 269 pp.
Dickson, Thomas Victor. See *Ideology.*
Dymally, Mervyn M., and Jeffrey M. Elliot. *Cuba in Transition: A New Force*

in the Western Hemisphere. San Bernardino, Calif.: Borgo Press, 1986. 160 pp.

González, Edward, and David Ronfeldt. *Castro, Cuba, and the World: Executive Summary.* Santa Monica, Calif.: Rand, 1986. 22 pp.

Hollander, Paul. See *Politics, Government, and Armed Forces.*

Kopilow, David J. *Castro, Israel, and the PLO.* Washington, D.C.: Cuban American National Foundation, 1985. 46 pp.

Kozar, Paul Michael. See *Politics, Government and Armed Forces.*

Moore, Carlos. *El Caribe y la política exterior de la revolución cubana, 1959–1963.* Puerto Rico: Centro de Investigaciones del Caribe y América Latina (Documento de Trabajo no. 19), 1985. 22 pp.

———. "Le Castrisme et l'Afrique noire, 1959–1972: calcus ethniques et contraintes stratégiques à la base de la politique interventionniste de Cuba castriste en Afrique noire." Thèse de doctorat d'Etat des lettres, Université de Paris VII, 1983. 24 + 1,175 pp.

Ratliff, Helga. *Follow the Leader in the Horn.* Washington, D.C.: Cuban American National Foundation, 1986. [On Cuban policy in Africa.]

Ratliff, William E. *Following the Leader in the Horn: The Soviet-Cuban Presence in East Africa.* Miami: Cuban American National Foundation. 1985. 22 pp.

Reagan on Cuba. Washington, D.C.: Cuban American National Foundation, 1986.

Smith, Wayne S. *Selected Essays on Cuba.* Washington, D.C.: School of Advanced International Studies, Johns Hopkins University, 1986. 97 pp.

Tokatlián, Juan G., ed. *Cuba—Estados Unidos: dos enfoques.* Bogotá: CEREC and Grupo Editor Latino Americano, 1984. 247 pp.

U.S. Department of State. *Warsaw Pact Economic Aid to Non-Communist LDCs, 1984.* Washington D.C.: Department of State, 1986. 27 pp. [Deals in part with Cuban foreign aid to LDCs.]

Articles and Papers

Bray, Majorie Woodford, and Donald W. Bray. "Cuba, the Soviet Union, and Third World Struggle." In *Cuba: Twenty-Five Years of Revolution, 1959–1984,* ed. Sandor Halebsky and John M. Kirk, 352–71. New York: Praeger, 1985.

Castro, Fidel. "Dette extérieure et Nouvel Ordre économique international." *Recherches Internationales* 16, 93–119.

Coll, Alberto R. "Functionalism and the Balance of Interests in the Law of the Sea: Cuba's Role." *American Journal of International Law* 79, no. 4 (October 1985), 891–911.

Cova, Johnny. "Cuba: un número clave en la combinación del Caribe." Presented at the annual Meeting of the Caribbean Studies Association, Caracas, Venezuela, May 1986.

Cross, Sharyl. "The United States and Cuba in the 1970s." In *José Martí and the Cuban Revolution Retraced,* ed. Johannes Wilbert, 49–59. Los Angeles: UCLA Latin American Center Publications, 1986.

Cypher, Dorothea. "The Effects of Culture on Cuban Influence in Grenada." In *American Intervention in Grenada: The Implications of Operation "Urgent Fury,"* ed. Peter M. Dunn and Bruce W. Watson. Boulder, Colo.: Westview, 1985.

Daly Hayes, Margaret. "Girding for the Long Run: Recommendations and Options for Coping with Soviet/Cuban Strategy in the Caribbean Basin." In *Grenada and Soviet/Cuban Policy: Internal Crisis and U.S./OECS Intervention,* ed. Jiri Valenta and Herbert J. Ellison. Boulder, Colo.: Westview, 1986.

Domínguez, Jorge I. "Cuba in the 1980s." *Foreign Affairs* 65, no. 1 (Fall 1986), 110–35.

———. "Grenadian Party Paper: Revealing an Imaginary Document." *Caribbean Review* 15, no. 2 (Spring 1986), 16–20.

———. "Report to the Political Bureau, Central Committee, Communist Party of Cuba, from the Special Task Force on the U.S. Imperialist Agression Against Grenada." In *Grenada and Soviet/Cuban Policy: Internal Crisis and U.S./OECS Intervention,* ed. Jiri Valenta and Herbert J. Ellison. Boulder, Colo.: Westview, 1986.

Domínguez, Jorge I., and Juan Lindau. "The Primacy of Politics: Comparing the Foreign Policies of Cuba and Mexico." In *How Foreign Decisions Are Made in the Third World,* ed. Bahgat Korany. Boulder, Colo.: Westview, 1985.

Drekonja Kornat, Gerhard. "Cuba: desde el debate sobre los incentivos hasta la campaña africana." *Mundo Nuevo* 12, nos. 25/26 (July–December 1984), 16–27.

Duncan, W. Raymond. "Castro and Gorbachev: Politics of Accommodation." *Problems of Communism* 35, no. 2 (March–April 1986), 45–57.

———. "Funciones de Cuba en el ámbito de la comunidad socialista: ¿a la vanguardia de los intereses del Tercer Mundo?" In *Cuba—Estados Unidos: dos enfoques,* ed. Juan G. Tokatlian, 77–109. Bogotá: CEREC and Grupo Editor Latino Americano, 1984.

"Entrevista a Ricardo Alarcón, Viceministro de Relaciones Exteriores de Cuba." *Cuadernos de Nuestra América* 2, no. 4 (July–December 1985), 316–20.

Erisman, H. Michael. "Cuba's Foreign Policy: Post-Dependency Impulses and Security Imperatives." *Harvard International Review* (December 1986).

Falcoff, Mark. "Bishop's Cuba, Castro's Grenada: Notes Toward an Inner History." In *Grenada and Soviet/Cuban Policy: Internal Crisis and U.S./OECS Intervention,* ed. Jiri Valenta and Herbert J. Ellison. Boulder, Colo.: Westview, 1986.

Fernández, Damián J. "Cuban Foreign Policy: Scholarship and Double Standards." *Journal of Inter-American Studies* 28, no. 2 (Summer 1986), 147–53.

Fourie, Deon. "Cuban presence in Angola." *Unisa. Latin American Report* 2, no. 1 (March 1986), 51–54.

Frechette, Myles R. "Cuba en los años ochenta." In *Cuba—Estados Unidos: dos enfoques,* ed. Juan G. Tokatlian, 45–58. Bogotá: CEREC and Grupo Editor Latino Americano, 1984.

González, Carmen. "La política exterior norteamericana hacia el Africa austral: el primer mandato de Reagan." *Cuadernos de Nuestra América* 3, no. 5 (January–June 1986), 107–23. [Concerns Cuban military presence in Angola.]

González, E. "The Cuban and Soviet Challenge in the Caribbean Basin." *Orbis: A Journal of World Affairs* 29 (Spring 1985), 73–94.

Grabendorff, Wolf. "La percepción euro-occidental sobre las relaciones internacionales de Cuba." Presented at the Instituto Superior de Relaciones Internacionales (ISRI), Havana, March 1985.

Hernández, Rafael. "La política de los Estados Unidos hacia Cuba y la cuestión de la migración." *Cuadernos de Nuestra America* 2, no. 3 (January–June 1985), 75–100.

Insulza, José Miguel. "Cuban-Soviet Relations in the New International Setting." In *Soviet-Latin American Relations in the 1980s,* ed. Augusto Varas. Boulder, Colo.: Westview, 1986.

LeoGrande, William M. "Cuba." In *Confronting Revolution. Security Through Diplomacy in Central America,* ed. Morris J. Blachman, William M. LeoGrande, and Kenneth Sharpe, 229–55. New York: Pantheon Books, 1986.

―――. "Cuba's Policy Toward Central America." Occasional Paper no. 12. *Cuba After the Third Party Congress. Selected Essays,* 35–51. Washington, D.C.: Central American and Caribbean Program, School of Advanced International Studies, Johns Hopkins University, 1986.

León, Laureano, Germán Sánchez, José Luis Rodríguez, and Luis Suárez Salazar. "El encuentro sobre la deuda externa de América Latina y el Caribe." *Cuadernos de Nuestra América* 2, no. 3 (January–June 1985), 282–96. [Roundtable discussion.]

Leonov, N. "USSR–Cuba: Fraternal Cooperation in Action." *International Affairs* [Moscow] 11 (1984), 22–29.

Martínez Salsamendi, Carlos. "El papel de Cuba en el Tercer Mundo: América Central, el Caribe y Africa." In *Cuba—Estados Unidos: dos enfoques,* ed. Juan G. Tokatlian, 127–98. Bogotá: CEREC and Grupo Editor Latino Americano, 1984.

Moura, Gerson. "Brasil-Cuba: enfirm, o reatamento." *Brasil. Perspectivas Internacionais* 2, no. 10 (April–June 1986), 1–4.

Olaciregui, Demetrio. "Fidel, Cuba y la unidad latinoamericana." *Tareas* [Panama] 61 (July–August 1985), 121–24.

Pastor, Robert A. "Does the United States Push Revolutions to Cuba? The Case of Grenada." *Journal of Inter-American Studies* 28, no. 1 (Spring 1986), 1–34.

Paulo Evaristo, Cardenal Ars, Archbishop of São Paulo. "Carta a Fidel Castro." *Tareas* 62 (September–December 1985), 9–12. [On foreign debt.]

Pérez, Silvia N. "La participación de Cuba en la comunidad socialista y su ejemplo para el Tercer Mundo." In *Cuba-Estados Unidos: dos enfoques,* ed. Juan G. Tokatlian, 112–26. Bogotá: CEREC and Grupo Editor Latino Americano, 1984.

Reagan, Ronald. *Reagan on Cuba.* Miami: Cuban American National Foundation, 1985. 50 pp.

Roett, Riordan. "La política exterior de Cuba y los Estados Unidos." In *Cuba-Estados Unidos: dos enfoques,* ed. Juan G. Tokatlian, 59–74. Bogotá: CEREC and Grupo Editor Latino Americano, 1984.

———. "La política exterior de Cuba y los EEUU." *Nueva Sociedad* 69 (1985), 133–40.

Skoug, Jr., Kenneth N. See *Documents.*

Smith, Wayne S. "La relación entre Cuba y Estados Unidos: pautas y opciones." In *Cuba-Estados Unidos: dos enfoques,* ed. Juan G. Tokatlian, 31–44. Bogotá: CEREC and Grupo Editor Latino Americano, 1984.

Sujostat, Alexandr. "USRR-Cuba: colaboración y comprensión mutua." *América Latina* 1 (1986), 86–88.

Szulc, Tad. "La posición hemisférica de Cuba mejora a pesar de los obstáculos de EE.UU." *Diálogo Social* [Panama] 180 (July 1985), 31–32.

Trachtenberg, M. "The Influence of Nuclear Weapons in the Cuban Missile Crisis." *International Security* 10 (Summer 1985), 137–63.

Valdés, Nelson P. "Report Redux: Thoughts on the Imaginary Document." *Caribbean Review* 15, no. 2 (Spring 1986), 21–23.

Valenta, Jiri, and Virginia Valenta. "Revolution in Grenada: The USSR, Cuba, and Eastern Europe: Leninism in Grenada." In *Grenada and Soviet/Cuban Policy: Internal Crisis and U.S./OECS Intervention,* ed. Jiri Valenta and Herbert J. Ellison. Boulder, Colo.: Westview, 1986.

Yamashkin, Piotr. "Cuba-Angola: el internacionalismo en acción." *América Latina* 1 (1986), 43–48.

Yopo H., Boris. "Cuba: la política exterior en 1985. ¿Hacia una definitiva reinserción latinoamericana?" in *Anuario Políticas Exteriores Latinoamericanas, 1985,* Santiago de Chile: PROSPEL, 1986. [Programa de Seguimiento de las Políticas Exteriores Latinoamericanas—PROSPEL]

———. "Soviet Military Assistance to Cuba and Nicaragua, 1980–1984." In *Soviet-Latin American Relations in the 1980s,* ed. Augusto Varas. Boulder, Colo.: Westview, 1986.

———. "La política exterior de Cuba: realismo y principios en un contexto internacional adverso." In *las políticas exteriores latinoamericanas frente a la crisis.* Buenos Aires: Grupo Editor Latinoamericano, 1985. 452 pp.

General

Books and Monographs

Elliot, Jeffrey M., and Mervyn M. Dymally. *Fidel by Fidel: A New Interview with Dr. Fidel Castro Ruz, President of the Republic of Cuba.* San Bernardino, Calif.: Borgo Press, 1985.

Gómez y Toro, Bernardo. *Revoluciones, Cuba y Hogar.* Santo Domingo: Editorial Alfa & Omega, 1986. 348 pp.

Neila Vilas, Xosé. *A prensa galega de Cuba.* Sada, Spain: EDC, 1985. 171 pp.

Rodríguez, Carlos Rafael. *Palabras en los setenta.* Havana: Ciencias Sociales, 1985. 208 pp. [Essay]

Suchlicki, Jaime, Antonio Jorge, and Damián Fernández, eds. *Cuba: Continuity and Change.* Coral Gables, Fla.: University of Miami, 1985. 189 pp. [Contributors include Luis Aguilar, Andrés Suárez, Jorge Salazar, Antonio Jorge, Jaime Suchlicki, Carlos Ripoll, Enrique Baloyra, Reinaldo Sánchez, Justo Carrillo and Raúl Moncarz.]

Articles and Papers

Iznaga, Alcides. "Como cambian los tiempos caballero." *Bohemia* 78, no. 40 (October 3, 1986), 34–35.

Kaye, Jacqueline. "The Flight from Disorder." In *José Martí: Revolutionary Democrat*, ed. Christopher Abel and Nissa Torrents. London: Athlone Press/Durham: Duke University Press, 1986.

Martínez Heredia, Fernando. "Ciencias sociales e insurrección." *Casa de las Américas* 26, 154 (January–February 1986), 160–63.

Otero, Lisandro. "La identidad latinoamericana entre la represión y la protesta." *Casa de las Américas* 26, nos. 155–56 (March–June 1986), 177–79.

Rivero, Eliana. "Toward a Definition of Contemporary Cuban Culture." Presented at the annual meeting of the Latin American Studies Association, Boston, October 1986.

Shatunóvskaya, Irina. "Cuba: país de amigos." *América Latina* [USSR] 8 (1985), 75–79.

Soley, Lawrence C., and John S. Nichols. "Castro and Clandestine Broadcasting in the Caribbean." In *Clandestine Radio Broadcasting*, 163–89. New York: Praeger, 1986.

Stuart, Angelica. "Impressions of the Cuban Revolution." *Latin American Perspectives* 11, no. 3 (Summer 1984), 141–48.

Villareal, Alonso. "Reflexiones sobre una 'Entrevista Urgente' a Fidel Castro en torno al General Noriega." *Panorama Centroamericano/Reporte Político* 6 (August 1986), VIII/12. [Addendum]

History

Books and Monographs

Adam y Silva, Ricardo. *La gran mentira*, 2d ed. Miami: Universal, 1986. 315 pp.

Alvarez Ruiz, Aladio, and José Albuerne Rivera. *Martí Conspirador.* Miami: Universal, 1986. 79 pp.

Aparicio Laurencio, Angel. *¿Es historia el libro que Hugh Thomas escribió sobre Cuba?* Madrid: Catoblejas, 1985. 80 pp.

Betancourt, Enrique C. *Apuntes para la historia. Radio, televisión y farándula en la Cuba de ayer . . .* Miami: Universal, 1986. 457 pp.

Calendario manual y guía de forasteros de la isla de Cuba para el año de 1795. Miami: Universal, 1985. 146 pp.

De Santa Cruz y Mallén, Francisco Xavier (Conde de San Juan de Jaruco). *Historia de familias cubanas.* Vol. 7. Miami: Universal, 1986. 416 pp.

———. *Historia de familias cubanas,* Vols. 8–10. Miami: Universal, 1986–1987.

Estrade, Paul. *Les clubs fémenins dans le Parti Revolutionnaire Cubain (1892–1898).* Paris: Université de Paris, 1986. 42 pp.

Fernández, Alfredo Antonio. *La última frontera 1898.* Havana: Editorial Letras Cubanas, 1985. 272 pp.

Fernández, José B. *Los abuelos: historia oral cubana.* Miami: Universal, 1986.

Fernández Rubio, Angel. *El proceso de institucionalización de la revolución cubana.* Havana: Editorial Ciencias Sociales, 1985. 72 pp.

Fitzgerald, Frank Thomas. See *Politics, Government, and Armed Forces.*

Franzbach, Martin, ed. *Kuba. Materialien zur Landeskunde.* 2d rev. and enl. ed. Frankfurt am Main, R.F.A., 1986. 113 pp.

Freston, Paul Charles. See *Ideology.*

González, Margarita. *Bolívar y la independencia de Cuba.* Bogotá: El Ancora Editores, 1985. 141 pp.

González, Servando. *Historia herética de la revolución Fidelista.* San Francisco, Calif.: Ediciones El Gato Tuerto, 1986. 160 pp.

González Casanova, P., ed. *Historia del movimiento obrero en América Latina.* Mexico: Siglo XXI, 1985. [Vol. 1 deals in part with Cuba.]

González Casanova, P., ed. *Historia política de los campesinos latinoamericanos.* Mexico: Siglo XXI, 1985. [Vol. 1 deals in part with Cuba.]

Infiesta, Ramón. See *Biography.*

Kothe, Julia. "Revolutionsgeschichtliche Studien zur Vorbereitung und zur ersten Etappe der 2. kubanischen Unabhangigkeits-revolution von 1895 (1892–1896) unter besonderer Berucksichtigung der Linken und des Gewichtes der proletarischen Revolutionskomponente." Dissertation A., Universität Rostock [East Germany], 1984. 199 pp.

Kuethe, Allan J. *Cuba, 1753–1815.* Ithaca, N.Y.: Cornell University Press, 1986. 232 pp.

Lecuyer, Marie-Claude. *Inmigration blanche à Cuba: L'experience galicienne (1853–1855).* Le Mirail: Université de Toulouse, 1987.

Llerena, Mario. *The Unsuspected Revolution.* Ithaca, N.Y.: Cornell University Press, 1986. 324 pp.

Luciano Franco, José. *Apuntes para una historia de la legislación administrativa colonial en Cuba, 1511–1800.* Havana: Ciencias Sociales, 1985. 426 pp.

McGinty, Patrick Eugene. "Intelligence and the Spanish American War." Ph.D. diss., Georgetown University, 1983. 479 pp. *DAI* 46, no. 1 (July 1985), 246-A, UM8505718.

Morales, Salvador. *Martí en Venezuela, Bolívar en Martí.* Caracas: Centauro, 1985. 306 pp.

Moya, Rogerio. *La muerte espera.* Havana: Letras Cubanas, 1985. 222 pp.

Pascual-Sanz, Fabriciano. *Historia de Cristóbal Colón.* Guatemala: La Helvetia, 1986. 522 pp.
Pérez Jr., Louis A. *Cuba Under the Platt Amendment, 1902–1934.* Pittsburgh: University of Pittsburgh Press, 1986, 448 pp.
Rodríguez Demorizi, Emilio. See *Biography.*
Salvucci, Linda Kerrigan. "Development and Decline: The Port of Philadelphia and Spanish Imperial Markets, 1783–1823." Ph.D. diss., Princeton University, 1985. 382 pp. *DAI* 46, no. 10 (Apr. 1986), 3139-40-A, UM8529048. [Deals in part with Cuba.]
Serráno, Carlos. *Anarchisme et Independence National à Cuba la fin du XXXe.* Cahier no. 1. Université de Paris, 1986. 99 pp.
Souza, Benigno. See *Biography.*
Stubbs, Jean. See *Labor and Unions.*
Suchlicki, Jaime. *Cuba: From Columbus to Castro.* 2d ed. Elmsford, N.Y.: Pergamon, 1986. 272 pp.
Vitier, Cintio. *Los papeles de Jacinto Finale.* Havana: Letras Cubanas, 1984. 114 pp.
Vyfhuis, Leslie Patricia. "Pressure Groups and Public Opinion: Their Effect on Foreign Policy during the Spanish-American War of 1898." M.A. thesis, Queen's University, Kingston, 1981. *Canadian Theses on Microfiche Service* no. 52936.
Wilbert, Johannes, ed. *José Martí and the Cuban Revolution Retraced.* UCLA, Latin American Studies, vol. 62. Los Angeles: UCLA Latin American Center Publications, 1986. 76 pp. [Proceedings of conference.]

Articles and Papers

Abel, Christopher. "Concluding Perspectives." In *José Martí: Revolutionary Democrat,* ed. Christopher Abel and Nissa Torrents. London: Athlone Press; Durham, N.C.: Duke University Press, 1986.
———. "Martí, Latin America, and Spain." In ibid.
Aldana Martínez, Jorge. See *Economics, Industry, and Planning.*
Alvarez-Ríos, René. "Crisis de la esclavitud abolicionismo." Presented at the conference "1886–1986 Centenaire de l'extinction définitive de l'esclavage à Cuba," Maison de l'Amérique Latine, Paris, November 1986.
Barcía, María del Carmen. "Táctica y Estrategia de la burguesía esclavista de Cuba ante la abolición de la esclavitud." Ibid.
Bosch Quidiello, Patricio. "Mambises gaditanos." *Cádiz Iberoamérica* 3 (1985), 59–61.
Brotherson, Festus, Jr. "Cuba: The New Regime of 1959 and Alternative Revolutionary Outcomes." In *José Martí and the Cuban Revolution Retraced,* ed. Johannes Wilbert, 25–35. Los Angeles: UCLA Latin American Center Publications, 1986.
Bustos, Manuel. "Los inicios de comercio con América." *Cádiz Iberoamérica* 3 (1985), 11–15.
Cairo, Ana. "La Revolución del 30: una aproximación historiográfica." Re-

vista de la Biblioteca Nacional José Martí 27, no. 1 (January–April 1985), 91–105.
Cross, Sharyl. See *Foreign Relations*.
Darío Molinari, Ramón. "Ramón Power, un puertorriqueño en las cortes de Cádiz." *Cádiz Iberoamérica* 3 (1985), 69–72.
De Armas, Ramón. "José Martí abolicionista." Paper presented at the conference "1886–1986 centenaire de l'extinction définitive de l'esclavage à Cuba," Maison de l'Amérique Latine, Paris, November 1986.
———. See also *Language and Literature*.
De la Torre, Mildred. "Apuntes sobre la historiografía del pensamiento cubano del siglo XIX (1959–1984)." *Revista de la Biblioteca Nacional José Martí* 27, no. 1 (January–April 1985), 19–39.
Del Vas Mingo, Marta Milagros. "El derecho de patronato en los proyectos abolicionistas cubanos." Presented at the conference "1886–1986 centenaire de l'extinction définitive de l'esclavage à Cuba," Maison de l'Amérique Latine, Paris, November 1986.
Duharte, Rafael. "La rebeldía esclava y la abolición de la esclavitud en Cuba." Ibid.
Durnerin, James. "L'abolition du patronato à Cuba en 1886: les débats à Madrid." Ibid.
Fernández Retamar, Roberto. "The Modernity of José Martí." In *José Martí: Revolutionary Democrat*, ed. Christopher Abel and Nissa Torrents. London: Athlone Press; Durham, N.C.: Duke University Press, 1986.
Figueroa, Loida. "Los combatientes puertorriqueños en las guerras de Independencia de Cuba." *Revista de Historia* (Puerto Rico) 1, no. 2 (July–December 1985).
García Alvarez, Alejandro. "El testimonio: su divulgación en Cuba revolucionaria." *Revista de la Biblioteca Nacional José Martí* 27, no. 1 (January–April 1985), 107–18.
García More, Rafael. "Abolición e independencia." *Bohemia* 78, no. 41 (October 10, 1986), 68–72.
Guerra, Félix. "Caminar hacia la Sierra Maestra (II). De la historia del hacha y del fuego." *Bohemia* 78, no. 37 (September 12, 1986), 49–52.
———. "Un brigadista en la Sierra. Seis historias del 61." *Bohemia* 78, no. 41 (October 10, 1986), 52–55.
Hidalgo Paz, Ibrahím. "Notas acerca de la historiografía martiana en el período 1959–1983." *Revista de la Biblioteca Nacional José Martí* 27, no. 1 (January–April 1985), 63–78.
Ibarra, Jorge. "El movimiento abolicionista cubano en Oriente y Camagüey en la década de 1860." Presented at the conference "1886–1986 centenaire de l'extinction définitive de l'esclavage à Cuba," Maison de l'Amérique Latine, Paris, November 1986.
Kula, Marcin. "Rozwazania o zakresie pojecia na przykladzie wydaren na Kubie w 1933 roku" [Revolution: What does it mean—as exemplified by what happened in 1933 in Cuba]. In *O spoleczenstwie i teorii spolecznej*.

Ksiega poswiecona pamieci Stanislawa Ossowskiego, ed. Edmund Mokrzycki, Maria Ofierska, and Jerzy Szacki, 329–36. Warsaw: PWN, 1985.

Lepkowski, Tadeusz. "Cuba 1869: desafectos al gobierno e insurrectos." *Estudios Latinoamericanos* (Warsaw), 9 (1983), 125–48.

Le Riverend, Julio. "Problemas de la formación agraria de Cuba (Siglos XVI–XVII)." *Revista de la Biblioteca Nacional José Martí* 27, no. 1 (January–April 1985), 177–201.

López-Alves, Fernando. "The New Radicalism of the 1960s." In *José Martí and the Cuban Revolution Retraced,* ed. Johannes Wilbert, 37–48. Los Angeles: UCLA Latin American Center Publications, 1986.

Martínez, I. Concepción. "Exilio y preparativos de la expedición." *Bohemia* 78, no. 38 (September 19, 1986), 76–78.

Montenegro González, Augusto. See *Politics, Government, and Armed Forces.*

Morin, Claude. "Productivité rentabilité de l'esclavage à Cuba." Presented at the conference "1886–1986 centenaire de l'extinction définitive de l'esclavage à Cuba," Maison de l'Amérique Latine, Paris, November 1986.

Nodal, Roberto. "The Black Man in Cuban Society: From Colonial Times to the Revolution." *Journal of Black Studies* 16, no. 3 (March 1986), 251–67.

Paute, Jean-Pierre. "Musique et societé esclavagiste à Cuba." Presented at the conference "1886–1986 centenaire de l'extinction définitive de l'esclavage à Cuba," Maison de l'Amérique Latine, Paris, November 1986.

Pérez, Louis, Jr. See *Bibliography and Information Science.*

Pérez Guzmán, Francisco. See *Bibliography and Information Science.*

Pérez Menéndez, Alicia, and Lilian Vizcaíno González. See *Bibliography and Information Science.*

Pérez Miranda, Roberto. "Evolución histórica de la flota de travesía cubana." *Transporte y Vías de Comunicación* 6, no. 4 (December 1985), 357–62.

Pollitt, Brian H. See *Economics, Industry, and Planning.*

Portuondo Zúñiga, Olga. "La historiografía cubana acerca del período 1510–1868 en XXV años de Revolución." *Revista de la Biblioteca Nacional José Martí* 27, no. 1 (January–April 1985), 119–39.

Poskonina, L. S. See *Bibliography and Information Science.*

Poumier-Taquechel, María. "Les suicides d'esclaves." Presented at the conference "1886–1986 centenaire de l'extinction définitive de l'esclavage à Cuba," Maison de l'Amérique Latine, Paris, November 1986.

Rosenberg, Jonathan. See *Politics, Government, and Armed Forces.*

Santí, Enrico Mario. "José Martí and the Cuban Revolution." In *José Martí and the Cuban Revolution Retraced,* ed. Johannes Wilbert, 13–23. Los Angeles: UCLA Latin American Center Publications, 1986.

Sarrachino, R. "José Maceo en su periplo gaditano." *Cádiz Iberoamérica* 3 (1985), 62–64.

Schulman, Ivan M. "Void and Renewal: José Martí's Modernity." In *José Martí: Revolutionary Democrat,* ed. Christopher Abel and Nissa Torrents. London: Athlone Press; Durham: Duke University Press, 1986.

Scott, Rebecca J. "Gradual Abolition and the Dynamics of Slave Emancipation in Cuba, 1868–86." In *Readings in Latin American History. Volume II*, ed. John J. Johnson, Peter Bakewell, and Meredith D. Dodge. Durham, N.C.: Duke University Press, 1985.

———. "Postemancipation Society in Cuba, 1880–1899. A Comparative Perspective." Presented at the conference "1886–1986 centenaire de l'extinction définitive de l'esclavage à Cuba," Maison de l'Amérique Latine, Paris, November 1986.

Socarrás Matos, Martín. "Cádiz, cuna del transporte comercial cubano." *Cádiz Iberoamérica* 3 (1985), 29.

Szulc, Tad. "Fidel Castro's Years as a Secret Communist." *New York Times Magazine* (October 19, 1986), 47ff.

Tornero, Pablo. "Economía y análisis demográfico: la esclavitud en Cuba en el período de la formación azucarera (1765–1817)." Presented at the conference "1886–1986 centenaire de l'extinction définitive de l'esclavage à Cuba," Maison de l'Amérique Latine, Paris, November 1986.

Winocur, Marcos. "La bourgeoisie face à la révolution cubaine. Une ruse de l'histoire." *Amérique Latine* [Paris] 21 (January–March 1985), 75–81.

Zanetti, Lecuona. See *Bibliography and Information Science*.

Ideology

Books and Monographs

Dickson, Thomas Victor. "Cuba's Attitude toward the United States as Indicated by Its Use of Propaganda Symbols." Ed.D. diss., Oklahoma University, 1984. 221 pp. *DAI* 46, no. 12 (June 1986): 3523-A, UM8603537.

Freston, Paul Charles. "The Revolutions in Cuba and Nicaragua: The Lessons for Christian Social Ethics in Latin America." M.C.S. thesis, Regent College, 1983. *Canadian Theses on Microfiche Service* no. 59690.

Grullón Jiménez, Juan I. *La filosofía de José Martí*. Santo Domingo: Editorial Santo Domingo, 1986. 217 pp.

Horowitz, Irving Louis, ed. *Cuban Communism*. 6th ed. New Brunswick, N.J.: Transaction Books, 1986. 850 pp.

Jothe, Julia. See *History*.

Krause Peters, Monika. "Vorbereitung der jungen Generation auf Liebe, Ehe und Familie in der Republik Kuba (unter besonderer Berücksichtigung der Rolle der Kubanischen Frauenfoderation FMC)." Dissertation A, Universität Rostock [East Germany], 1983. 277 pp.

Liss, Sheldom B. *Roots of Revolution: Radical Thought in Cuba*. Lincoln: University of Nebraska Press, 1987.

Mestas, Juan Eugenio. "José Martí: Su Concepto de la Clase Obrera." Ph.D.diss., State University of New York, Stony Brook, 1985. 209 pp. *DAI* 46, no. 8 (February 1986): 230A, UM8522090.

Muruchi Poma, Germán. "Der politokonomische Inhalt des revolutionaren Demokratismus José Martis und seine geschichtliche Bedeutung für den

antiimperialistischen Kampf der Volker Lateinamerikas am Ende des 19. Jahrhunderts." Dissertation A, Universitat Leipzig [East Germany], 1985. 4 + 151 + 9 pp.
Pérez-Stable, Marifeli. See *Politics, Government, and Armed Forces*.
Ripoll, Carlos. *Harnessing the Intellectuals: Censoring Writers and Artists in Today's Cuba*. Washington, D.C.: Cuban American National Foundation, 1985. 55 pp.
Sánchez de Bustamente, Antonio. *La filosofía clásica alemana en Cuba, 1841–1898*. Havana: Ciencias Sociales, 1984. 142 pp.
Smith, Guadalupe Ramos. "Kritik der positivischen Schule von Ferri und ihre Bedeutung für die Strafgesetzgebung und Strafrechtstheorie in Kuba." Dissertation, Humboldt-Universität zu Berlin [East Germany], 1983. 119 + 201 + 11 pp.
Torres-Cuevas, Eduardo. *El alma visible de Cuba*. Havana: Ciencias Sociales, 1985. 326 pp.
Vásquez-Viaña, Humberto. *Antecedentes de la guerrilla del Ché en Bolivia*. Research Paper Series. Stockholm: Institute of Latin American Studies, University of Stockholm, 1986. 79 pp.

Articles and Papers

Cavallini, Massimo. "La revolución es una obra de arte que debe perfeccionarse." *Pensamiento Propio* 4, no. 33 (May–June 1986), 39–43.
Del Monte Horruitiner, Gladys, and Manuel Gómez Morales. "Los especialistas jóvenes y el trabajo cultural." *Temas* 7 (1985), 105–28.
Fernández, Frank. "En el golfo de la indolencia." *Guáncara Libertaria* 7, no. 27 (Summer 1986), 4–6. [Critique of Castroism].
García Galló, Gaspar Jorge. "La revolución cubana confirma el carácter científico marxista de socialismo real." *Unión*, 1984, no. 1, pp. 73–81.
Gersteinberg, B. "Acerca del problema del 'eclecticismo' filosófico en la ilustración cubana." *Lateinamerika* 20, no. 1 (1985), 101–11.
Ibarra, Jorge. "Martí and Socialism." In *José Martí: Revolutionary Democrat*, ed. Christopher Abel and Nissa Torrents. London: Athlone Press; Durham, N.C.: Duke University Press, 1986.
Kapcia, Antoni. "Cuban Populism and the Birth of the Myth of Martí." In ibid.
Kirk, John M. "José Martí and His Concept of the *intelectual comprometido*." In ibid.
———. "José Martí y su concepto del intelectual comprometido." *Anuario del Centro de Estudios Martianos* 8 (1985), 117–135.
López, Della Luisa. "Ernesto Che Guevara: aspectos de su pensamiento económico." *Economía y Desarrollo* 89 (November–December 1985), 87–111.
Maique, María E., Alicia Jardines, Caridad Pérez, and María E. Talavera. "Los jóvenes profesionales y la investigación de la cultura." *Temas* 7 (1985), 129–36.
Menéndez, Lázara, and Raquel Mendieta. See *Anthropology and Archaeology*.
Mirónov, Vladímir. See *Biography*.

Nápoles Padrón, Elsa, Marina Alexandrova, and Carlos Alvarez de Zayas. See *Education*.
Santí, Enrico Mario. See *History*.
Serbín, Andrés. "Cuba: entre la ideología y el pragmatismo." *Nueva Sociedad* [Caracas] 3 (May–June 1985), 8–12.

Labor and Unions
Books and Monographs

Fuller, Linda Olsen. "The Politics of Workers' Control in Cuba, 1959–1983: The Work Center in the National Arena." Ph.D. diss., University of California, Berkeley, 1985. 526 pp. *DAI* 46, no. 9 (March 1986): 2828-A, UM8524953.
González Casanova, P., ed. See *History*.
Gutiérrez, Tania. "Tareas fundamentales para el diseño del ambiente laboral en el proceso de industrialización de Cuba." Ph.D. diss., Facultad de Arquitectura, ISPJAE [Cuba] and Hochschule Für Architektur und Bauwesen Weimar (Escuela Superior de Arquitectura y Planificación) [East Germany], 1985.
Martínez Andueza, Francisco J. "Beitrag der wissenschaftlichen Arbeitsorganisation zur vollen Nutzung des Arbeitsvermogens der Arbeiter in den Maschinenbaubetriebeb Kubas." Dissertation A., Technische Hochschule Magdeburg [East Germany], 1984. 170 pp.
Miranda Fernández, Lucinda. See *Biography*.
Okuneva, M. *La clase obrera en la Revolución cubana*. Moscow: Naúka, 1985. 152 pp.
Riesgo, Rodolfo. *Cuba: el movimiento obrero y su entorno sociopolítico*. Miami and Caracas: Saeta Ediciones, 1985. 251 pp.
Stubbs, Jean. *Tobacco on the Periphery: A Case Study of Cuban Labour History, 1860–1958*. New York: Cambridge University Press, 1985. 203 pp.

Articles and Papers

Fuller, Linda. "Changes in the relationship between the Unions, Administration, and the Party at the Cuban Workplace, 1959–1982." *Latin American Perspectives* 13, no. 2 (Spring 1986), 6–32.
———. "The State and the Unions in Cuba since 1959." In *Labor and Politics in Latin America*, ed. Edward Epstein. Boston: Allan and Unwin, 1987.
Peláez, María J. "Hacia la organización sindical." *Bohemia* 78, no. 40 (October 3, 1986), 68–71.

Language and Literature
Books and Monographs

Abaroa, Leonardo. *Con estas otras manos*. Havana: Unión, 1985. 98 pp. [Short stories]

Abreu Felippe, José. *Poesía cubana contemporánea. Antología.* Madrid: Catoblejas, 1986. 283 pp. [Poetry]
Alberto, Eliseo. *La fogata roja.* Havana: Editorial Gente Nueva, 1985. 304 pp. [Novel]
Alonso, Dora. *El valle de la pájara pinta.* Havana: Casa de las Américas, 1985. 108 pp. [Poetry]
Alvarez Jané, Enrique. *Me planto.* Havana: Unión, 1984. 168 pp.
Arango, Angel. *Coyuntura.* Havana: Unión, 1984. 124 pp. [Science fiction]
Ares, Mercy, et al. *Características nacionales de la literatura cubana.* Miami: Universal, 1986. 92 pp.
Augier, Angel. *Acción y poesía en José Martí.* Havana: Editorial Letras Cubanas, 1985. 422 pp.
Barnet, Miguel. *Canción de Rachel.* Havana: Letras Cubanas, 1985. 150 pp. [Narrative]
Barroso, Bonita C. *Con Cuba en la garganta.* Barcelona: Ediciones Rondas, 1986. 30 pp. [Poetry]
Benítez-Rojo, Antonio. *El mar de los tres trópicos.* Hanover, N.H.: Ediciones del Norte, 1987. [Essays on Cuban culture and literature.]
Bertot, Lillian D. "Linguistic and Stylistic Approaches to the Poetry of José Lezama Lima." Ph.D. diss., University of Florida, 1984. 128 pp. *DAI* 46, no. 3 (September 1985), 712-A, UM8509903. [In Spanish]
Bordao, Rafael. *Proyectura.* Madrid: Catoblejas, 1986. 72 pp. [Poetry]
Bravo-Villasante, Carmen. *Cuentos populares de Iberoamérica.* Houston: Arte Publico Press, 1985. 170 pp. [Includes folktales from Cuba.]
Brene, José R. *Pasado a la criolla y otras obras.* Havana: Letras Cubanas, 1984. 368 pp.
Cabrera, Lydia. *Anagó: Vocabulario Lucumí.* Miami: Universal, 1986. 326 pp. [On the Yoruba spoken in Cuba.]
Campoamor, Fernando G. *El hijo alegre de la caña de azúcar.* Havana: Científico Técnica, 1985. 152 pp.
Camps, David. *En el viaje sueño.* Havana: Unión, 1984. 204 pp.
Canet, Antonio. See *Art Cinema, Music, and Theater.*
Carpentier, Alejo. *Obras completas de Alejo Carpentier, Vol. IX: Crónicas 2: Arte, Literatura, y Política.* Mexico City: Siglo XXI, 1986.
Carvalho, André. *Cubalibre.* Havana: Casa de las Américas, 1986. 170 pp. [Novel]
Casaus, Victor. *De un tiempo a esta parte.* Havana: Letras Cubanas, 1984. 150 pp. [Poetry]
Cerda, Carlos. "Método realista y configuración no mimética en la novela de José Donoso, Casa de Campo." Dissertation A., Humboldt-Universität zu Berlin [East Germany], 1983. 185 + 26 + 11 pp.
Chao, Ramón. See *Biography.*
Collazo, Conrado. "La poética de lo fragmentario en José Lezama Lima." Ph.D. diss., State University of New York, Stony Brook, 1984. 296 pp. *DAI* 46, no. 4 (October 1985), 992-A, UM8513531.

Collazo, Miguel. *Estancias*. Havana: Unión, 1985. 92 pp. [Novel]
Da Rocha, María Emilia Pereira. "Aspectos históricos de el Otoño del Patriarca." Ph.D. diss., Texas Tech University, 1985. 416 pp. *DAI* 46, no. 6 (December 1985), 1604-A, UM8517797.
De la Nuez, René. *El caballo de Troya*. Havana: Letras Cubanas, 1985. 84 pp. [Novel]
Del Castillo, Amelia. *Agua y Espejos (Imágenes)*. Miami: Universal, 1986. 70 pp.
Delgado-Sánchez, Joaquín. *El Rumbo*. Miami: Universal, 1986. 118 pp. [Novel]
De los Santos, Alfonso. *Vísperas*. Havana: Letras Cubanas, 1984. 126 pp. [Novel]
Depestre Catony, Leonardo. *Consideraciones acerca del vocabulario cubano*. Havana: Ciencias Sociales, 1985. 60 pp.
Díaz Martínez, Manuel. *Poesía inconclusa*. Havana: Letras Cubanas, 1985. 154 pp.
———. *Mientras traza su curva el pez de fuego*. Havana: Unión, 1985. 156 pp. [Poetry]
Escobar Varela, Angel. *Allegro de sonata*. Havana: Editorial Unión, 1984, 52 pp. [Poetry]
Fernández, Roberto. *La vida es un special*. Houston: Arte Publico Press, 1985. 96 pp. [Novel]
———. *La montaña rusa*. Houston: Arte Publico Press, 1985. 184 pp. [Satire]
Ferreiro, Pilar A. *Cuentos rurales del siglo XX*. Havana: Letras Cubanas, 1984. 378 pp. [Short stories]
Foncueva, José A. *Escritos de José Antonio Foncueva*. Havana: Letras Cubanas, 1985. 335 pp.
Garabedian, Martha Ann. "Imagery and Experience in the Poetry of Oscar Hahn, José Emilio Pacheco, and Heberto Padilla: A New Expression of Reality in Three Contemporary Spanish American Poets." Ph.D. diss., University of Connecticut, 1984. 403 pp. *DAI* 45, no. 8 (February 1985), 2540-A, UM8425765.
Garzón Céspedes, Francisco. *Cantos a la revolución, al pueblo y al amor*. Havana: Editorial Letras Cubanas, 1985. 102 pp. [Poetry]
Glaze, Linda S. *Critical Analysis of Valle Inclan's Ruedo Ibérico*. Miami: Universal, 1985. 206 pp.
Goldaras, José Raul. *¡Salve América!* Miami: Universal, 1986. 61 pp. [Poetry]
Gómez de Avellaneda, Gertrudis. *Tradiciones*. Havana: Letras Cubanas, 360 pp.
González Bolaños, Aimée. *La narrativa de Félix Pita Rodríguez*. Havana: Editorial Letras Cubanas, 1985. 380 pp.
Gutiérrez, Mariela. *Los cuentos negros de Lydia Cabrera. Un estudio morfológico*. Miami: Universal, 1986. 148 pp.
Habana, Daniel. *Adios a la Paz*. Miami: Universal, 1986. 195 pp. [Novel]
Hampton, Janet Jones. "The Image of the Black Woman in the Spanish-

American Novel: A Study of Characterization in Selected Spanish-American Novels." Ph.D. diss., Catholic University of America, 1985. 197 pp. *DAI* 46, no. 5 (November 1985): 1292-A, UM8515068. [Deals in part with black women in Cuban novels.]

Hernández, Jorge Luis. *El jugador de Chicago.* Havana: Unión, 1984. 146 pp. [Short stories]

Hernández-Lima, Dinorah. "Versiones y re-versiones históricas en la obra de Guillermo Cabrera Infante." Ph.D. diss., University of Maryland, 1983. 200 pp. *DAI* 45, no. 10 (April 1985), 3140-A, UM8429918.

Herrera, Tirso R. *Amor sin fronteras.* Miami: Universal, 1986. 166 pp.

Jamís, Fayad. *La pedrada, selección poética.* Havana: Letras Cubanas, 1984. 192 pp.

Johnson, Maribel Dicker. "Thematic and Stylistic Development in Three Contemporary Cuban Novels." Ph.D. diss., University of Colorado, Boulder, 1984. 139 pp. *DAI* 46, no. 2 (Aug. 1985), 436-A, UM8508952.

Leyva, Waldo. *El polvo de los caminos.* Havana: Letras Cubanas, 1984. 60 pp. [Poetry]

Lorente, Luis. *Café nocturno.* Havana: Unión, 1985. 86 pp. [Poetry]

———. *Ella canta en La Habana.* Matanzas, 1985.

Lorenzo Luaces, Joaquín. *El becerro de oro.* Havana: Letras Cubanas, 1985. 90 pp.

Loynaz, Dulce María. *Poesías escogidas.* Havana: Letras Cubanas, 1984. 140 pp.

Machado Pérez, Eloy. *Caman Lloro.* Havana: Letras Cubanas, 1984. 106 pp. [Poetry]

Marquéz Ravelo, Bernardo. *Balada del barrio.* Havana: Letras Cubanas, 1984. 252 pp. [Novel]

Martí, José. *La Edad de Oro.* Havana: Editorial Gente Nueva, 1985. 240 pp. [Marti's children's stories.)

———. *Obras completas. Edición crítica. Tomo II.* Havana: Centro de Estudios Martianos, 1985. 351 pp.

———. *Poesía completa.* Havana: Editorial Letras Cubanas, 1985. 294 pp.

Martí, Tula. *Un azul desesperado.* Miami: Universal, 1986. 105 pp. [Essays on Cuban society.]

Martínez, Ricardo. *Siete cuentos de la Sierra.* Havana: Editorial Unión, 1985. [Stories]

Martín Farto, Miguel. *La carpa de las fiestas.* Havana: Gente Nueva, 1985. 36 pp. [Stories]

Mond, F. *¿Donde está mi Habana?* Havana: Letras Cubanas, 1985. 250 pp. [Science fiction]

Moya, Rogerio, and Raúl Rivero. *Estrictamente personal.* Havana: Unión, 1985. 276 pp. [Interviews]

Muller, Alberto. *Tierra metalizada.* Miami: Universal, 1986. 62 pp.

Navarro, Osvaldo. *El caballo de Mayaguardo.* Havana: Letras Cubanas, 1984. 168 pp. [Novel]

Núñez, Ana Rosa. *Antología de poesía infantil.* Miami: Universal, 1985. 180 pp.
Núñez Jiménez, Antonio. *Pedro en el laberinto de las doce lenguas.* Havana: Editorial Gente Nueva, 1985. 166 pp. [Story]
Otra Ruíz, Jesús. *Pensamiento martiano y otros fulgores.* Havana: Unión, 1985. 314 pp. [Essays]
Parrado, Gloria. *Triptico.* Havana: Unión, 1984. 190 pp. [Drama]
Pedraza, Jorge A. *Estampillas de colores.* Miami: Universal, 1986. 94 pp.
Pereira, Teresinka. *La literatura antillana.* Educa, 1985. 114 pp.
Pérez, Magaly. "Ernest Hemingway, the Gulf Stream and Cuba." Dissertation A., Universität Jena [East Germany], 1984. 133 pp.
Pichardo, Esteban. *Diccionario provincial casi rabozado de voces y frases cubanas.* Havana: Editorial Ciencias Sociales, 1985. 640 pp.
Pichardo, Francisco Javier. *Poesías escogidas.* Havana: Letras Cubanas, 1985. 115 pp.
Piedra, José. "The Afro-Cuban Esthetics of Alejo Carpentier." Ph.D. diss., Yale University, 1985. 434 pp. *DAI* 47, no. 1 (July 1986): 197-A, UM8601001.
Piedra, Juan Enrique. *Sangre Bajo las Banderas.* Miami: Universal, 1986. 101 pp. [Poetry].
Pita Rodríguez, Félix. *De sueños y memorias.* Havana: Letras Cubanas, 1985. 312 pp. [Essays]
———. *Recordar el futuro.* Havana: Editorial Letras Cubanas, 1985. 200 pp. [Poetry]
Poncet y de Cárdenas, Carolina. *Investigación y apuntes literarios.* Havana: Editorial Letras Cubanas, 1985. 120 pp. [Essays]
Rexach, Rosario. *Estudios sobre Martí.* Madrid: Nova-Scholar, 1985. 176 pp.
Robreño, Eduardo. *Como lo pienso lo digo.* Havana: Editorial Unión, 1985. 234 pp. [Stories]
Rocasolano, Alberto. *En años del reposo turbulento.* Havana: Unión, 1984. 100 pp. [On José Martí.]
Rodríguez, Antonio Orlando. *Cuentos de cuando La Habana era chiquita.* Havana: Unión, 1984. 128 pp.
Rodríguez Herrera, Mariano. *Desconocidas historias de viejos tiempos.* Havana: Unión, 1985. 116 pp. [Stories]
Ronet, Jorge, and Andrés Hernández-Alende. *Guacasi. Los símbolos del delirio.* Miami: Universal, 1986. 323 pp.
Rostagno, Irene. "Fifty Years of Looking South: The Promotion and Reception of Latin American Literature in the U.S." Ph.D. diss., University of Texas, Austin 1984. 269 pp. *DAI* 46, no. 4 (October 1985), 1011-A, UM8513292.
Saldaña, Excilia. *Cantos para un mayito y una paloma.* Havana: Unión, 1984. 96 pp. [Children's stories]
Sánchez, Herminda. *¡De pie!* Havana: Unión, 1984. 84 pp. [Drama]
Sánchez-Boudy, José. *Diccionario de cubanismos más usuales.* Vol. 3. Miami: Universal, 1986.

———. *Calendario soleda—Guaracha y látigo. (Poemas de Guao y Caimito).* Miami: Universal, 1986. 74 pp.

———. *Patrióticas.* Miami: Universal, 1986. 68 pp. [Poetry].

Solano, Nélida. *El mundo narrativo de José Soler Puig.* Havana: Editorial Letras Cubanas, 1985. 252 pp.

Solís, Cleva. *Los sabios días.* Havana: Unión, 1985. 144 pp. [Poetry]

St. John Troya. *La psiquis, la hoz.* Miami: Universal, 1986. 115 pp.

Torres, Omar. *Al partir.* Houston: Arte Publico Press, 1985. 160 pp. [Novel]

Turton, Peter. *José Martí: Architect of Cuba's Freedom.* London: Zed Press, 1986.

Vidal, Hernán. *Para llegar a Manuel Cofiño. Estudio de una narrativa revolucionaria cubana.* Minneapolis: Society for the Study of Contemporary Hispanic and Lusophone African Revolutionary Literatures and Institute for the Study of Ideologies and Literature, 1984.

Waibel, Leo, and Ricardo Herrera. *La taponimia en el pasaje cubano.* Havana: Ciencias Sociales, 1984. 100 pp.

Xenes, Nieves. *Poesías.* Havana: Letras Cubanas, 1984. 64 pp.

Zalamea, Luis. *Voces en el Desierto.* Miami: Universal, 1984. 77 pp. [Poetry]

Articles and Papers

Abaroa Hernández, Leonardo. "Humpty-Dumpty." *Bohemia* 78, no. 37 (September 12, 1986), 36–37.

———. "Presencia de la mar en la obra de Félix Pita Rodríguez." *Unión,* (1984), no. 3, pp. 119–31.

Acosta, Leonardo. "Dos novelas venezolanas de lo real maravilloso." *Casa de las Américas* 27, no. 157 (July–August 1986), 161–70.

Agramonte, Roberto. "Martí y el libro." *Círculo: Revista de Cultura* 15 (1986), 47–58.

Alba Buffill, Elio. "La ensayística de Humberto Piñera: filosofía y literatura." Ibid., 65–72.

Alfonso, Vitalina. "Ríe malicioso y lo sostiene una enorme reflexión." *Casa de las Américas* 16, nos. 155–56 (March–June 1986), 194–96.

Alonso, Alejandro G. "Firmo: Homo Sapiens brasileño." Ibid., 174–76.

Alpízar Castillo, Rodolfo. "Valores de la estructura 'Al + infinitivo' en el español de Cuba: intento de sistematización." *Anuario L/L* 14 (1983), 120–34.

Alvarez Conesa, Sigifredo. "Dibujo a tinta." *Unión* 1 (1984), 63–69. [Story]

Alvarez García, Imeldo. "En torno al tema de la LCB en nuestra literatura." *Unión,* 1985, no. 1, pp. 5–17.

Arango, Angel. "La joven ciencia-ficción cubana." *Unión,* 1984, no. 1, pp. 128–38.

Araujo, Nara. "Una nueva historia de las literaturas de la América Latina." *Casa de las Américas* 16, nos. 155–56 (March–June 1986), 196–199.

Arcos, José Luis. "Sobre *Poesía completa* (edición crítica) de José Martí." Ibid., 180–83.

Arias, Salvador. "La cuentista de Rafael Soler." *Anuario L/L* 14 (1983), 30–53.
Augier, Angel. "Presencia de Rubén Darío en poetas cubanos." *Revista de Literatura Cubana* 4, no. 6 (January–June 1986), 78–96. [Essay]
Barnet, Miguel. "La vida real." *Unión,* 1985, no. 1, pp. 18–23. [Story]
Blanc, Giulio V., "Enríquez el feroz." *Mariel Magazine* 1, no. 1 (1986), 21–22. [Story]
Callejas, Bernardo. "Máximo Gómez y José Martí: historia y literatura de campaña." *Santiago* 57 (March 1985), 59–110.
Campuzano, Luisa. "Quirón o del ensayo (Notas sobre la ensayista de la Revolución)." *Revista de la Biblioteca Nacional José Martí* 27, no. 1 (January–April 1985), 141–75.
Cirules, Enrique. "Bluefields." *Unión,* 1984, no. 4, pp. 136–45. [Story]
Clavijo, Uva. "Lo cubano en la obra de Alfonso Hernández Catá." *Círculo: Revista de Cultura* 15 (1986), 25–30.
Corfiño, Manuel. "El anzuelo dorado." *Unión,* 1984, no. 4, pp. 4–38. [Story]
Correa, Miguel. "La enormidad del hacha." *Mariel Magazine* 1, no. 1 (1986), 18–19.
Cristóbal Pérez, Armando. "¡Que vengan!" *Unión,* 1985, no. 1, pp. 113–29. [Story]
Cruz, Mary. "El romanticismo visto por Bachiller y Morales (1830 a 1838)." *Revista de Literatura cubana* 4, no. 6 (January–June 1986), 27–48. [Essay]
Cué Fernández, Daisy. "Ramón de Palma y sus leyendas indias." *Santiago* 57 (March 1985), 209–24.
Dávalos, Fernando. "Coincidencia Extraordinaria." *Bohemia* 78, no. 38 (September 19, 1986), 50–55.
De Armas, Emilio. "Bien, yo respeto, y el respeto de composición de los versos libres." *Revista de Literatura Cubana* 4, no. 6 (January–June 1986), 97–108.
De Armas, R. "La influencia de Cádiz en José Martí." *Cádiz Iberoamérica* 3 (1985), 65–68.
De la Torre, Rogelio A. "Martí y la generación del 98." *Círculo: Revista de Cultura* 15 (1986), 59–64.
Díaz Martínez, Manuel. "Realidad y fábula en Rafael Alcides." *Unión,* 1984, no. 4, pp. 183–86.
Dill, Hans-Otto. "Los *Cantos para soldados*—un ejemplo de poesía revolucionaria militante de Nicolás Guillén." *Unión,* 1984, no. 1, pp. 48–59.
Dorta Contreras, Antonio Juan. "Martí: traducir a Victor Hugo. Etica revolucionaria y creación." *Santiago* 57 (March 1985), 123–36.
Escalona Delfino, José Antonio. "Martí y el conocimiento científico." *Santiago* 57 (March 1985), 111–22.
Escanparter, José A., and Linda S. Glaze. "Carlos Felipe," "Matías Montes Huidobro," "José Triana." In *Dictionary of Cuban Contemporary Literature,* ed. Julio A. Martínez. Westport, Conn.: Greenwood Press, 1987.
Escanparter, José A., and Linda S. Glaze. "Dolores Prida," "José Corrales."

In *Dictionary of Hispanic Authors in the United States,* ed. Nicolás Kanellos. Westport, Conn.: Greenwood Press, 1987.

Feijoo, Gladys. "La madre de la novela *Cecilia Valdés* de Cirilo Villaverde." *Círculo: Revista de Cultura* 15 (1986), 79–84.

Feito, Francisco E. "Ramón Ferreira," "Justo Rodríguez Santos," "Nivaria Tejera," and "Eliseo Diego." In *Dictionary of Contemporary Cuban Literature,* ed. Julio A. Martínez. Westport, Conn.: Greenwood Books, 1987.

Fernández Pequeño, José M. "Explosión en Tallapiedra a la hora de la literatura policial revolucionaria." *Revista de Literatura Cubana* 4, no. 6 (January–June 1986), 109–20.

Fernández Retamar, Roberto. "José Martí en los orígenes del antimperialismo latinoamericano." *Casa de las Américas* 25, no. 151 (July–August 1985), 3–11.

———. "José Martí: Man of the Antilles." *Cimarrón* [New York] 1, no. 1 (Spring 1985), 5–12.

Fernández Santana, Isabel. "El archivo literario del Instituto de Literatura y Lingüística." *Anuario L/L* 14 (1983), 171–80.

Fornet, Ambrosio. "The Novel of the Cuban Revolution Today." Presented at the annual meeting of the Latin American Studies Association, Boston, October 1986.

García Riverón, Raquel M. "En torno al *Atlas lingüístico de Cuba.*" *Anuario L/L* 14 (1983), 73–90.

Gayol Mecías, Manuel. "La noche del Gran Godo." *Casa de las Américas* 26, no. 153 (November–December 1985), 103–09. [Story]

Giro, Radamés. "Visión panorámica de la guitarra en Cuba (1513–1958)." *Unión,* 1984, no. 4, pp. 76–98.

González, Reynaldo. "Lizandro Otero en la temporada de su madurez." *Unión,* 1984, no. 3, pp. 164–67.

González-Cruz, Luis F. "Frente al Espejo." In *Poesía cubana contemporánea: Antología,* ed. José Abreu Felippe. Madrid: Catoblejas, 1986. [Poetry]

Guillén, Nicolás. "Don Juan." *Unión,* 1984, no. 3, pp. 107–11. [On Juan Gualberto Gómez.]

Gutiérrez, Ignacio. "Kunene." *Unión,* 1984, no. 1, pp. 82–91. [Short drama]

Gutiérrez de la Solana, Alberto. "In memoriam de Lino Novás Calvo." *Círculo. Revista de cultura* 13 (1984), 7–10.

———. "Literatura y psicología: El bebedor de lágrimas de Alfonso Hernández Catá." *Círculo: Revista de Cultura* 15 (1986), 41–46.

———. "Novelística cubana: dédalo de soledad y terror." *Círculo. Revista de Cultura* 12 (1983), 17–29.

Heras León, Eduardo. "Cuestión de principio." *Unión,* 1984, no. 3, pp. 21–36. [Story]

Mejía Duque, Jaime. "Onelio Jorge Cardoso: los relatos y los días." *Unión* 3 (1984), 5–20.

Mesa de la Fe, Ana Gloria. "Presencia de la guerra civil española en la literatura cubana." *Anuario L/L* 14 (1983), 135–40.

Millet, José. "De la poesía de Samuel Feijóo: *El pájaro de las soledades.*" *Unión,* 1984, no. 3, pp. 149–63.
Montero, Reinaldo. "Félix, el feliz." *Bohemia* 78, no. 38 (September 19, 1986), 35–37.
Morales, Salvador. "Algo más que una semblanza: José Martí en la igualdad." *Unión,* 1984, no. 4, pp. 42–48.
———. "El bolivarismo de José Martí." *Tareas* [Panama] 60 (January–June 1985), 57–79.
Morejón, Nancy. "Presencia del mito en el Caribe." *Unión,* 1984, no. 3, pp. 99–106.
Muriel, Justo. "Este hombre generoso que no sabía odiar." *Guángara Libertaria* 7, no. 25 (Winter 1986), 20–23. [On Nicolás Salinas.]
Navarro, Desiderio. "Intertextualidad, canon, juego y realidad histórica en la poesía de Luis Rogelio Nogueras." *Casa de las Américas* 26, no. 154 (January–February 1986), 145–51.
Navarro, Noel. "Las clases sociales y su contexto en la narrativa cubana." *Unión* 1985, no. 1, pp. 90–112.
Núñez Jiménez, Antonio. "La palma real, símbolo de Cuba (II y final)." *Casa de las Americas* 26, no. 153 (November–December 1985), 32–53.
———. "La palma real, símbolo de Cuba (I)." *Casa de las Américas* 26, no. 152 (September–October 1985), 31–52.
Padrón Nordarse, Frank. "Con la buena voluntad del tiempo." *Revista de Literatura Cubana* 4, no. 6 (January–June 1986), 49–77. [Essay on time in Eliseo Diego's poetry.]
Pavón Tamayo, Luis. "La enajenación y la esperanza en *Los pasos perdidos.*" *Unión* 1984, no. 3, pp. 138–48.
Peraza Zarausa, Norma T. "Los emigrantes gallegos en Cuba: notas sobre sus inquietudes culturales." *Anuario L/L* 14 (1983), 141–45.
Piñera Llera, Humberto. "Hernández Catá y la 'mitología' de Martí." *Círculo: Revista de Cultura* 15 (1986), 9–22.
Prats Sariol, José. "Convocar a la exigencia." *Unión,* 1984, no. 4, pp. 146–51. [Essay]
Herlinghaus, Hermann. "Zum Problem der Kontinuitat im Romanschaffen Alejo Carpentiers." *Lateinamerika* 20, no. 2 (Spring 1985), 93–100. [Essay]
Hernández Morelli, Rolando. "Noticias, lugar y texto de 'Un niño de La Habana,' espécimen narrativo inédito de 1837." *Círculo: Revista de Cultura* 15 (1986), 79–84.
Hospital, Carolina. "Conflict and the Cuban American Writer." *Collegium* 4, no. 1 (August–September 1986), 35–37.
Iznaga, Diana. "Un testimonio sobre la guerra de los Diez Años: *Episodios de la Revolución Cubana,* de Manuel de la Cruz." *Anuario L/L* 14 (1983), 54–72.
Jiménez, Onilda A. "Texto y Contexto de *Los Perros Jíbaros* de Jorge Valls." *Círculo: Revista de Cultura* 15 (1986) 99–108.

Leante, César. "¿Existe una novela revolucionaria cubana?" *Cuadernos Hispanoamericanos*, February 1986, 137–43.
Le Riverend, Julio. "El antimperialismo en Cuba (1898–1920)." *Casa de las Américas* 26, no. 152 (September–October 1985), 129–35.
———. "Historia y ficción." *Revista de Literatura Cubana* 4, no. 6 (January–June 1986), 146–149. [Essay]
López Lemus, Virgilio. "La décima cubana. Notas sobre su desarrollo." *Revista de Literatura Cubana* 4, no. 6 (January–June 1986), 121–145.
López Oliva, Manuel. "Paisaje de vida y sueños en *La cueva del Muerto* de Marta Rojas." *Unión*, 1984, no. 3, pp. 40–50.
———. "Texts and Contexts in Cuban Plastic Arts." Presented at the annual meeting of the Latin American Studies Association, Boston, October 1986.
Machover, Jocobo. "José Lezama Lima: le pélerin immoble." *Amérique Latine* 24 (October–December 1985), 61–63.
Marinello, Juan. "Cartas a Manuel Navarro Luna." *Anuario L/L* 14 (1983), 181–96.
Martí, José. "Dos cartas inéditas de José Martí." *Santiago* 57 (March 1985), 241–47.
Martínez, Martha. "Julieta Campos o la interiorización de lo cubano." *Revista Iberoamericana* 132–33 (July–September 1985), 793–98.
Martínez Gordo, Isabel. "Sobre la hipótesis de un patois cubano." *Anuario L/L* 14 (1983), 161–70.
———. "José Lezama Lima, el ensayista." *Unión* 1 (1985), 146–60.
———. "El curso délfico." *Casa de las Américas* 26, no. 152 (September–October 1985), 20–25. [On José Lezama]
———. "La poesía, el crítico y el poeta." *Revista de Literatura Cubana* 4, no. 6 (January–June 1986), 150–55. [Poetry]
Prieto, Abel E. " 'Sucesiva o coordenadas habaneras': apuntes para el proyecto utópico de Lezama." *Casa de las Américas* 26, no. 152 (September–October 1985), 14–19.
Quiroga Clérigo, Manuel. "Miguel Barnet y üsu' gallego en La Habana." *Cuadernos Hispanoamericanos* 5 (May 1985), 168–70.
Repilado, Ricardo. "*Gallego*: el regreso del pícaro." *Unión*, 1984, no. 1, pp. 109–27.
Rodríguez, Carlos Rafael. "El amor y el cólera en tiempos de García Márquez." *Casa de las Américas* 26, nos. 155–56 (March–June 1986), 188–90. [Essay]
Rodríguez Rivera, Guillermo. "Del plagio, la teoría y la crítica." *Casa de las Américas* 27, no. 157 (July–August 1986), 142–50.
Saínz, Enrique. "En torno a 'La fuga de la tórtola' de José Jacinto Milanés." *Unión*, 1985, no. 1, pp. 165–73.
———. "Poesía completa de José Lezama Lima." *Casa de las Américas* 26, no. 152 (September–October 1985), 26–29.

Saldaña, Excilia. "Monólogo de la esposa." *Casa de las Américas* 26, no. 152 (September–October 1985), 86–100. [Poetry]
Souza, Raymond D. "Exile in the Cuban Literary Experience." In *Escritores de la diáspora cubana. Manual bibliográfico,* ed. Daniel Maratos and D. Hill Marnesba, 1–5. Metuchen, N.J.: Scarecrow Press, 1986.
Torrents, Nissa. "Imagen de la mujer en la obra de Alejo Carpentier." In *Hommage à Alejo Carpentier, 80 anniversaire,* 197–207. Bordeaux: Presses Universitaires de Bordeaux, 1985.
Valdés Bernal, Sergio. "¿Existía en el siglo XVIII una modalidad cubana del español?" *Anuario L/L* 14 (1983), 154–60.
Vidal, Manuel. "Despertar a la pintura." *Unión,* 1984, no. 1, pp. 92–94. [Story]
Vitalina, Alfonso. "Rie malicioso y lo sostiene una enorme reflexión." *Casa de las Américas* 26, nos. 155–56 (March–June 1986), 194–95.
Vitier, Cintio. "Martí y Darío en Lezama." *Casa de las Américas* 26, no. 152 (September–October 1985), 4–13.
Vladimir, Oleriny. "Trayectoria de la novela en Cuba y en Checoeslovaquia en los primeros años de la época socialista." *Revista de Literatura Cubana* 4, no. 6 (January–June 1986), 5–26.
Yáñez, Mirta. "El diablo son las cosas." *Unión,* 1985, no. 1, pp. 83–91. [Story]
Yannuzzi, Alberto. "El sentido nacional en la obra de José Antonio Ramos." *Círculo: Revista de Cultura* 15 (1986), 35–40.
Zaldívar, Rudel. "Chinea: escribe y contesta." *Unión,* 1985, no. 1, pp. 66–71.
Zambrano, María. "La Cuba secreta." *La Gaceta del Fondo de Cultura Economía.* 185 (May 1986), 12–15.

Law and Human Rights

Books and Articles

Escasena, José L. *La evolución de la legalidad.* Havana: Ciencias Sociales, 1984. 284 pp.
La legislación penal y algunas regulaciones administrativas. Havana: Ciencias Sociales, 1984. 302 pp.
Legislación Económica. See *Documents.*
Valladares, Armando. *Against All Hope: The Prison Memoirs of Armando Valladares.* New York: Alfred A. Knopf, 1986. 381 pp.
Valls, Jorge. *Twenty Years and Forty Days: Life in a Cuban Prison.* Maryknoll, N.Y.: Orbis Books, Maryknoll Fathers, 1986. 125 pp.

Articles and Papers

Coll, Alberto R. "Functionalism and the Balance of Interests in the Law of the Sea: Cuba's Role." *American Journal of International Law* 79 (October 1985), 891–911.
———. See also *Foreign Relations.*

Cores Trasmonte, Baldomero. "A constitución de Cuba e Porto Rico. Primero modelo autonómico español." *Estudios de Historia Social* (January–June 1984), 407–18.

Del Olmo, Rose. "Detención de narcotraficantes extranjeros en Cuba: los últimos 15 años." Presented at the annual meeting of the Caribbean Studies Association, Caracas, Venezuela, May 1986.

Fiszman, Sula. "Foreign Investment Law: Encouragement versus Restraint: Mexico, Cuba and the Caribbean Basin Initiative." *Hastings International and Comparative Law Review* 8, no. 2 (Winter 1985), 147–83.

"The Rights of Cuban Refugees Facing Indefinite Detention in the United States." *Vanderbilt Journal of Transnational Law* 17 (Fall 1985), 925–73.

Politics, Government, and Armed Forces
Books and Monographs

Annino, Antonio. *Dall'insurrezione al regime politiche di massa e strategie istituzionali in Cuba 1953–1965*. Milan: Franco Angeli, 1984.

Azicri, Max. See *Economics, Industry, and Planning*.

Carrillo, Justo. *Cuba 1933: estudiantes, yanquis y soldados*. Miami: University of Miami Press, 1985. 497 pp.

De Armas, Ramón. *Los partidos burgueses en Cuba neocolonial (1899–1952)*. Havana: Editorial Ciencias Sociales Cubanas, 1985. 278 pp.

Del Prado, Wilfredo. *Cuba: Destiny as Choice*. Miami: Universal, 1986. 191 pp.

Fitzgerald, Frank Thomas. "Politics and Social Structure in Revolutionary Cuba: From the Demise of the Old Middle Class to the Rise of the New Professionals." Ph.D. diss., State University of New York, Binghamton, 1985. 494 pp. *DAI* 46, no. 8 (February 1986): 2459-A, UM8521036.

Harnecker, Martha. *Estrategia y revolución. La estrategia de Fidel y la formación del ejército político de la revolución*. Lima: Editorial Horizonte, 1985. 82 pp.

Hollander, Paul. *Political Hospitality and Tourism: Cuba and Nicaragua*. Washington, D.C.: Cuban American National Foundation, 1986.

Iglesias, Alex. "Active Resistance as a Major Method of Coping in a Communist Political Prison." Ph.D. diss., University of Florida, 1984. 170 pp. *DAI* 46, no. 3 (September 1985), 998–999B, UM8509939. [Concerns 96 men who served prison sentences in a political prison in communist Cuba.]

Kozar, Paul Michael. "The Politics of Deterrence: A Comparative Assessment of American and Soviet Defense Policy, 1960–1964." Ph.D. diss., Georgetown University, 1984. 306 pp. *DAI* 46, no. 1 (July 1985): 256-A, UM8505713. [Includes some information about the Cuban missile crisis.]

Marshall, Peter, and Barry Lewis. See *Economics, Industry, and Planning*.

Pérez-Stable, Marifeli. "Politics and Conciencia in Revolutionary Cuba." Ph.D. diss., State University of New York, Stony Brook, 1985. *DAI* 46, no. 10 (April 1986): 3169-A, UM8527939.

Ra'anan, Uri, Francis Fukuyama, Mark Falcoff, Sam C. Sarkesian, and Richard H. Shultz, Jr. *Third World Marxist-Leninist Regimes: Strengths, Vulnerabilities, and U.S. Policy.* Elmsford, N.Y.: Institute for Foreign Policy Analysis, Inc., Pergamon, 1986. 110 pp.

Ratliff, Helga. See *Foreign Relations.*

Roses, Lorraine Elena. *Voices of the Storyteller: Cuba's Lino Novás Calvo.* Contributors to the Study of World Politics, no. 14. Westport, Conn.: Greenwood Press, 1986. 155 pp.

Sloan, John W. See *Economics, Industry and Planning.*

Subervi-Velez, Federico Antonio. See *Cubans Abroad.*

Suchlicki, Jaime, ed. *Problems of Sucession in Cuba.* Coral Gables, Fla.: University of Miami Press, 1985. 105 pp. [Includes articles by Edward González, Jorge I. Domínguez, Enrique Baloyra, León Gouré, Ambler H. Moss, Jr., and Jorge Mas Canosa.]

Taber, Michael, ed. *The Fight Against Bureaucracy in Cuba.* New York: Pathfinder Press, 1985. 400 pp.

Torrás, Jacinto. *Jacinto Torrás, obras escogidas.* Havana: Editora Política, 1984. 490 pp.

Wilbert, Johannes, ed. See *History.*

Articles and Papers

Azicri, Max. "Cuba After Twenty-Six Years." *Contemporary Marxism* 14 (1986).

Domínguez, Jorge I. "Blaming Itself Not Himself: Cuba's Political Regime After the Third Party Congress." *Cuba After the Third Party Congress. Selected Essays,* 1–10. Washington, D.C.: Central American and Caribbean Program, School of Advanced International Studies, Johns Hopkins University, Occasional Paper no. 12, 1986.

Falkoff, Mark. "Cuba as a Marxist-Leninist Regime." *Cuban Update,* Summer 1986, 7 pp.

Fields, Gary. See *Economics, Industry, and Planning.*

López-Alves, Fernando. See *History.*

Montenegro González, Augusto. "Política y fuerzas militares en Cuba precastrista." *Universitas Humanística* [Bogotá] 14, no. 24 (July–December 1985) 167–68.

———. "Política y fuerzas militares en Cuba precastrista." Presented at the 45th Congreso Internacional de Americanistas, Bogotá, Colombia, July 1985.

Oostiende, Gert J. "La burguesía cubana y sus caminos de hierro." *Boletín de Estudios Latinoamericanos y del Caribe* 37 (December 1984), 99–115.

Packenham, Robert A. See *Economics, Industry, and Planning.*

Rosenberg, Jonathan. "Cuba Today and in the Future." In *José Martí and the Cuban Revolution Retraced,* ed. Johannes Wilbert, 61–72. Los Angeles: UCLA Latin American Center Publications, 1986.

Vandenbroucke, Lucien S. "Anatomy of a Failure: The Decision to Land at the Bay of Pigs." *Political Science Quarterly* 99, no. 3 (1984), 471–91.

Religion

Books and Monographs

Betto, Frei. *Fidel y la religión.* Bogotá: Oveja Negra, 1986. 344 pp.
———. *Fidel Castro y la Religión.* Mexico City: Siglo Veintiuno, 1986.
———. *Fidel Castro e a religião: Coversas com . . .* São Paulo: Brasiliense, 1985. 384 pp.
Cabrera, Lydia. See *Anthropology and Archaeology.*
Crahan, Margaret E. *The Church and Revolution: Cuba and Nicaragua.* Bundoora, Victoria [Australia]: Institute of Latin American Studies, 1986. 30 pp.
Ramos, Marco Antonio. *Panorama del Protestantismo en Cuba.* Miami: Ediciones Caribe, 1986. 668 pp.
Rosado, Caleb. "Sect and Party: Religion under Revolution in Cuba." Ph.D. diss., Northwestern University, 1985. 384 pp. *DAI* 46, no. 11 (May 1986): 3495-A, UM8600908.

Articles and Papers

Batista, Israel. "No se puede escapar a un proceso de cambio tan profundo." *Pensamiento Propio* 4, no. 26 (September–October 1986), 38–40. [Interview about protestantism in Cuba.]
Betto, Frei. "Sobre Fidel y la religión." *Casa de las Américas* 26, nos. 155–56 (March–June 1986), 21–24.
De Céspedes, Carlos M. "The Catholic Church in Cuba Today." In *Cuba After the Third Party Congress. Selected Essays,* 73–80. Washington, D.C.: Central American and Caribbean Program, School of Advanced International Studies, Johns Hopkins University, Occasional Paper no. 12, 1986.
Herrera, María Cristina. "The Cuban Church Today: A 'Vivencia.' " In ibid., 53–72.
Kirk, John M. "A 'Secular' Perspective on Church-State Relations in Cuba: *Fidel y la religión.*" Presented at the Canadian Association of Latin American and Caribbean Studies, Université de Montréal, October 1986.
———. "Between God and the Party: The Church in Revolutionary Cuba, 1969–1985." *Canadian Journal of Latin American and Caribbean Studies* 11, no. 21 (1986), 93–109.
———. "In Search of an Identity: The Church in Revolutionary Cuba." Presented at the University of California, San Diego, October 1986.
———. "Liberation Theology, Cuban-Style." *International Conference on Liberation Theology.* Vancouver, B.C.: Simon Fraser University, 1986.
"Lo que quiere ser la iglesia cubana." *Mansaje Iberoamericano* 244 (March 1986), 10–13.
"Presente y futuro de la iglesia en Cuba." Ibid., 6–9.
Rendon, Thomas. "The Cuban Church Reborn." *The Other Side,* July–August 1986.

Rojas, Marta. "*Fidel y la religión:* un libro para aprehender." *Casa de las Américas* 26, nos. 155–56 (March–June 1986), 184–87.
Sigmund, Paul E. "Fidel and the Friars: Castro Confesses to Friar Betto." *Caribbean Review* 15, no. 2 (Spring 1986), 30–31.

Science and Technology
Books and Monographs

Gutiérrez, Jorge. *Los cactos nativos de Cuba.* Havana: Editorial Científico Técnica, 1984. 52 pp.
Mayea Silveiro, Sergio. "Biologie, Okologie and Bekampfung von Kartoffelkrankheiten in Kuba." Dissertation B, Universität Rostock [East Germany], 1984. 236 + 21 pp.
Reynoso, Alvaro. *Selección de textos.* Havana: Ciencias Sociales, 1985. 352 pp.
Rodríguez Valdés, José Antonio. "Appraisal of Transport Technologies: Methods and Application on the Example of Fertilizer Transhipment in Cuba." Ph.D. diss., The Main School of Planning and Statistics, Warsaw, 1986.

Articles and Papers

Castillo Asencio, Orlando. "Calidad de la reparación de los vehículos automotores." *Transporte y vías de Comunicación* 3 (September 1985), 275–79.
Hernández Gutiérrez, Dimas Néstor. "Metodología para elaborar la norma de consumo de piezas de repuesto en la reparación general de los automóviles." *Transporte y Vías de Comunicación* 3 (September 1985), 256–63.
Marrero Osorio, Sergio A., and Luis R. Ramos Rodríguez. "Evaluación de laboratorio del acoplamiento eléctrico cubano para automóviles Lada." *Transporte y Vías de Comunicación* 6 (December 1985), 309–18.
Miliá, I., F. Cruz, A. Serra, and J. Matutes. "Caracterización de serpentinas cubanas por varias técnicas físicas." *Revista Cubana de Física* 5, no. 1 (1985), 48–60.
Pérez Rodríguez, Omar. "Desarrollo de la base de reparación de vagones en Cuba." *Transporte y Vías de Comunicación* 6 (December 1985), 384–91.
Soto Pau, Filipe. "Método de evaluación para las pruebas de filtros de aceites de producción nacional." *Transporte y Vías de Comunicación* 3 (September 1985), 249–55.
Suárez Torres, Juan O., and Pablo Zamora Rodríguez. "Problemas en la explotación de tractores en la agricultura cubana." *Transporte y Vías de Comunicación* 6 (December 1985), 296–308.

Sociology
Books and Monographs

Abel, Christopher, and Michael Tijaddle, compilers. *Caribbean Societies: Collected Seminar Papers.* Vol. 2. London: Institute of Commonwealth Studies, 1985. [Contains papers on Cuba.]

De Santa Cruz y Mallén, Francisco Xavier. See *History*.
Prieto, Yolanda. See *Cubans Abroad*.

Articles and Papers

Aguirre, B. E. "The Conventionalization of Collective Behavior." *American Journal of Sociology* 90, no. 3 (1984), 541–66.

Alert, Anja. "Zur aktuellen gesellschaftlichen Entwidklung in Kuba." *Jahrbuch Asien, Afrika, Lateinamerika* [Berlin], October 1984, 200–06.

Arbena, Joseph. "Sport in Revolutionary Societies: Cuba and Nicaragua." In *Sport and Society in Latin America*, ed. Joseph Urbina. Westport, Conn.: Greenwood Press, 1987.

Eckstein, Susan. "Restratification After Revolution: The Cuban Experience." In *Crisis in the Caribbean Basin*, ed. Richard Tardanico. Beverly Hills, Calif.: Sage, 1986.

Mertsálov, Anatoli. "La juventud cubana, constructora de la nueva sociedad." *América Latina* [USSR] 8 (1985), 21–24.

Moore, Carlos. "Congo or Carabalí? Race Relations in Socialist Cuba." *Caribbean Review* 15, no. 2 (Spring 1986), 12–15, 43.

Statistics

Books and Monographs

Comité Estatal de Estadísticas. *Anuario demográfico de Cuba 1984*. Havana: Comité Estatal de Estadísticas, 1984. 217 pp.

———. *Boletín estadístico mensual de Cuba, agosto–diciembre de 1985*. Havana: Comité Estatal de Estadísticas, 1985. 122, 122, 122, 121, 144 pp.

———. *Boletín Estadístico de Cuba, Marzo 1986*. Havana: Comité Estatal de Estadísticas, 1986.

———. *Cuba en cifras 1984*. Havana: Comité Estatal de Estadísticas, 1985. 126 pp.

———. *Cuba en cifras 1985*. Havana: Comité Estatal de Estadísticas, 1986. 126 pp.

———. *Cuba. Quarterly Economic Report*. Havana: Banco Nacional de Cuba/Comité Estatal de Estadísticas, 1985. 31 pp.

———. *Evolución de la fecundidad de la mujer cubana en el período 1959–1984*. Havana: Comité Estatal de Estadísticas, 1985. 110 pp.

———. *La economía cubana 1985*. Havana: Comité Estatal de Estadísticas, 1986. 32 pp.

———. *Principales aspectos demográficos de la población cubana en el año 1985. Evolución de la población cubana en el quinquenio 1981–1985 y su consideración con el de 1976–1980. Evolución perspectiva de la población para el quinquenio 1986–1990*. Havana: Instituto de Investigaciones Estadísticas, 1986. 102 pp.

Pérez, Magaly, and Noemí Pascal. *Estadística sobre la mujer cubana*. Havana: Editorial Letras Cubanas, 1985. 40 pp.

Articles and Papers

Hernández, Osvaldo. "La importancia de la estadística para el movimiento obrero." *Revista Estadística* 8, no. 17 (December 1985), 48–57.

Piña, Luis, and Jorge D'Espaux. "Consideraciones generales sobre las pérdidas de muestreo y sus aplicaciones al control de inventarios." *Economía y Desarrollo* 91 (March–April 1986), 109–17. [On sampling techniques and their applications to inventory control.]

Women

Books and Monographs

Colectivo de especialistas de salud pública. *La mujer cubana y la salud pública.* Havana: Editorial Letras Cubanas, 1985. 40 pp.

Comité Estatal de Estadísticas. *Evolución de la fecundidad de la mujer* . . . See *Statistics.*

Leahy, Margaret E. *Development Strategies and the Status of Women: A Comparative Study of the United States, Mexico, the Soviet Union, and Cuba.* Boulder, Colo.: Lynne Rienner Publishers, 1986. 164 pp.

Navarro, Dalia. *La mujer cubana en el deporte.* Havana: Editorial Letras Cubanas, 1985. 32 pp.

Pérez, Magaly, and Noemí Pascal. See *Statistics.*

Ponce Ortiz, María. *La mujer cubana en la educación superior.* Havana: Editorial Letras Cubanas, 1985. 56 pp.

Prieto, Yolanda. "Reinterpreting an Immigration Success Story: Cuban Women, Work, and Change in a New Jersey Community." Ph.D. diss., Rutgers University, 1984. 326 pp. *DAI* 46, no. 3 (September 1985): 804-05-A, UM8507143.

Articles and Papers

Anker, Richard. "Comparative Survey." In *Working Women in Socialist Countries: The Fertility Connection,* ed. Valentina Bodrova and Richard Anker, 1–22. Geneva: International Labor Organization, 1985.

Azicri, Max. "Women in Cuba." In *Women's Studies Encyclopedia,* ed. Helen Tierney. Westport, Conn.: Greenwood Press, 1987.

Castro, Fidel. *Fidel Castro habla a las mujeres de América Latina.* Buenos Aires: Anteo, 1985. [Closing speech of the "Encuentro sobre la situación de la mujer en América Latina y el Caribe," June 7, 1985.]

Eng, Luisa. *La mujer cubana en la revolución educacional.* Havana: Editorial Letras Cubanas, 1985. 72 pp.

Farnós Morejón, Alfonso. "La transición demográfica en Cuba: Los roles económicos y sociales de las mujeres." In *Algunas características de la reciente evolución de la fecundidad en Cuba,* ed. Raúl Hernández Castellón, Alfonso Farnós Morejón, and Fernando González Quiñonez. Havana, 1985.

Farnós Morejón, Alfonso, Fernando González Quiñonez, and Raúl Hernández. "Cuba." In *Working Women in Socialist Countries: The Fertility Connection,* ed. Valentina Bodrova and Richard Anker. Geneva: International Labor Organization, 1985.

González Quiñonez, Fernando. "Fecundidad y Empleo Femenino en Cuba." In *Algunas características de la reciente evolución de le fecundidad en Cuba,* ed. Raúl Hernández Castellón, Alfonso Farnós Morejón, and Fernando González Quiñonez. Havana, 1985.

Ortíz Díaz, María Dolores. "Las primeras mujeres universitarias en Cuba." *Revista Cubana de Educación Superior* 5, no. 1 (1985), 126–31.

Stubbs, Jean. "Women and Agricultural Cooperatives in Cuba." Presented at the annual meeting of the Latin American Studies Association, Boston, October 1986.

Torrents, Nissa. See *Language and Literature.*

Contributors

LOURDES CASAL, late of Rutgers University, Department of Social Psychology

ISABEL CASTELLANOS, Assistant Professor of Modern Languages, Florida International University, Miami, Fla. 33199

JORGE CASTELLANOS, Professor Emeritus, Marygrove College, Detroit, Mich. 48221

VIRGINIA R. DOMÍNGUEZ, Assistant Professor of Anthropology, Duke University, Durham, N.C. 27706

MANUEL R. GÓMEZ, President, Cuban-American Committee, 400 First St. NW, Washington, D.C. 20001

EDWARD J. MULLEN, Professor of Spanish, University of Missouri, Columbia, Mo. 65211

MARIFELI PÉREZ-STABLE, Assistant Professor, Program of Politics, Economics, and Society, State University of New York, Old Westbury, N.Y. 11771

YOLANDA PRIETO, Assistant Professor of Sociology and Director, School of Social Science and Human Services, Ramapo College, Mahwah, N.J. 07430

WILLARD W. RADELL, JR., Associate Professor of Economics, Indiana University of Pennsylvania, Indiana, Pa. 15701

SERGIO G. ROCA, Professor of Economics, Adelphi University, Garden City, N.Y. 11530

ANDREW ZIMBALIST, Professor of Economics, Smith College, Northampton, Mass. 01063

PITT LATIN AMERICAN SERIES
Cole Blasier, Editor

ARGENTINA
Argentina in the Twentieth Century
David Rock, Editor

Discreet Partners: Argentina and the USSR Since 1917
Aldo César Vacs

Juan Peron and the Reshaping of Argentina
Frederick C. Turner and José Enrique Miguens, Editors

The Life, Music, and Times of Carlos Gardel
Simon Collier

BRAZIL
The Film Industry in Brazil: Culture and the State
Randal Johnson

The Politics of Social Security in Brazil
James M. Malloy

Urban Politics in Brazil: The Rise of Populism, 1925–1945
Michael L. Conniff

COLOMBIA
Gaitán of Colombia: A Political Biography
Richard E. Sharpless

Roads to Reason: Transportation, Administration, and Rationality in Colombia
Richard E. Hartwig

CUBA
Army Politics in Cuba, 1898–1958
Louis A. Pérez, Jr.

Cuba Between Empires, 1878–1902
Louis A. Pérez, Jr.

Cuba, Castro, and the United States
Philip W. Bonsal

Cuba in the World
Cole Blasier and Carmelo Mesa-Lago, Editors

Cuba Under the Platt Amendment
Louis A. Pérez, Jr.

Cuban Studies, Vol. 16
Carmelo Mesa-Lago, Editor

Cuban Studies, Vol. 17
Carmelo Mesa-Lago, Editor

Intervention, Revolution, and Politics in Cuba, 1913–1921
Louis A. Pérez, Jr.

Revolutionary Change in Cuba
Carmelo Mesa-Lago, Editor

The United States and Cuba: Hegemony and Dependent Development, 1880–1934
Jules Robert Benjamin

MEXICO

Essays on Mexican Kinship
Hugo G. Nutini, Pedro Carrasco, and James M. Taggart, Editors

The Mexican Republic: The First Decade, 1823–1832
Stanley C. Green

The Politics of Mexican Oil
George W. Grayson

Voices, Visions, and a New Reality: Mexican Fiction Since 1970
J. Ann Duncan

US POLICIES

Cuba, Castro, and the United States
Philip W. Bonsal

The Hovering Giant: U.S. Responses to Revolutionary Change in Latin America
Cole Blasier

Illusions of Conflict: Anglo-American Diplomacy Toward Latin America
Joseph Smith

Puerto Rico and the United States, 1917–1933
Truman R. Clark

The United States and Cuba: Hegemony and Dependent Development, 1880–1934
Jules Robert Benjamin

The United States and Latin America in the 1980s: Contending Perspectives on a Decade of Crisis
Kevin J. Middlebrook and Carlos Rico, Editors

USSR POLICIES

Discreet Partners: Argentina and the USSR Since 1917
Aldo César Vacs

The Giant's Rival: The USSR and Latin America
Cole Blasier

OTHER NATIONAL STUDIES

Barrios in Arms: Revolution in Santo Domingo
José A. Moreno

Beyond the Revolution: Bolivia Since 1952
James M. Malloy and Richard S. Thorn, Editors

Black Labor on a White Canal: Panama, 1904–1981
Michael L. Conniff

The Origins of the Peruvian Labor Movement, 1883–1919
Peter Blanchard

The Overthrow of Allende and the Politics of Chile, 1964–1976
Paul E. Sigmund

Panajachel: A Guatemalan Town in Thirty-Year Perspective
Robert E. Hinshaw

Peru and the International Monetary Fund
Thomas Scheetz

Rebirth of the Paraguayan Republic: The First Colorado Era, 1878–1904
Harris G. Warren

SOCIAL SECURITY

The Politics of Social Security in Brazil
James M. Malloy

Social Security in Latin America: Pressure Groups, Stratification, and Inequality
Carmelo Mesa-Lago

OTHER STUDIES

Adventurers and Proletarians: The Story of Migrants in Latin America
Magnus Mörner, with the collaboration of Harold Sims

Authoritarianism and Corporatism in Latin America
James M. Malloy, Editor

Authoritarians and Democrats: Regime Transition in Latin America
James M. Malloy and Mitchell A. Seligson, Editors

Constructive Change in Latin America
Cole Blasier, Editor

Female and Male in Latin America: Essays
Ann Pescatello, Editor

Latin American Debt and the Adjustment Crisis
Rosemary Thorp and Laurence Whitehead, Editors

Public Policy in Latin America: A Comparative Survey
John W. Sloan

Selected Latin American One-Act Plays
Francesca Colecchia and Julio Matas, Editors and Translators

The State and Capital Accumulation in Latin America: Brazil, Chile, Mexico
Christian Anglade and Carlos Fortin, Editors

Transnational Corporations and the Latin American Automobile Industry
Rhys Jenkins